COMMON CENTS

COMMON CENTS

How to Succeed with Activity-Based Costing and Activity-Based Management

REVISED EDITION

PETER B. B. TURNEY

McGraw-Hill

New York Chicago San Francisco Lisbon London Madrid
Mexico City Milan New Delhi San Juan Seoul
Singapore Sydney Toronto

The **McGraw·Hill** Companies

1 2 3 4 5 6 7 8 9 0 DOC/DOC 0 9 8 7 6 5

ISBN 0–07–144037–2

This publication is designed to provide accurate and authoritative information in regard to the subject matter covered. It is sold with the understanding that the publisher is not engaged in rendering legal, accounting, or other professional service. If legal advice or other expert assistance is required, the services of a competent professional person should be sought.

—From a declaration of principles jointly adopted by a committee of the American Bar Association and a committee of publishers.

McGraw-Hill books are available at special quantity discounts to use as premiums and sales promotions, or for use in corporate training programs. For more information, please write to the Director of Special Sales, Professional Publishing, McGraw-Hill, Two Penn Plaza, New York, NY 10121–2298. Or contact your local bookstore.

 This book is printed on recycled, acid-free paper containing a minimum of 50% recycled, de-inked fiber.

Library of Congress Cataloging-in-Publication Data

Turney, Peter B. B.
  Common cents : how to succeed with activity-based costing and activity-based management/ by Peter B.B. Turney.— rev. ed.
    p. cm.
  ISBN 0–07–144037–2 (hardcover : alk. paper)
1. Activity-based costing. I. Title.
  HF5686.C8T83 2005
  657'.42—dc22

2004023290

CONTENTS

PREFACE TO REVISED EDITION

Common Cents burst onto the scene in 1991. It was a time of intense interest in activity-based costing (ABC) and activity-based management (ABM) following the emergence of these management methods in the latter half of the nineteen eighties.

Common Cents captured the spirit and substance of those pioneering years. It documented the results of numerous case studies and ABC implementation projects from 1986 to 1991. Grounded in these experiences, it was the first book to describe the theory, practice, and results of ABC and ABM.

After seven printings over 14 years, it is safe to say that *Common Cents* is a classic. It has inspired many organizations in their quest for the ABC performance breakthrough. I am not surprised at the extensive use of the book at companies like IBM, AT&T, Lucent Technologies, and Chrysler. After all, most of the examples in the first edition were about manufacturing companies, and ABC was used to help close the performance gap with Japanese manufacturing companies.

What is surprising is the extent to which *Common* Cents has been used by nonmanufacturing companies. For example, the U.S. Army base at Fort Riley used *Common Cents* to guide its ABC implementation efforts.

I really shouldn't be surprised because ABC works in all types of organizations and in all parts of the value chain. And you won't be surprised to learn that the diverse interest in *Common Cents* and ABC was a major factor in my decision to revise the book.

The decision to write the revised edition of *Common Cents* was an easy one. The book is still selling well, and the concept and methods are as relevant today as they were in 1991. But the world has changed, and it was clear that the book would benefit from an update.

In 1991 the emphasis was on "world class" and Japanese management practices. Today's management agenda includes strategy mapping, the balanced scorecard, lean manufacturing, six sigma, business process management, outsourcing, financial returns from information technology outlays, controlling government spending, performance budgeting, and so on. Today's ABC is involved in all of these initiatives, and *Common Cents* explains how.

ABC is more popular today than it has ever been. In 1991 it was used primarily in manufacturing companies. Today it is used in all sorts of organizations: financial services, utilities, telecommunications, aerospace and defense, supply chain, packaged goods, distribution, software, health care, government agencies, and the military. The revised edition has examples from these sectors.

Information technology has progressed considerably since 1991. Many organizations have implemented enterprise resource planning (ERP) systems that provide integrated databases of financial and nonfinancial information. Some of these systems also provide enhanced analytic and reporting capabilities. The widespread use of the Internet is another major change, one that makes it easier to collect and distribute information in an ABC system.

ABC has benefited from these developments. ABC is now an analytic tool that sits on top of corporate databases. It pulls financial and operational data from these databases, models their relationships, and reports financial business intelligence to management. This helps create a sustainable and accessible ABC system.

Some of the most exciting developments relate to the ABC method and the way in which it is applied. Resource planning, activity-based budgeting, time-based ABC, customer profitability systems, and ABC analytics are new or have been enhanced over the last decade. These developments increase the value proposition from ABC by adding new applications, creating new ways to increase profit or reduce cost, and reducing the cost and time of implementation. The revised edition has new material on these topics.

There is an ongoing transition from the stand-alone ABC system to an integrated performance management system. ABC's contribution to these new systems extends beyond historical information for decision making. These new uses include supplying performance measures for balanced scorecards, feeding cost information into equipment management systems, supporting detailed process analyses, and simulating the financial and process impact of decisions. The final chapter of this book previews these new performance management systems.

An inevitable question is this: Is the development and application of ABC complete, or is there more to come? I would like to answer this by telling a story from 1988. I'm in a limousine, heading back to the airport from a conference where I'd given a presentation. I'm sitting in the back of the limousine with Professor Mansfield (now deceased), who at the time was on the faculty of the University of Pennsylvania and was one of the world's leading authorities on technology diffusion. In the back of the car, he said, "Peter, it's 1988. You just started on this ABC work. How long will it take for it to be completely installed in the world?" And I looked at him, and off the top of my head said, "Ten years?" Then he said, "Peter, you're wrong. It will take twenty years."

A decade and a half after Professor Mansfield's prescient observation, I have to agree that he was right. There are at least five to ten years to go in this field before we can say, "Mission accomplished." If you think this means a new edition of *Common Cents* or a sequel, you may well be right!

—**Peter B. B. Turney**

COMMON CENTS

COMMON CENTS

PART ONE

Why You Need Activity-Based Costing

Dealing with today's business challenges is hard enough even when you have all the right information. But if you're responding to wrong financial information, you could well be in a losing battle.

In Chapter 1 you'll see how flawed cost information can sabotage your competitive and financial position by encouraging you to set the wrong priorities and focus on the wrong problems. You'll see how it can lead you to

- Set the wrong prices
- Sell the wrong products and services
- Focus on the wrong markets
- Serve the wrong customers
- Design costly products and services
- Cut cost but fail to *reduce* cost
- Fail to control government spending
- Make incorrect sourcing decisions

In Chapter 2 you'll learn why accounting systems do not provide the relevant and accurate information needed in today's challenging business environment. Accounting systems are reasonably good for external reporting, but they can be misleading—even dangerous—for internal decision making.

CHAPTER 1

The Need for ABC Information

Unreliable cost information is an open invitation to disaster. Cost information is used in making a wide range of strategic and operational decisions. So, if you have erroneous cost information, you are wide open to a variety of competitive problems or missed opportunities.

Take the following examples of the use of cost information:

- Managing the profitability of products and services
- Managing the profitability of customers and markets
- Managing the cost of processes
- Identifying ways of cutting cost
- Making decisions about outsourcing

The question is, if you are making decisions like these with erroneous cost information, will you have problems or missed opportunities in your organization?

Well, you really can't know for sure without doing an activity-based costing (ABC) study. Organizations that have implemented ABC, however, have found a variety of problems and opportunities. Based on their experience, let's take a closer look at some of the possible problems that can result from faulty cost information.

SETTING THE WRONG PRICES

Selling something for less than it costs can be common sense. Or it can be the wrong move.

There are all kinds of "common cents" reasons for selling a product or service at a loss. Retailers, for example, may underprice a selected product temporarily. They use this underpriced product as a "loss leader" to boost customer traffic through the store. The basic premise is that increased traffic generates greater overall sales volume.

Organizations may also use a similar underpricing strategy on a broader basis to establish, protect, or regain market share. It's common sense when it's well informed and intentional—and when it works.

Unintentional losses, however, are always the wrong move. No company stays in business long by selling the majority of its products for less than they cost. Yet this is exactly what more and more companies are doing with more and more of their products.

To put the problem into a dollar-and-cents perspective, consider this one simple example. It's one of many from companies that have implemented ABC.

The company made a product at a cost of $2 per unit—at least, that was the product cost that the company's conventional costing system assigned. So management wisely priced the product for a nice "profit" at a competitive $4 per unit.

But guess what. There was no profit on the product. In fact, each sale resulted in a $498 loss! It was as if the company were wrapping dollar bills around the product each time it was shipped to a customer.

The company had its priorities wrong. It was devoting its energy to the wrong customers. The right customers were being served by someone else.

The company was also devoting little effort to cutting the cost of this product. In reality, there were many opportunities to improve.

Now you are probably saying to yourself, "How could this be?"

Simple: Because of this product's low sales volume, at a $4 price, it failed to cover its costs of production and distribution by a wide margin. A more appropriate ABC study revealed that the product actually cost $500—not $2—to make and distribute.

That's a 25,000 percent product costing error!

It would be nice if this example were an isolated product costing aberration. But it's not. Costing inaccuracies—and other strategic errors— are quite common when companies with a variety of products or high

FIGURE 1−1

ABC as a Percent of Conventional Cost

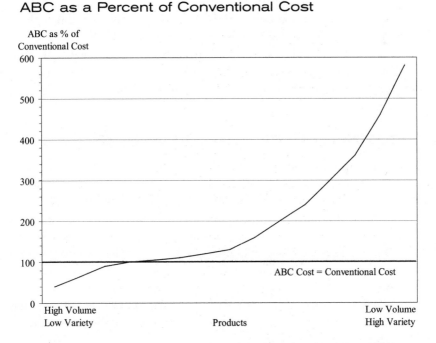

Product costs reported by conventional systems often differ substantially from the more accurate activity-based costing (ABC) results, as shown in this comparative example from a Nortel assembly plant. Using the conventional costing data can result in severe errors in product strategies.

overhead use conventional cost systems. While these inaccuracies typically aren't as dramatic as 25,000 percent, they can still be quite significant.

The curve in Figure 1–1 shows a profile common to many companies. Notice that the true cost of many products—primarily the low-volume, high-variety ones—is up to 600 percent greater than the conventional cost. The costs of high-volume, lower-variety products err in the other direction. Their true cost drops by 10 to 80 percent, which is perhaps an even more significant correction for highly competitive products.

Substantial costing inaccuracies in either direction lead to unintentional competitive mistakes. Pricing errors lead to economic losses. Producing and selling the wrong products (to the wrong customers) weakens the company in the marketplace. Focusing cost-reduction efforts on the wrong products and the wrong costs makes it difficult to compete with low-cost offshore producers.

You can't afford competitive mistakes—especially in today's global economy. You need every advantage you can get in order to compete with Japanese, Indian, Chinese, and other tough competitors, including other U.S. companies. Cost systems that send you the wrong signals can put you on a crisis course from which recovery is difficult.

FOCUSING ON THE WRONG MARKETS

Cost is an important determinant of marketing focus. Consequently, it's only natural that managers devote their attention and resources to the markets they perceive as the most profitable. And it's the cost system that reports the profitability of the products that are sold into these markets. Managers chase profits, but profits can be phantoms of the cost system.

The business of Mueller-Lehmkuhl, for example, was to combine two products—attaching machines and fasteners—and market them to customers as a package. The firm rented the machines to customers at a deliberately low price. This established a very competitive position. Then, to generate profits, the fasteners were priced to cover their cost and the remaining cost of the machines.

On the surface, everything seemed fine. Customers were happy and loyal.

However, Mueller-Lehmkuhl's cost system assigned too much cost to the labor-intensive fasteners. (Overhead was assigned using direct labor hours). This made these fasteners appear quite costly and unprofitable. So, over the years, Mueller-Lehmkuhl put little marketing effort into these "expensive" and "low-profit" fasteners. Consequently, the company walked away from some profitable markets.[1]

SERVING THE WRONG CUSTOMERS

Have you ever checked to see how much profit you are actually making from each customer? If you did this check with conventional cost information, everything would probably appear fine. However, if you were to do an ABC study of customer profitability, you might be shocked to see the differences. Some customers cost more than they are worth! Here's why.

It's common to find that different customers need different levels of support. Some customers buy standard products infrequently, but in high volumes. They rarely call your customer-support department, since their own engineers do all the necessary training and solve most field problems.

Other customers, however, may buy nonstandard products. Moreover, their purchases are often frequent and in low volumes. They may constantly change their orders and expect a rapid response when they call. Plus, the complexity of the nonstandard products often requires a heavy engineering effort. As a result, these customers make frequent calls to the sales, order entry, and customer service departments.

Customers for nonstandard products demand a lot. But these are just the customers that marketing focuses most of its efforts on. This seems to make good sense because the cost system reports high profitability for these customers. They're the ones ordering the low-volume, specialty products that look really profitable. Plus, the additional costs incurred to service these customers are buried in departmental overhead accounts.

But are these customers really generating profits? To answer this question, let's take a look at some real-life examples.

Cost to Manufacture

A small machine shop ran three shifts a day, seven days a week. But it was making very little money.

The shop's major customer—a Fortune 100 company that the machine shop considered its bread and butter—provided 50 percent of the sales volume. But profitability was a different matter, as an ABC study revealed.

The major customer ordered high-precision machined parts in small lots. This required

- Long setups
- Intense engineering support
- Heavy programming support
- Substantial sales support
- More order activity
- More scrapped units
- Special packaging requirements
- More inspection
- Higher inventory

Unfortunately, the additional costs of these activities were not assigned to the major customer that required them. Instead, the conventional cost system spread the costs across the machine shop's entire customer base. As a result, the major customer enjoyed subsidized pricing. More disastrously, though, the machine shop's number-one customer was actually its number-one loser.

Without this knowledge, the company missed some opportunities to better address this major customer. There were opportunities to reprice products to offset some of the additional costs. There were opportunities to redirect marketing effort toward profitable customers. There were opportunities to reduce the cost of serving the major customer through a program of continuous improvement.[2]

All these opportunities were lost because of an inappropriate cost system that focused management's attention elsewhere.

Cost to Serve

Distorted manufacturing costs are not the only reason why unprofitable customers are hidden. It may be because the cost of serving customers varies from one customer to another.

The Deluxe Corporation (a major supplier of checks) found this out by applying ABC to its cost-to-serve activities (such as order-processing activities). The ABC analysis revealed that some banking customers were highly unprofitable. These customers used Deluxe's traditional high-cost distribution channels of mail and telephone. Other customers—primarily those that used the Internet for transmitting orders—were quite profitable.

Armed with this knowledge, Deluxe was able to institute new marketing programs for banking customers and to negotiate new contracts to migrate customers to profitability.

DESIGNING COSTLY PRODUCTS
AND SERVICES

Inaccurate or missing cost information can also prevent companies from realizing the benefits that can be gained from *world-class* design.

In the last two decades, we've learned a lot about designing world-class products. Today's products are designed faster and brought to market in a fraction of the time it used to take. Getting product part counts down seems to have reached the proportions of a national sport. And, thanks to world-class design, many companies have increased product quality while bringing costs down.

In fact, the opportunity for cost reduction via product design is enormous. For example, Ford Motor and others have estimated that as much as 60 to 80 percent of the cost over a product's life cycle is locked in by the time product design is completed. This rises to 90 to 95 percent by the time the design of the production process is completed (see Figure 1–2). So design alone offers tremendous cost-reduction opportunities.

The question is, are you getting the leverage on cost that's possible with world-class design? More to the point, are your product and service designers able to apply the principles of world-class design? Or are they being frustrated by inaccurate or missing cost information that may lead them to do exactly the opposite?

Costly Product Design

Inaccurate cost information thwarted the design efforts of an electrical accessories manufacturer. This company was on the path toward world-class performance. Lead times were down. Quality was up. Inventory levels were plummeting. The next step was to design products using

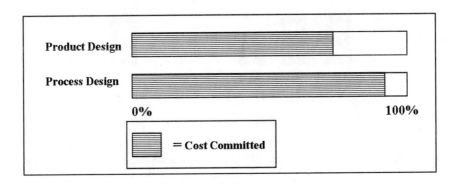

FIGURE 1–2

The Critical Role of Design

Most product costs are locked in during design. Thus, the earlier you start thinking about cost reduction, the more leverage you'll have.

world-class principles—low part counts, common parts, modular sub-assemblies, short time to market, and so on.

The design engineers understood the principles of world-class design. However, they were frustrated by a cost system that pushed them in exactly the opposite direction.

A case in point was a simple little brass strip. This strip was used to connect wires to a grounding circuit in several of the company's products. Connections were made via holes drilled in each strip (see Figure 1–3)[3]; depending on the product, the strip could require from one to three holes.

It was possible to design a single strip with three holes (the solution on the right in Figure 1–3). Such a strip could be used universally in all products. This approach made sense to the engineers because they would have only one part number, rather than three. Not only was this consistent with world-class goals of reducing parts inventory counts, but it seemed possible that one universal part would cost less than three variants.

Did their intuition make sense? Yes, if you look at the impact on activity of one versus three parts:

- Only one part would have to be ordered, not three.
- Only one part would have to be received, stored, and released to the shop floor.

FIGURE 1–3

Costing Product Design Options

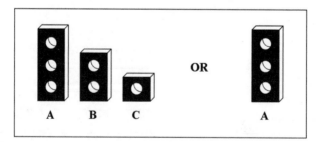

Source: WCI Ltd.

How much can a simple wire-connection strip cost? Should you make individual strips for one-, two-, and three-wire applications, or should you make a universal three-hole strip? Conventional costing says that option C in the alternative on the left costs less for single-wire connections because it consumes less material and direct labor. Should you design to that or to the world-class goals that focus on reduced parts inventory?

- Only one part, not three, would have to be stored and maintained in the database.
- Just one part would need to be changed in the future, not three.
- It would be necessary to forecast volume for only one part.
- Forecasting was more likely to be wrong for three parts than for one, particularly if lead times were long.
- Less inventory would be carried with one part than with three.
- Scheduling part production would be easier with one part instead of three.

Unfortunately, the existing cost system torpedoed engineering's world-class intuition. The cost system said that a single strip was more expensive than three different strips (parts A, B, and C in the alternative on the left of Figure 1–3). After all, the three-hole strip required more material and direct labor than the one- and two-hole strips. And, to make things worse, the cost system assigned all overhead based on material and direct labor (which were a small portion of total cost).

It was difficult for engineering to fight this cost system. Its projection of product cost was considered to be an important performance measure for the company. In world-class design versus conventional costing, world-class design lost an uphill battle to convention. The company also lost an opportunity to cut costs on numerous activities associated with the connection strip. And that was for one simple part. How many other opportunities do you think were lost to conventional costing?

Costly Service Design

Service companies don't suffer from distorted cost information the way manufacturing companies do. This is because they usually don't have cost accounting systems (because they have no need to value inventory). But they do suffer from the lack of accurate cost information.

Take the case of the retirement plans division of an insurance company. This division designed a retirement plan and sold the plan to its customers. This plan was thought to be profitable until an ABC study revealed that the cost of designing the product exceeded the revenues generated from its sale. This was before the costs of delivering and administering the product were taken into account!

Armed with accurate ABC costs, the division redesigned and repriced the product for profitability as well as customer service.

CUTTING COST BUT FAILING TO REDUCE COST

When hard times hit, the gut reaction of many Western companies is to reach for the knife. We've all seen the headlines: "Company X lays off 5,000 workers." "Company Y cuts white-collar employees by 20 percent."

Does this cost cutting really work? In the short run, it does save money. But over time, people are rehired and costs creep back up. In some cases, the same people who were laid off come back as consultants. How can this be?

The typical cost report tells you *what* you are spending, but it doesn't tell you *why* you are spending it. So when you slash overhead costs, you're cutting the *result*, not the *cause*. Consequently, you're more likely to damage the quality of your products and services than to reduce costs permanently.

It's rather like visiting a weight-loss clinic. You lose 60 pounds in six weeks through a crash course of dieting and exercise. But once the course is over, you return to your regular high-calorie diet and sedentary lifestyle. Not surprisingly, your weight creeps back up. You can't keep the fat off until you give up a fat lifestyle.

The way to reduce costs permanently is to change the way you perform the work. Unfortunately, conventional cost information *does not* tell you how to do this. Nor does it encourage you to do it. As a result, crash cost-cutting efforts often fail to restore a company to lasting health.

As we will soon find out, ABC provides a wealth of information about the activities and processes in which cost is incurred. This information helps to pinpoint the targets for cost reduction and reveal the *changes in process* that are needed to cut cost permanently.

NOT CONTROLLING GOVERNMENT SPENDING

In its early years, ABC was used primarily by profit-making companies. But the benefits of ABC have also been realized by not-for-profit and government organizations such as the military, federal government departments, and state and local government agencies.

The common issue for these organizations is doing more with less. This reflects the intense budget pressure on government today.

Unfortunately, conventional government accounting systems do little to promote cost efficiency. This is because government accounting systems do not reveal the sources or causes of overspending.

Take the case of a military supply process. This process was responsible for providing a major military base with supplies as varied as televisions for servicemen's families and shells and spare parts for tanks.

The supply process was complex, repetitive, time-consuming, and costly. The base's accounting system provided no insights into the sources and causes of these costs. It was only in response to new information from an ABC study that opportunities were identified and improvements made.

MAKING INCORRECT SOURCING DECISIONS

One source of competitive advantage is to focus on what you know best. Processes that are central to your business—such as the research on proprietary technologies—are maintained in-house. Those that are commodity processes—such as the manufacture of routine parts and back-office accounting processes—are outsourced. These nonstrategic processes can be handled by a third party—so long as the cost and quality are right.

This sounds good in theory, but in the absence of good cost information, you may not always make the right decision (Figure 1–4). Let's look at the role that inaccurate or incomplete cost information can play in the outsourcing of manufacturing parts and processes.

Outsourcing Manufactured Parts

How does your company decide which parts to manufacture and which to source from outside? If you source from outside, is a local or an offshore supplier best?

Assuming that the part is nonstrategic, the biggest decision factor for some companies is the outside supplier's price. Quality and service may receive a sideways glance, but outside price versus the cost of manufacturing internally is often the final arbiter.

What does your cost system tell you about the cost of manufacturing a part in-house? It tells you what the material and direct labor costs are. But does it load overhead onto the part based on the amount of direct labor? If it does, the in-house cost will inevitably be higher than the price charged by an offshore supplier located in a country with low direct labor costs.

Experience tells us, however, that the price quoted by an outside supplier is a small fraction of the total cost of getting a part to its destination on time and in a condition fit to use. Even if we include the additional

FIGURE 1-4

Costing Sourcing Options

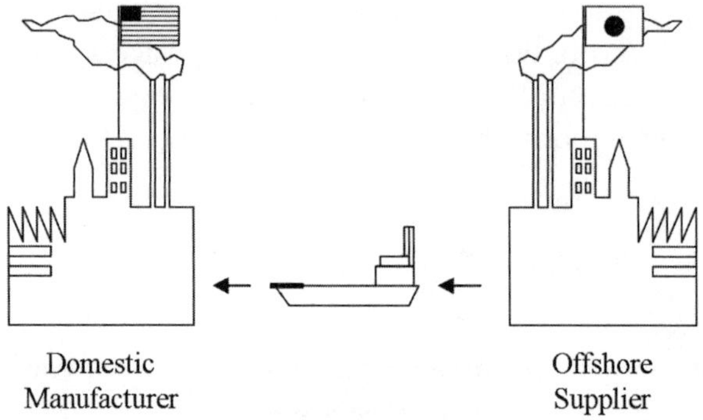

Domestic
Manufacturer

Offshore
Supplier

Outsourcing is often a viable manufacturing strategy. Too often, however, the decision to source from outside is based on faulty or incomplete cost data. Contrary to expectations, costs may go up while quality and service go down.

transportation costs, there are other hidden costs that are easily over-looked. They typically include ordering, expediting, handling, storage, and quality.

Let's take a closer look at these hidden costs in terms of acquiring a part from a supplier that's 5,000 miles away. Here's some of what you're up against.

Ordering activities. Distance increases the hidden costs of procure-ment and reduces supplier responsiveness. Order lead times are in weeks or even months. Requirements must be forecast well in advance of actual use, with the added risk that the forecast will be wrong.

In contrast, a simple technique to trigger orders for parts can be used with local suppliers. This is the *kanban*. It's a visible signal, such as the return of an empty container, indicating that a new order should be filled. *Kanban* is part of a "pull" system where the frequency and size of orders are determined by the demand of the next process (and ultimately the needs of customers).

A pull system simplifies the material procurement process. It eliminates activities such as inspection, receiving, and storing, and it reduces overall costs.

Expediting activities. Forecasting errors provide lots of work for expediters. In addition to the cost of the expediters themselves, there's the cost of air freight and special handling.

Storage activities. Long lead times inevitably translate into more inventory, with all the costs of storing and handling that inventory.

Quality activities. The best quality is achieved when customers and suppliers are closely linked. Close linkage is difficult, however, at a distance of 5,000 miles.

If the offshore supplier produces defective parts, it may be weeks before these parts make their way through the shipping and inventory pipeline. By this time, there may be thousands of defective parts in the warehouse or on the boat.

Sorting out such a mess isn't easy. It's not uncommon to put engineers and managers on planes to resolve the quality problems at the supplier's plant.

There are situations in which the price quoted for offshore supply is so low that it more than offsets the hidden costs. But can you be sure that you've always made the right decision? To gain some insight, let's look at a real-life example of sourcing from Mexico.

The Case of the Mexican Subassembly

A midwestern U.S. company was looking for ways to reduce cost. This company sold products into a marketplace that had recently been invaded by foreign competition. Its customers had lost 60 percent of their business to the Japanese and other offshore manufacturers in just a few short months.

Losing the lion's share of its business so quickly was life-threatening. Survival required major surgery.

Transplanting assembly work to Mexico seemed to be an obvious way to reduce cost. Labor rates in Mexico were about 50¢ per hour at the time. By comparison, rates in the Midwest exceeded $8 per hour, even for fairly unskilled work.

So the company picked a subassembly requiring a lot of hand work and sent it to Mexico. The economics were compelling. Not only should labor costs come down by over 90 percent, but overhead should plummet as well. (The drop in the subassembly's cost would occur because the cost system added manufacturing overhead as a percent of direct labor.)

The outsourcing was handled like this: Parts were shipped to the company's midwestern location by suppliers. The parts were "kitted" (that is, the parts were boxed, with each box containing the specific components needed for a single subassembly), and the kits were shipped to Mexico. After assembly in Mexico, the completed subassemblies were shipped back to the Midwest.

How did things work out? Did cost go down by 90 percent? Did the company become more competitive?

Well, there were some unanticipated problems.

For example, there was the extra work required by the company's procurement staff. Keeping track of all those parts arriving in the Midwest, in shipment to Mexico, in the Mexican plant, and in shipment

---

GLOBAL SUPPLY CHAINS

As long as cost, quality, and timeliness are consistent with competitive requirements, it makes sense to source globally. Each part of the supply chain should be located for maximum performance.

Coordinating global supply chains requires a specific process that streamlines activities, eliminates wasted time, and prevents poor quality. If managed correctly—including the use of business intelligence such as activity-based costing—global supply chains can provide low-cost performance.

On the other hand, a supply chain that is not optimized may not be competitive. Interestingly, many companies are resorting to inventory buffers, multiple suppliers, and other ways of "hedging their bets" in response to an increasingly complex and underperforming distribution system.

This response can only lead to higher cost, lower quality, and poor response. I wonder if these companies have access to activity-based business intelligence. If not, they may not be aware of their deteriorating performance.

Activity-based business intelligence can help companies determine which processes, product elements, and service elements should be outsourced. This intelligence can help them choose the right supply chain parameters to ensure low cost and efficiencies.

In the twenty-first century, supply chains are global—just as markets are global. High performance companies are those that use business intelligence to make sourcing choices that improve profit performance.

back to the Midwest turned out to be a major headache. The company set up a special group in procurement just to keep track of all this movement.

Another problem was the quality of the subassemblies, which was poor. Many of the subassemblies required rework when they arrived in the Midwest. A special group of engineers was assigned to the problem, and a special rework group was established in the company's midwestern plant to correct the problems.

What happened to cost? Well, procurement staff and engineers are quite costly. They require salaries, benefits, and resources to support them. Overall cost went *up*, not down.

A visible symptom of all the extra work was an additional seven weeks to complete a customer order. The company had lost one of the main advantages of domestic manufacture—short lead times and flexible response. The company's customers weren't happy about this either.

The irony was that the company's conventional cost system predicted that costs would go down, not up. If direct labor went down, overhead (according to the cost system) would go down, too. But the conventional labor-based cost system missed all the additional activity (and associated cost) required to service the Mexican plant.

Fortunately, the company recognized these inaccuracies and omissions before it was too late. It brought the subassembly operation back home to the Midwest. Costs went back down, and both quality and customer service improved substantially. Along with this, the company built an ABC system to provide improved cost information for future decisions.

Outsourcing Processes

You would think that outsourcing a process would be pretty straightforward. Review the income statement, identify the high-cost areas, determine that a particular process is not "strategic," and solicit bids from outside vendors. The difficulty is that accounting information does not provide any information about the underlying process and its appropriateness for outsourcing.

Take the case of the aerospace company that wanted to outsource its payroll department. This department employed about 60 people to process 40,000 checks each week.

This was a high-cost area that was just waiting to catch the attention of the accountants. To make matters worse, the lowest third-party bid was *40 percent* lower in cost per check processed.

This was an open-and-shut situation for outsourcing—or so it would seem. Yes, it was a high-cost process. Yes, the internal cost was higher than the outside vendor's price. But did the quality of the outside vendor match the internal quality? Also, did the internal process have the potential to match the costs of the third-party vendor?

An ABC study of the payroll process revealed the sources and causes of cost. It showed that a few simple changes would reduce cost by 40 percent, with further opportunities for progress.

Did this new ABC information change the decision? The answer is yes, even though payroll was deemed nonstrategic. Not all such stories have a happy ending, but in this case the enthusiasm of the people working in the payroll department coupled with the insights from ABC convinced management to keep payroll in-house.

SUMMARY

Incorrect cost information can put you on a crisis course from which you may never recover. It may lead to problems you can ill afford in today's competitive environment. You may focus on the wrong priorities and solve the wrong problems.

The ways you can be led astray are many, but they include

- Setting the wrong prices
- Selling the wrong products and services
- Focusing on the wrong markets
- Serving the wrong customers
- Designing costly products and services
- Cutting cost but failing to reduce cost
- Not controlling government spending
- Making incorrect sourcing decisions

Even worse, your cost system may tell you not only to stay on one of these courses, but to increase your speed, too. The faster you go, the further behind you get.

KEY TERMS

ABC.   Activity-based costing.
Activity-based costing (ABC).   A method of measuring the cost and performance of activities, products, and customers. In product costing

applications, for example, ABC allows costs to be apportioned to products on the basis of the actual activities and resources consumed in producing, marketing, selling, delivering, and servicing the product.

Conventional cost system.   An older, traditional cost system that uses direct material and labor consumed as the primary means of apportioning overhead. This was adequate when the overhead cost of indirect activities was a small percentage of the direct labor consumed in actually making products. But today, automation has reduced direct labor substantially, leaving indirect activities as a far more significant cost factor. For this and other reasons, using direct labor as a primary apportioning device can cause significant costing distortions and poor strategic decisions.

REFERENCES

1 Robin Cooper, "You Need a New Cost System When ...," *Harvard Business Review*, January-February 1989, pp. 77–82.

2 Peter B. B. Turney and James M. Reeve, "The Impact of Continuous Improvement on the Design of Activity-Based Cost Systems," *Journal of Cost Management*, Summer 1990, pp. 43–50.

3 The source of Figures 1–3 and 1–4 was Paul Collins of World Class International, Ltd.

CHAPTER 2

The Limitations of Managing with Accounting Information

What is wrong with accounting information? Not a great deal if your purpose is financial reporting, because this is the purpose for which accounting systems were created.

Yes, there have been scandals. Enron was the biggest of them all. There have been well-publicized restatements of earnings for major companies like MCI, creating embarrassment for accounting firms as well as potential liability.

And there is definitely room for improvement. For example, financial statements should include additional disclosures about nonfinancial issues. These disclosures include profit and loss information about different segments of the business as well as performance information by major business process—disclosures made possible by the methods described in this book.

But those scandals and restatements are related to financial reporting, not to the use of financial information for internal purposes. Generally speaking, for external purposes, financial accounting systems work reasonably well.

Our focus here is the use (and misuse) of financial information for management decision-making purposes. Financial systems were not designed to provide useful, accurate information for internal use. So it is not surprising that financial accounting information has limited utility for internal decision making.

The difficulty in most organizations is that prior to activity-based costing (ABC), the financial system was the *only* system that provided financial information. If you wanted to understand the details of financial performance or to analyze the financial impact of a decision, the only information was according to generally accepted accounting principles.

Let's take a closer look at why the limits of accounting information are so important today.

MANAGING IN THE NEW MILLENNIUM

Managing today is different from managing 20 years ago. The world is more competitive, with new opportunities and new risks. New management practices and methods of organization are pervasive. We measure success in different ways. Information technology has transformed the way we do business.

These changes increase the *value* of accurate, useful financial information. They also increase the *penalty* for using inaccurate and misleading financial information.

The New Competitive Environment

Global competition was not part of our lexicon before the 1980s. Now major sectors of the economy are dominated by foreign competitors.

The pace of technological change has accelerated rapidly. Products once took years to develop and stayed on the market for decades. Now products are routinely replaced every 18 months or even faster.

Productivity is accelerating as organizations leverage the investments they made in technology during the 1990s. No one can afford to stand still while competitors take advantage of business-to-business (B2B) Internet supply chains, outsource back-office processes to low-cost countries, and make other competitive changes.

Expectations of corporate accountability are heightened today. Companies are expected to be "green," to comply with a strict code of business ethics and practices, to enhance the quality of life in the communities in which they operate, and to adhere to acceptable labor practices.

Terrorist threats, antiglobalization demonstrations, wars, stock market bubbles, and the like are part of today's world. They are a reality over which we have little control.

The lesson from all this? You need business intelligence—not financial accounting information—at your fingertips. You need business intelligence so that you can change your plans intelligently and fast. However, if you use financial information from the accounting system, you may make the wrong choices and suffer the consequences—going out of business, downsizing, reorganizing, laying off workers, outsourcing, and so on—you know the score.

New Business Practices

Survival—let alone success—in this new competitive environment is no longer assured by "business as usual." Successful organizations have a new way of managing and a new standard of performance.

New management practices have transformed the requirements for business intelligence. These practices demand timely and accurate information about resources, processes, outputs, and customers—information that is not found in accounting systems. They include

- *Lean organizations.* Lean organizations are customer-focused organizations. Their products and services, and the processes that supply them, delight their customers with high quality, excellent service, flexible response, and high value. They do this without extraneous product or service features and without activities that are not valued by the customer. They utilize advanced management practices, including continuous improvement, just-in-time process flow, people involvement, quality function deployment (QFD), and supply-chain management. They are agile in the face of continually, and unpredictably, changing customer opportunities.

- *Six sigma.* Sigma (σ) is a statistical term used to denote the amount of variability in a process, product, or service. The six sigma method is used to design or redesign processes to remove the sources of variability and increase quality. Developed by General Electric, six sigma is widely used to improve quality and increase customer value.

- *Balanced scorecard.* The balanced scorecard is a carefully selected set of performance measures derived from the organization's strategic plan and strategy map. To provide balance in strategy execution, performance measures are grouped into customer, business improvement, organizational health, and financial perspectives. The balanced scorecard corrects the tendency to focus narrowly on measures from the financial accounting system.

- *Information technology.* Information technology has enabled vast changes in the way organizations function. Supply-chain management systems, for example, have transformed product logistics. The Internet has transformed the ordering of products and services, mining data about these orders, and also the customer experience.
- *Business process management (BPM).* BPM combines information technology with process tools, such as six sigma or ABC, to modify core processes in order to reduce cost and time. These methods create sustained reductions in process cost and time.

These new business practices are changing the way leading organizations work. Leading organizations now follow different principles of organization, process, and measurement. These principles include

- Strategic focus
- Customer value
- Process
- Quality
- Measurement (relevance, consistency, timeliness, accuracy, and balance)
- People involvement
- Learning

Leading organizations are focused around a sound strategy. Their purpose is to execute the chosen strategy successfully in order to create a defined result. Their task is to deploy their resources and align their activities in the pursuit of success.

Leading organizations are attuned to their customers' desire for value. They emphasize activities that add value for their customers and delete activities that are not value-adding. Non-value-adding activities—such as rework of quality problems—add time, waste, and delay, but do not improve the customer's outcome.

Leading organizations emphasize process over form. A process is a linked chain of activities that collectively deliver value to the customers. The activities in a process flow horizontally across an organization; they do not match the vertically aligned boxes of the organization chart. Managing processes rather than boxes on the organization chart is the key to managing customer value.

Quality is a given in leading organizations. Customers do not value products or services that fail to meet their requirements. Nor are customers willing to pay for poor quality. Six sigma (no more than two defects per million) is the minimum quality standard of companies such as Motorola.

Leading organizations pay attention to what and how they measure. And for good reason. What you measure is what you get. If you measure the wrong things, you get the wrong results. Let's take a look at the key measurement principles:

- *Relevance.* Measures must be relevant to the chosen strategy. Improving the measure should enhance strategic success.
- *Validity.* The measure should be a valid representation of the goal you want to meet. For example, if the measure improves, does this mean that you will be closer to meeting the goal?
- *Consistency.* Measures should be consistent with modern business practices. A measurement of process quality is consistent, but an accounting measure that encourages decisions that *reduce* quality is not.
- *Timeliness.* Measures must be reported within the time frame required to make a decision. A relevant measure is of no value if it is late.
- *Accuracy.* Measures must be accurate. They must measure what they purport to measure; otherwise they will introduce error into the system.
- *Balance.* Measures must provide balance across the organization's perspectives. Short-term financial considerations, for example, should be balanced with the need to grow and to prepare for future success. Balance ensures that long-term success is not sacrificed for short-term results.
- *Low cost of measurement.* The cost of measurement should not exceed the value received from the information. A high cost of measurement is unpopular with management, which complains about the effort and cost of measurement.

Leadership comes from the top, but participation comes from the grass roots of the organization. Leading organizations involve their people in everything they do. People embody knowledge and capability. It is through people that systems and technology are combined to provide value to customers.

Developing intellectual property (such as software) and growing the knowledge and capability of the organization's people and systems are key characteristics of leading organizations. Through continuous learning, these organizations build their intellectual property, human resources, information systems, and performance management systems into a competitive weapon and financial asset.

ACCOUNTING MEASURES NOT DESIGNED FOR INTERNAL BUSINESS INTELLIGENCE

Unfortunately, accounting systems provide limited business intelligence. Let's look at three aspects of accounting systems—the general ledger, variance reporting systems, and cost accounting systems.

General Ledger

The general ledger is the central repository of financial accounting information. Depending on the organization, this information will comply with the rules of generally accepted accounting principles (GAAP), government accounting standards, utility reporting standards, or some other such system.

While the general ledger may comply with these rules, it was not designed to provide business intelligence for the modern organization. Here are some of the challenges:

- *Accounts versus activities.* Accounting systems report information on salaries, supplies, depreciation, and other accounts. They provide no information about the activities that make up the work of the organization. Without this information, management cannot assess the value of these activities, nor understand the cost and other measurement attributes of these activities.

- *Functions versus processes.* Accounting systems organize account information according to the functions on the organization chart. They report the cost of *departments* but not of *processes.* Because processes cut horizontally across functions, it is not easy to correct for this deficiency without installing an ABC system.

- *Verifiability and conservatism versus economic value.* Accounting rules emphasize verifiability and conservative valuation rather than economic cost. The costs of building intellectual capital and growing human resources, for example, are expensed rather than capitalized. This creates a massive distortion for companies like Microsoft that have built their business on these intangibles.

- *Noneconomic fixed-asset accounting.* Fixed-asset accounting is another victim of rule making. Depreciation calculations follow arbitrary accounting conventions and rarely have any economic meaning. Government organizations don't compute depreciation—the cost of fixed assets is usually omitted from operating budgets. How can you understand (and manage) the cost of an asset over its life cycle using distorted or missing information?

- *Legal entity versus business entity.* Accounting systems organize financial data according to legal entity. Entity A and entity B will each have their own accounting system and reports. But what if A sells to B, who packages A's product and sells it to C? A and B are jointly serving the customer C, but their accounting systems are independent, so they can't see each other's costs. Would it not be useful to view A and B's activities as a single business? This would allow A and B to collaborate and manage their joint process. (Thank goodness we can build *virtual* ABC models to resolve this problem.)

Variance Reporting Systems[1]

Accounting systems in manufacturing companies may include variance reporting systems. These systems are designed to flag areas of cost that are higher than standard, allowing management to take action to correct the underlying problem. Their existence owes much to the influence of Frederick Taylor and the scientific management movement in the early part of the twentieth century. Do these systems work in modern organizations? The answer is no, and here's why:

- *Measurement of direct labor.* Direct labor is the cost of people who touch the product during its manufacture. It is the focal point of variance reporting systems. This may have made sense 100 years ago, when direct labor accounted for as much as half of product cost.

  Setting direct labor standards today puts the measurement focus on a cost that has mostly disappeared as a result of technical and organizational change. It takes the focus away from the myriad nondirect labor activities inside and outside of production that account for most of the cost in a modern manufacturing company.

- *High cost of measurement.* Variance reporting systems can be quite costly to maintain. One company, for example, measured direct labor for each of 60 operations in the assembly of its products. These 60 operations took less than four minutes *total* and represented a fraction of the average product's cost. The cost of measuring the variances was *more than* the cost of the product.

- *Misdirected cost-reduction efforts.* In many cases, variance reporting systems allocate overhead to products as a percentage of direct labor. This percentage may be very high—in the hundreds of percent—because the majority of the cost in modern manufacturing organizations is overhead. This creates the *appearance* of a causal relationship, with overhead being dependent on direct labor cost. As a result, production and engineering may incorrectly focus on the reduction of direct labor in the mistaken belief that overhead cost will also go down. In some cases, overhead has gone *up* because of these mistaken efforts.

- *Negative impact on quality.* Using financial variances to evaluate performance can have a negative impact on key performance metrics, such as quality. For example, a purchase-price variance may encourage the purchasing department to change suppliers in order to reduce purchase costs. This may improve the performance of the purchasing department—but at the cost of reduced product quality and disrupted production.

  This kind of scenario occurred at the Tektronix Oscilloscope Group. Purchasing reduced the purchase price of a part by changing suppliers. The cost "saving" was significant for purchasing—it represented about half of the target favorable purchase-price variance for the year. But the quality of parts from the new supplier was poor. The parts did not fit. Considerable time was spent reworking the parts to make them fit, and production was disrupted. The purchasing department looked good, but the financial performance of the division as a whole (and the satisfaction of its customers) suffered.

- *Unwanted output and poor quality.* Using labor standards to evaluate direct labor efficiency creates an incentive to build products. Managers may lengthen production runs to report favorable overhead efficiency variances. Product piles up in the warehouse, and quality decreases because of the extra time it takes to discover defects.

It doesn't matter that there's no customer for the output. "Efficiency" is up. But overall cost is higher and customer satisfaction is diminished.

Cost Accounting Systems

Manufacturing companies use cost accounting systems to report the cost of inventory and cost of sales—as required for financial reporting purposes. Service organizations such as banks, hospitals, and insurance companies don't "manufacture" products. They don't maintain inventories of their services, so they don't need a product cost system for financial reporting purposes. As a result, service companies don't have manufacturing-style cost accounting systems.

You might think that manufacturing companies are therefore better informed than their service counterparts. Unfortunately, this is not true, because the product costs reported by cost accounting systems are often inaccurate and incomplete. Experience shows that reported product costs often err by hundreds or even thousands of percent.

The problem is in the underlying methodology of conventional cost systems. They adhere to the assumption that *products cause cost*. Each time a unit of the product is manufactured, it's assumed that costs are incurred.

This assumption does make sense for certain types of cost. For example, the cost of activities performed directly on the product unit, such as direct labor, fits this assumption.

Direct labor activities are performed directly on a valve, housing, circuit board, or other product unit. If the number of units produced goes up, more units must be assembled, and the cost of direct labor will go up, too.

The assumption does not work, however, with activities that aren't performed directly on the product units. For example, some activities are performed on batches of products. When you set up a machine to produce a type of part, you produce a batch of the parts rather than an individual unit. Conventional cost systems deal with units, not batches.

Other activities are performed for a product type. When you change engineering specifications on a product, for example, all future product units are affected, not just a single unit. Again, this doesn't fit into the unit methodologies and assumptions of conventional costing.

The correct assumption—one that fits what's really happening—is that activities cause costs, and products (and customers) create the need to perform activities. But this assumption requires a very different type of cost system, as the next chapter shows.

For now, let's continue our investigation of why conventional cost systems report inaccurate product costs. Fundamentally, it's because they try to assign cost directly to product units rather than assigning cost to activities first, then from activities to product units.

Figure 2–1 is a case in point. Products A and B are different. Product A is a mature product. Its technology is quite simple. As a result, it requires little inspection effort. However, it does require quite a lot of direct labor for assembly.

In contrast, product B is a new product. It's a complex product that requires a lot of inspection time, although the amount of labor required to assemble it is less.

The conventional cost system assigns overhead cost to products A and B using direct labor hours. Direct labor hours is a measure of the activity that is performed directly on each unit of products A and B. It's also a commonly used costing measure in conventional cost systems.

FIGURE 2–1

Conventional Costing Breaks Down When Products Differ

Product A	Product A
100 units	**Conventional:**
1 inspection hour	$3 \times \$120 = \$360/100 = \$3.60$
3 direct labor hours	**ABC:**
	$1 \times \$100 = \$100/100 = \$1$
Product B	**Product B**
100 units	**Conventional:**
5 inspection hours	$2 \times \$120 = \$240/100 = \$2.40$
2 direct labor hours	**ABC:**
	$5 \times \$100 = \$500/100 = \$5$
Inspection overhead = \$600	
Cost per direct labor hour = \$120	
Cost per inspection hour = \$100	

Direct labor hours, for example, *do not* accurately measure the cost of inspecting products A and B.

The problem is that the inspection effort is determined by the relative complexity of the products, not by the amount of direct labor. In fact, direct labor is negatively correlated with complexity in this example.

Product A, the simpler product, requires less inspection effort than B, but more direct labor time. Therefore, product A is overcosted by the conventional cost system. Product B, which requires more inspection effort but less direct labor time, is undercosted.

What if we assign cost based on the number of inspection hours? Would that be a better measure?

The number of inspection hours required for each product is a direct measure of the inspection effort. Thus, it provides a more accurate measure of how much of the cost of this activity each product consumes. (Inspection hours is an example of the type of measure used in ABC, as the next chapter explains.)

The extent of conventional costing inaccuracy can be demonstrated by calculating the inspection cost of each product. The results of this are shown in Figure 2–1. Notice that product A's cost falls by 72 percent and product B's cost increases by 108 percent. The relative cost of the two products is the reverse of what it was before.

The example in Figure 2–1 is typical of the inaccuracies reported by conventional cost systems. When inaccuracies are removed by introducing an ABC system, it's quite common to see shifts in cost ranging from drops of 10 to 30 percent to increases of several hundred (or even thousand) percent. Not surprisingly, such large shifts in cost lead to drastic reappraisals of product mix and pricing strategy.

Conventional cost systems often report the cost of products to fractions of a penny. For example, the cost of a product may be reported as

$$\$5.258637$$

Carrying product costing to such precision is a tribute to the power of computers and the accountant's traditional desire for exactness.

It's a brave manager who challenges the accuracy of such a precise number. *But keep in mind that precision doesn't necessarily mean accuracy.* Computers always compute with great precision. But if you put in inaccurate numbers or use the wrong computational methodology, all you get is precision without accuracy.

So how much should you trust the $5.258637 that your conventional cost system gives you? Too often the first digit is wrong. Worse yet, the decimal point is often in the wrong place, too.

HOW WELL DOES YOUR COST SYSTEM WORK?

Try this in your company. Call the accountants and ask them to give you the overhead or burden rate. Write down the unit of measure—it may well be dollars per labor hour or dollars per machine hour.

Then ask the question, "When was this rate last updated?" The answer may surprise you. It is common to find that cost system burden rates have not changed for five years or more.

Now take a look at the unit of overhead measure—labor hours or machine hours. If two products use the same number of labor hours, should they cost the same? What about packaging, setups, material moves, and other activities that may be different between the two products?

If you determine that the two products should not cost the same, the next question is, "How large is the costing error?" Without a modern activity-based costing system in place, it is difficult to know for sure.

You can, however, estimate the errors using your knowledge of the process. Bear in mind, however, that experience shows that managers understand the direction of the error but almost always underestimate its magnitude.

Which companies are most likely to have large inaccuracies in reported product costs? It's those with large amounts of overhead and high diversity.

In recent years, the importance of overhead has increased tremendously. Knowledge workers, particularly engineers and software specialists, have replaced much of the direct labor force in many plants. In some cases, overhead outside the plant—engineering, marketing, and distribution—has increased to the point where it exceeds direct labor. Figure 2–2 illustrates this trend.*

The more overhead there is, the greater the chance for distortion in reported costs. As a rule of thumb, overhead that exceeds 15 percent of total costs may cause inaccuracies in conventional systems.

But overhead is not the only factor. Diversity—products or services that differ from one another—is another important factor. Diversity results from differences in the design, maturity, volume, or scope of the

* Companies with a global supply chain should remember that their material cost includes overhead incurred by first- , second- , and third-tier suppliers.

FIGURE 2-2

The Importance of Overhead Cost

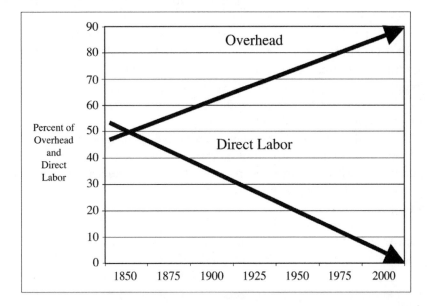

The relative importance of direct labor and overhead have changed over the past 130 years. Thus, yesterday's cost systems, which focus on direct labor, must give way to cost systems that focus on overhead.

product or service. Each difference makes a product unique and gives it a unique cost.

As an example of diversity, consider a valve manufacturer that makes valves of different sizes in iron or brass. This diversity exists to meet different customer needs. A hospital, as another example, has patient diversity. One patient may be in the hospital for a triple heart bypass, while another is in for gallbladder removal. Each product or service requires different activities or different amounts of the same activities and therefore incurs a different overall cost.

You can easily visualize the effects of diversity by looking at the opposite case. Think about the company that makes only *one* product and has only *one* product cost. All products are identical, and therefore they must cost the same.

For an example of this, let's go back to the 1920s, to the Ford Motor Company's Rouge River Plant. At that time, Ford made only one product—

the black Model T. Ford's cost system was very simple, but quite effective in costing these automobiles. One person counted the cars coming out of the plant. This count was then divided into the total cost of running the plant over the period of the count.

The Ford Motor Company today is a very different company from what it was in the 1920s. Ford offers its customers millions of choices of product and option configurations. Henry Ford's cost accounting system could not have coped with this level of diversity. Even a modern conventional cost accounting system would fail to report accurate product costs for such a diverse product set.

In addition to product diversity, modern organizations have areas of activity (and cost) that were unimportant in the 1920s. These include distribution, marketing and sales, research, human resources, and information systems. In many cases, these nonproduction costs exceed the cost of production.

What does cost accounting have to say about these costs? The answer is nothing. Costs that are incurred outside of the plant are not inventoried under accounting rules and are excluded from product cost.

This is a costly omission because of the size of these costs—nonproduction costs typically exceed production cost—and because of hidden differences in the cost and profitability of customers, distribution channels, markets, and so on that consume these costs in different ways.

To understand the importance of measuring nonproduction costs, we need the help of ABC. In the case of Dayton Technologies, ABC revealed the hidden differences in product and customer costs. Figure 2–3

FIGURE 2–3

The Importance of Product and Customer Profitability Analysis

Customer	Sales $	ABC Product Margin	% Margin	All Related Customer Costs	Net ABC Customer Margin	Net Margin %
Customer A	$2,312,470	$828,517	36%	$524,784	$303,734	13.13%
Customer B	$4,937,170	$872,710	18%	$162,752	$709,958	14.37%

This ABC analysis from Dayton Technologies shows the importance of accurate product and customer costs. Compare the product and net margin for customer B. Does the inclusion of customer-related costs change your mind about the value of this customer?

shows the result of the analysis and confirms the importance of including both production *and* nonproduction costs in the analysis.

Figure 2–3 shows two views of profitability for two customers. Based on an accurate assignment of product cost, customer A has an ABC product margin twice that of customer B. Including customer-related costs, however, provides a completely different picture. Customer A consumes much more design and special ordering costs than does customer B, and thus is actually *less* profitable than customer B.

Without knowing the difference in the cost to serve each customer, it might be tempting to offer more discounts and engineering and order services to customer A. Knowing the difference in cost to serve might lead to new, more profitable strategies for dealing with each customer.

To sort out the costs of different products and customers, you need an ABC system. If you don't have one, and you are a manufacturing company, you will be making decisions based on inaccurate and incomplete cost information.

Inaccurate product costs make it difficult to correctly choose which products to sell, how to price those products properly, and how to design them for low cost. Not knowing the cost to serve customers can send you chasing after the wrong customers and markets.

The price of using inaccurate and incomplete information can be very high, even deadly in some cases. But, on the other hand, how much does it cost to get accurate information?

Happily, the answer is not much—*if you use the right system.*

THE DEATH SPIRAL

Conventional cost accounting adheres to the requirement that all manufacturing costs be attached to the products produced. This *full absorption* of costs can be dangerous to a company's health.

Full absorption creates an incentive to produce even when there are no customers in sight. Production triggers the attachment of cost to units. If these units disappear into a warehouse, the cost disappears with them. But are your customers happy, and are you making money?

Sounds similar to the problem of unwanted output and poor quality resulting from direct labor efficiency, doesn't it?

But things can get much worse with full absorption.

What happens if you don't have enough products to absorb the cost? Let's say you dropped some products or outsourced parts to the Far East. What happens if you have no other products or parts to take up the slack?

In these circumstances, full absorption can lead to a "death spiral." It works like this.

An uncompetitive product is dropped, but not all of its costs go away. You can't close part of the plant, turn off half the boiler, or saw machines in half. Also, it may take months to reduce engineering and other staff.

Now, what happens to that leftover *unabsorbed* cost?

Simple: It gets dumped into the unfortunate remaining products. So now their reported costs go up.

Up pops another "uncompetitive" product—the next candidate for outsourcing. This product is dropped. But some of its costs remain and are reassigned to other products. So the cycle repeats itself, taking profits and competitiveness into a downward spiral as products are plucked away.

It doesn't take many cycles of the death spiral before there's nothing to do but close the plant. Even if the plant doesn't close, it may be badly wounded. Plus, many jobs are lost and sent overseas unnecessarily. (It doesn't have to happen this way. Chapter 3 will show how the unabsorbed costs can be identified as *idle-capacity costs* and isolated from product costs.)

When seen in its entirety, the death spiral seems to be too obvious a trap for anyone to fall into. But don't bet on it. It happens more often than you'd like to think. Take a look at what happened in the case of an electronics plant.

It's quite sobering to walk into this plant. It's one of the plants where a large company manufactures electronic products. It's a huge plant, occupying over 750,000 square feet. But a lot of the space is currently unused.

Most of the workforce is gone. Some of the jobs and products that once flowed off the assembly lines have been taken over by some far-off "Asian tiger." Other jobs are victims of new technology—some new electronics products require half the labor of the products they replaced.

This is an all too familiar story in U.S. electronics plants. What happened? And what was the role of cost information?

It started back when the plant employed about 5,000 people. This was a time of turmoil for the parent company. It was coping with the aftershocks of rapid technological change and global competition.

As a result of these new forces, the plant saw a drop in market share for its products. This forced a layoff of over 2,500 employees in just one year.

A key problem for the plant was that the overhead cost was difficult to eliminate as volume went down. The direct workforce could be reduced in step with volume. Laying off management and technical people, how-

ever, took more time. And other overhead costs—such as the costs of space, heating, and maintenance—just didn't go away.

The result was that volume decreased by half, but overhead went down by only a third. This dramatically increased the overhead cost per unit of production—by 25 percent over the previous year.

This led to a dramatic cost increase for some products. The unit cost of one product, for example, went up by 25 percent, that of another by 40 percent.

This created a further problem for the plant. Since it was one of several plants located around the world, the parent company was constantly evaluating the issue of sourcing. Where in its manufacturing network should any given product be produced?

Answering sourcing questions was a complex issue that required consideration of product design, manufacturing technology, quality, and strategy in addition to cost. Cost was a key issue, however, because the plant went head to head with low-cost plants located in Asia. It was also important because of the drop in the plant's market share resulting from increased competition.

The company had a staff group that made recommendations for sourcing. This group required that every plant make calculations on a full-cost, *fully absorbed* basis.

This put the plant at a significant disadvantage because it had to spread the costs of all the excess capacity over fewer remaining products. In other words, the costs of manufacturing associated with activities and assets *not used* by the current products were included in the calculated product costs.

As a result, the plant lost its highest-volume product within one year. This product was considered too costly to manufacture after its overhead rate increased by 65 percent.

The plant's response? It launched an *Excellence* program to introduce *world-class manufacturing* into the plant. Using just-in-time, focused factory, and other world-class concepts, the aim was to make the plant *world class* within a year. To do this, the program focused on cutting throughput times, improving quality, reducing cost, and focusing totally on the needs of its customers.

The Excellence program had immediate success. Throughput time on one product, for example, was reduced from three to four weeks under the old functional approach to 1 hour and 50 minutes on the first day of the new Excellence program. Asset turnover doubled as work-in-process inventories fell. Quality improved dramatically—about 99 percent of the products met customer quality standards by the following year.

These dramatic improvements were recognized when the plant received a national productivity award. The plant was also featured in business publications as one of the top plants in the United States and one of the best hopes that U.S. manufacturing could become competitive with the rest of the world.

Unfortunately, volume fell another 30 percent in year two. As a result, overhead cost per unit increased 36 percent over the previous year. This was despite the dramatic improvements in the plant's manufacturing capabilities and efficiencies (Figure 2–4).

Year four saw the plant in a holding pattern. Market share increased for some key products. The additional volume—and continued improvements in efficiency—caused the overhead cost per unit to fall. Optimism increased.

FIGURE 2–4

The Death Spiral

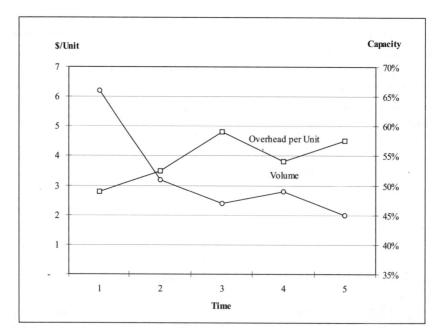

"Doing it right" doesn't guarantee survival. This electronics plant struggled to stay in business despite winning awards for quality, productivity, and service. The culprit? It was a cost system that unfairly penalized products for excess plant capacity.

However, the plant was actually fighting a rear-guard action. It was now below 50 percent capacity, and overhead cost per unit was still increasing despite continued improvements in quality and productivity. This cost increase was enough to push several products into the loss-making column. Another major product was pulled from the plant and moved offshore.

Much energy was expended to keep all remaining products by demonstrating the plant's ability to produce them efficiently. Emphasis was placed on strategic advantages in quality and service, particularly the ability to manufacture and ship product to customers on a timely basis. (After all, products manufactured at this plant for the U.S. market didn't have to spend six weeks on a boat from the Far East.)

Would year five be the last flutter in the death spiral, or would the plant manage to survive for another year?

The bad news is that the plant has continued to lose products to offshore plants.

The good news is that the plant was able to continue operating. Some new products were introduced to replace current products. The plant introduced some innovative ways of distributing its products that reduced cost and improved customer service. Low-technology work (not suited to the plant's manufacturing capability) was moved to a new satellite plant in Mexico.

This plant did survive. What's frightening about this story, however, is that one of the best plants in the United States had to fight for survival. It's a story of a world-class plant in a losing battle with improper cost information.

SUMMARY

Managing organizations requires good-quality information about the contribution of each part of the organization to overall financial health. This information helps management make appropriate decisions about product and service offerings, prices, levels of customer service, and other strategic factors.

The value of accurate and relevant financial information has increased with changes in management practices, technology, and information systems. Rapid change and a brutal competitive environment further increase the value of this information.

Conventional sources of financial information—the general ledger, variance reporting systems, and cost accounting systems—may be useful for financial reporting purposes, but they are unable to provide accurate relevant information for management decision making.

This inability is not academic. There is an accumulated body of evidence showing that reliance on financial accounting information can damage an organization's financial strength and competitive ability. The death spiral example described in the chapter shows what can happen when management relies on poor-quality financial information.

The only solution available is to create a set of financial and nonfinancial information using entirely different measurement principles. This solution is called activity-based costing, and it is introduced in the next several chapters.

KEY TERMS

Balanced scorecard.   Goals and performance measures derived from the organization's strategic plan and strategy map. Goals and performance measures are grouped into perspectives, including financial, customer, internal business process, and organizational health and learning.

Business process management (BPM).   A method of improving the performance of business processes by combining information technology with management methods such as six sigma and activity-based costing.

Cost accounting system.   A financial accounting method for costing manufactured products to allow the proper recording of cost in the inventory and cost of sales accounts.

Death spiral.   The sequential outsourcing or dropping of products in response to inaccurate cost information.

Flexibility.   The ability to respond to changing customer needs quickly.

Full absorption.   A requirement in financial accounting that all overhead costs, even those associated with unused capacity, be assigned to existing products.

General ledger.   A database of financial accounting information. The general ledger classifies financial information according to rules such as generally accepted accounting principles (GAAP), government accounting standards, or utility reporting standards.

Just in time (JIT).   (1) The determination of workload based on the use of output by the next activity; (2) continuous improvement.

Lean organization.   A customer-focused organization with high standards of quality, service, response, and value.

Quality function deployment (QFD).   The design of products and processes based on customer requirements.

Six sigma.   A method used to design or redesign processes to remove the sources of variability and increase quality. Sigma (σ) is a statistical term used to denote the amount of variability in a process, product, or service.

Variance reporting system.   A system designed to flag costs that are higher than standard, allowing management to take action to correct the underlying problem.

World class.   An organization that has achieved high standards of business performance and is continuously improving its ability to meet its customers' needs.

REFERENCES

1 Peter B. B. Turney and Bruce Anderson, "Accounting for Continuous Improvement," *Sloan Management Review*, Winter 1989.

PART TWO

Why Activity-Based Costing Is the Solution

OK, you're convinced.

Accounting information is not a good source of business intelligence and may be actively dangerous. For example, the consequences of conventional costing—such as selling the wrong products, mispricing products, or failing to cut costs—are not acceptable in today's competitive world.

So what's the solution?

It's something called activity-based costing—or simply ABC for short.

ABC is not an upgrade of conventional approaches. It's too late for upgrades; the problem is too serious for "business as usual" solutions. What's needed is a radically different approach to costing—the ABC approach.

ABC is a methodology for providing information that helps organizations improve their financial performance. In Part 4 of this book you'll see how ABC is used in an activity-based improvement program.

For now, let's focus on the method itself. To do this, Part 2 answers the following questions:

- What is ABC?
- How does ABC correct the deficiencies of conventional cost systems?
- What problems and opportunities are revealed by ABC?
- Why is ABC consistent with the business practices of leading organizations?

CHAPTER 3

The ABC Innovations

Cost information should reveal problems to tackle and opportunities to exploit. But, as the previous chapters show, that's not always the case. Conventional cost systems *actually* hide problems and fail to identify opportunities.

Relying on conventional cost information is similar to the situation in Figure 3–1. Conventional cost information is like the sea that hides dangerous rocks. On the surface, all appears calm and smooth; there's no inkling of unprofitable products and customers, and there's no hint of waste in the operations. And, like the unwary mariner, the good ship *Enterprise* sails on, oblivious to the dangers lurking below.

What the ship's officers need to do is look below the surface of misinformation and find business intelligence. This would reveal the rocks of high-cost processes, unprofitable products and services, and unprofitable customers and markets. These are the things that sink the ships of enterprise in today's competitive world.

And nearby lurk sharks of all kinds. Some may be hungry competitors looking for the opportunity to bite off parts of your organization. Others may be hostile asset strippers or hungry conglomerates. Trouble is like the smell of blood to these sharks. Underperforming organizations are their feeding grounds.

Can the aspiring high-performance enterprise be saved from these perils?

Yes. It can.

FIGURE 3−1

Rocks and Sharks

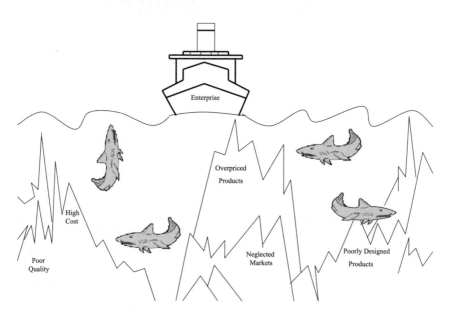

Submerged rocks and sharks are hidden problems and opportunities. ABC information is business intelligence that helps organizations reveal and identify the problem rocks, improve their competitive position, and avoid getting eaten by sharks.

Part of the solution is to provide activity-based information about the rocks lurking below the surface. This *business intelligence* reveals those tasty morsels that are so prized by the sharks of competition. Which products, services, and customers are unprofitable? Which products are improperly priced? Which profitable products, services, and customers are being neglected? What opportunities are there for reducing the cost of products, services, and processes?

To answer such questions—to avoid the rocks and sharks—today's organization needs a high-performance navigation system. Activity-based costing (ABC) is just such a system. ABC allows you to identify problems and plot a safe course to solutions and opportunities. It does this by providing intelligence about activities and cost objects.

Activities are descriptions of the work that goes on in an organization. Entering the details of a customer order at a computer terminal, setting up a machine, inspecting a part, helping a welfare client, issuing a driver's license, and shipping a product are examples of activities.

Cost objects are the reasons for performing activities. They include products, services, customers, clients, and other strategic factors. Entering the details of a customer order at a computer terminal (the activity), for example, is performed because a customer (the cost object) wishes to place an order.

Activities and cost objects are basic to the ABC concept. This chapter shows you how ABC enables organizations to

- Report more accurate cost information
- Provide useful information about activities

You will also find out

- What ABC reveals about the rocks and sharks that lie in wait for the unwary
- How well ABC fits the business intelligence needs of aspiring high performance organizations

It's also important to realize that navigation by ABC information is imperative whether times are good or bad. The tide is in during boom times, covering up the rocks and sharks. Don't wait until the recession hits and the tide is out. You may already be on the rocks, with the sharks tearing you to pieces.

HOW ABC GIVES YOU ACCURATE COST INFORMATION

The underlying assumption of ABC is quite different from that of conventional costing. Conventional costing assumes that products cause cost. ABC is more realistic. As shown in Figure 3–2, ABC assumes that activities cause cost and that cost objects create the demand for activities.

As an example of how activities and cost objects work, let's say you're involved in auditing the quality of printed circuit boards. Auditing product quality is an activity. It involves checking the thickness of the circuits, the placement and sizes of holes and pads, and the flatness of the board.

FIGURE 3-2

The ABC Assumption

The basic assumption of ABC is very simple: Work is performed to create products, deliver services, and satisfy customers. Work requires resources—such as people—and the incurrence of cost. This may be a simple concept, but it's exactly the way your organization and every other organization functions.

Auditing product quality requires various resources. These include the individuals doing the work, the equipment and software to measure and record the checks made on the boards, and floor space for the work.

Auditing product quality is performed on boards received from the finishing department. Receiving a batch of boards from finishing is the trigger that initiates the work associated with the activity. The boards themselves are the cost objects that demand activity (more boards means that auditing product quality must be performed more frequently).

ABC's underlying assumption makes intuitive sense when it is applied to an activity such as auditing product quality. But why does it make a difference in the accuracy of reported cost information? To understand this, let's take a closer look at how ABC helps in costing the quality-auditing activity.

The First Innovation: Assigning Costs to Activities

The first innovation of ABC is the assignment of costs to the activity. This assignment is based on measurements of resources used. These measurements are called *resource drivers*.

For auditing product quality, the cost of the people doing the work is assigned based on determinations of who is doing the work, how much of each person's time is spent on auditing boards, and their salaries, taxes, and benefits. Figure 3–3 shows the costs assigned to the auditing product quality.

In contrast, in a conventional cost system, costs are assigned to departments or cost centers. The costs of auditing product quality, for example, would be buried in the costs of the finishing, or quality control department.

In most cases, activities *are not defined* in conventional cost systems. You can learn about the cost of the quality control department, but you'll rarely find any information about the cost of an activity within the departmental accounts.[1] This is unfortunate, because knowledge of activity costs helps focus attention on the structure, flow, and performance of the process. Departmental costs, however, highlight the cost of "functional silos" rather than processes.

Knowing what each activity costs helps in identifying important activities—those with the greatest potential for cost reduction. Knowledge

FIGURE 3−3

The Cost of the Activity Auditing Product Quality

Test equipment depreciation	$58,000
Salaries, taxes, and benefits	88,000
Space	61,000
Supplies	6,500
Fixtures	120,000
Total activity cost	$333,500
Number of boards tested	667,000
Cost per board	$0.50

Cost information directs attention to high-cost activities and confirms that savings have been achieved subsequent to improvement.

of activity cost also allows you to model the impact of cost-reduction actions and to subsequently confirm that savings were achieved.

The Second Innovation: Assigning Costs to Cost Objects

ABC's second innovation is the way in which costs are assigned to cost objects. *ABC assigns activity costs to cost objects based on activity drivers that accurately measure consumption of the activity.*

An *activity driver* is a measure of the consumption of an activity by a cost object (such as a product, service, or customer). The number of hours devoted to each product by engineers, for example, measures each product's consumption of engineering activity.

In the case of auditing product quality, for example, "number of batches" best measures the consumption of the activity by each type of board. This is because the activity is performed on only one board in each batch received.

Figure 3–4 shows how this works for two different types of printed circuit boards. The activity driver "number of batches" assigns twice as much ABC cost to board B as it assigns to board A. This is correct, because board B is audited twice, whereas board A is audited only once.

The audit cost per batch in Figure 3–4 is the same for both products ($50). This assumption is correct if the audit of each board takes roughly the same length of time and uses the same resources regardless of the product checked.*

If this is not true (if, for example, board A requires significantly more checking time because it has more holes), then a different activity driver should be used. "Number of holes checked," for example, might be a better activity driver, because it would capture variations in effort from one board type to another.

Now, let's take a moment to look at how conventional costing treats the auditing product quality example.

Conventional costing uses direct labor hours as the activity driver. Direct labor hours is a measurement of the "touch labor" needed to produce a unit of the product.

In Figure 3–4, the cost assigned to board B by direct labor hours is half that assigned to board A. This is because board B uses half the direct labor hours of board A.

---

* The cost per batch is computed by the ABC model. It is based on the cost of resources assigned to the activity divided by the number of batches processed.

FIGURE 3-4

Accurate Product Costs

Quality Auditing Acitivity		
Cost per batch		$50
Cost per direct labor hour		$25
	Product A	**Product B**
Number of direct labor hours	4	4
Number of batches produced	1	2
Conventional costs (DLH)	$100	$50
ABC costs (batches)	$50 ✓	$100 ✓

✓ Accurate product cost

ABC assigns cost to products based on their use of activities, which is cost per batch in this example. The result is accurate product costs.

This would be correct, however, only if the amount of direct labor correlated well with the number of batches. In this case, it doesn't, so the two products are miscosted by substantial margins. Board A is overcosted by 100 percent, and board B is undercosted by 50 percent.

The inaccuracy in conventional costing for this example is no accident. It results from limitations in the activity driver used to assign cost; direct labor hours (DLHs) *do not* accurately measure the use of the auditing product quality activity by the products.

ABC corrects for this inaccuracy by choosing an activity driver that does accurately measure cost consumption by each product. In this case, the driver is the number of batches. However, it could have been the number of holes checked, the number of checking hours, or the number of direct labor hours if the facts had been different.

In short, ABC is generally superior to conventional costing because it provides more accurate product costs. This occurs because ABC uses *more activity drivers* and *more types* of activity drivers than conventional costing. Like a toolkit that contains a wide range of tools, ABC uses different activity drivers to fit different circumstances.

The Number of Activity Drivers

ABC systems have multiple activity drivers. Conventional systems, on the other hand, usually have only one activity driver, although occasionally they have as many as three.

More activity drivers allow ABC to "do it more ways" than conventional cost systems. Most organizations have many activities that are consumed in different ways. It's unlikely that one activity driver (such as direct labor hours) can capture this diversity even in a small organization.

Types of Activity Drivers

Another fundamental innovation of ABC is the recognition that there are different levels of activity in most organizations. Different activity levels require different types of activity drivers (Figure 3–5).[2]

Let's start by looking at three levels of activities that exist in many organizations. These are *primary* activities that are assigned directly to cost objects. The first examples of activities are from a manufacturing company:

- *Unit* activities are performed on units of the product. Tapping threads in a metal elbow is an example of a unit activity.

FIGURE 3-5

Activity and Driver Levels for a Manufacturing Company

Activity	Activity Driver
Unit	
Assembly	Direct labor hours
Stamping	Machine hours
Batch	
Moving material	Number of moves
	Time per move
Inspecting first piece	Number of runs
	Time per inspection
Product	
Modifying product design	Engineering hours
Programming CNC machines	Programming hours

ABC recognizes that activities relate to cost objects at different levels and that different levels require different activity drivers.

- *Batch* activities are performed on batches of products rather than individual product units. Setting up a machine to produce a batch of products and inspecting the first piece of the batch are examples of batch activities.
- *Product* activities benefit all units of a particular product. An example is preparing a numerical control (NC) program for a product.

Accurate assignment of the cost of unit activities is accomplished by using measures of the product unit. The number of direct labor hours needed to tap threads in a metal elbow, for example, accurately measures operator effort.

Unit activity drivers are the *only* activity drivers found in conventional cost systems. Direct labor hours, machine hours, material cost, and product units are all used as unit activity drivers.

The problem is that unit activity drivers do not cost nonunit activities accurately. You need batch activity drivers for batch activities and product activity drivers for product activities.

Let's see why this is the case.

In Figure 3–6, making tools and dies is a product activity; it benefits all the units of each product type produced. The cost of this activity ($1,000) is assigned to the two products using a *unit activity driver* (the number of units) and a *product activity driver* (the number of products).

Under ABC in Figure 3–6, the product activity driver assigns an equal amount of cost ($500) to each product. This assumes that manufacturing tools and dies for each product requires the same amount of effort.

Product B, however, is a low-volume product, so its cost per unit ($10) is much higher than that of product A ($2.50). This makes sense, because product A is able to spread its activity cost over a larger number of units ($500/200).

Under conventional costing, the unit activity driver assigns cost directly to the product units. This has two results. First, each unit receives an identical amount of cost ($4). Second, product A has more product units than product B, so in total, product A receives the lion's share of the cost ($4 × 200).

Both of these conventional costing results are wrong. *It's the products that benefit equally, not the units.* The high-volume product shouldn't pick up more cost simply because it's successful.

ABC avoids these conventional costing errors by picking activity drivers that match the type of activity. Setting up a machine to produce a

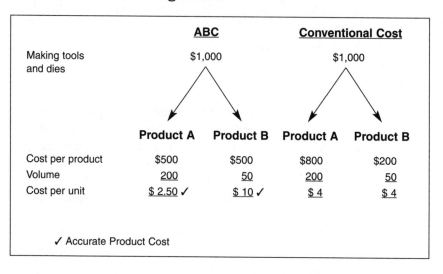

FIGURE 3-6

Accurate Cost Assignment

ABC first traces the costs associated with the product type to the product type. These product-level costs are then assigned in a second step to the units of the product type. In this example, the high-volume product correctly receives less cost per unit than the low-volume product.

batch of parts is costed using the number of setup hours or the number of production runs. Changing the engineering specifications of a product is costed using the number of engineering change notices or the number of engineering change hours.

Activities and activity drivers in service organizations are different from those in manufacturing companies. But they can also be grouped into unit, batch, and product (service) levels. Figure 3–7 provides examples of activities and drivers in a bank's loan application process.

Assignment to Customers

ABC's activity cost assignment innovation works just as well for customers as it does for products and services. The difference is that the cost of customer activities is assigned to customers rather than products or services.

Examples of customer activities are processing customer orders and providing engineering and logistic support. Activity costs are assigned to customers using activity drivers such as the number of customer orders

FIGURE 3-7

Activity and Driver Levels for a Loan Application Process in a Bank

Activity	Activity Driver
Unit	
Process loan application	Number of loan applications
Analyze loan application	Number of loan applications
Batch	
Loan applications accumulated by type	Number of batches by loan type
Service	
Design imaging routine for loan type	Software design hours
Design loan product	Marketing hours

Service organizations are no different than manufacturing organizations. Their activities and activity drivers are unique, but they fit the same framework as any other organization.

and the number of customers. Alternatively, activity cost is assigned to customers based on the time taken to meet each customer's unique needs.[3]

Activity costs vary from one customer to another—sometimes inadvertently and sometimes by design. For example, a customer who asks for an insurance quote over the phone is more costly to service than one who uses the Internet.

ABC makes customer profitability analysis possible. It provides new perspectives on service to customers, and it opens up opportunities for analysis and action that don't exist in conventional cost systems.

Experience with ABC shows how valuable customer profitability analysis can be. In most companies, customer profitability varies significantly from customer to customer and market to market. It is therefore important to know which customers are profitable and what distinguishes a profitable from an unprofitable customer.

The reader will find many examples of the use of ABC to determine customer profitability in this book. Chapter 10 is dedicated to the topic.

Secondary Activities

Not all activities are primary activities and directly associated with products, services, or customers. Human resource activities, for example, do not directly benefit products, services, or customers. Instead, the human resource department supports other activities in the organization by maintaining employment records, hiring staff, and carrying out other activities related to human resource management. These activities are called *secondary* activities.

It's easy to cost secondary activities. For example, you can measure how much time is spent by human resource personnel on each human resource activity. So the cost of a career counselor can be assigned accurately to the career counseling activity.

But you can't assign the cost of secondary activities directly to cost objects. The career counselor, for example, doesn't provide career counseling to products and customers.

The solution is to assign the cost of human resource activities to the activities they support. This can be done based on the relative amount of time spent, the number of employees serviced, or some other direct measurement of the service provided.

The final step is to assign the cost of the primary activity—including its share of the support activity cost—to the cost objects. This is done using an activity driver that accurately measures the use of the primary activity by the cost object.

Some secondary activities do not support other activities. Public relations and charitable activities, for example, are difficult to associate with internal customers (they are not used or consumed). How should

---

THE IMPORTANCE OF SECONDARY ACTIVITIES

In today's global economy, companies are consolidating, outsourcing, and managing secondary activities as a source of competitive advantage. Companies are investing in software, hardware, communications, and other resources to provide world-class support services such as customer support and technical support.

The cost of these secondary activities is significant for many companies, yet they are often excluded from costing models because they cannot be traced directly to products. This is unfortunate, because secondary activity costs can impact outsourcing decisions such as whether to locate a call center in Toronto or Bangalore. They also allow profit assessments of products and customers that use the secondary activities.

these costs be handled in the ABC model? One solution is to allocate them to other activities. Inevitably, the result will be somewhat arbitrary. A preferred solution is not to assign their cost to other activities or cost objects. (Fortunately, the majority of secondary activities do support internal customers and can be assigned in a meaningful way).

Assignment of secondary activities is a source of intelligence about an increasingly important component of modern business organizations. It provides useful economic information about strategic support services and avoids the inaccurate allocations of conventional costing systems.

The Third Innovation: Information about Activities

The third innovation of ABC is the improved quality of information about activities. In addition to cost information, you find nonfinancial information about the work that is being done.

For example, government and other nonprofit organizations are interested in knowing how much of their cost is devoted to core activities. A core activity is one that relates directly to the mission of the organization. Helping welfare clients find housing, for example, is a core activity in a government housing agency.

Core activities differ from enabling activities—activities that support core activities. Preparing paychecks for housing counselors is an enabling activity because it supports the core activity of providing housing to welfare clients.

ABC can provide useful information to managers about core and enabling activities. When core activities are tagged with a "core" or "enabling" attribute in the ABC model, they can be reported to management by type. Managers can examine these reports and identify opportunities to eliminate enabling activities and redirect efforts to mission critical work.

Electric utilities use ABC to distinguish between activities that support the core regulated business and those that support unregulated energy services. Supplying power to residential and business customers is usually regulated and subject to cost-plus pricing rules. Nonregulated business—such as supplying Internet service over power lines—is not subject to electric power regulations (although it may be subject to different regulations).

It is helpful to electric utilities to tag their activities in the ABC model as regulated or unregulated. This ensures that only the cost of regulated activities are associated with the regulated revenue stream. Reports can also be prepared on the cost and profitability of unregulated energy services.[4]

ABC can also provide useful information for continuous improvement programs. Attributes for cost drivers, performance measures, and non-value-added can be added to activities in the model. Figure 3–8 shows examples of these types of information for the auditing product quality activity.

The number of holes in the circuit boards and the density of the circuitry determine how much effort is required to perform the activity (more holes and greater density require more work). These determining factors are called *cost drivers*.

It's also important to know how well the activity is carried out. Indicators of the results achieved through an activity are called *performance measures*.

The primary performance measure for auditing product quality is the frequency of warranty returns. This measure should be zero if the audit is done right every time. A second measure is how often the checker's inspection mark is missing from a board. A batch that isn't stamped as having been checked will be returned by the customer.

FIGURE 3–8

Information about Performance

Auditing Product Quality Activity

Type of activity:
- Non-value-added

Cost drivers:
- Number of holes
- Density of circuitry

Performance measures:
- Percent of boards returned
- Percent of boards not marked

In addition to the costing benefits of ABC, nonfinancial information, such as that shown here, permits judgments about performance.

The ABC analysis in Figure 3–8 shows that the auditing product quality activity is a *non-value-added* activity. A non-value-added activity is one that *does not* contribute to the value received by the customer.

The purpose of the auditing product quality is to catch defects in the printed circuit boards. The defects can then be corrected prior to shipment of the boards to the customer.

This is a valuable contribution as long as the quality of prior processes is suspect. But the customer does not value the auditing per se. Instead, the customer values the quality of the boards.

A better solution is to improve the quality of prior processes so much that the auditing activity is no longer necessary to ensure that the customer receives a quality product. At that point, the auditing product quality activity can be discontinued without any negative impact, and cost is reduced.

Providing nonfinancial information such as this may be the most important contribution of ABC. Its purpose is to help improve the activity. It is, after all, better to improve or eliminate work than to assign the cost of unnecessary work to products or customers more accurately.

ABC supplies a powerful combination of nonfinancial and cost information. These two types of information help in managing—and improving—the performance of the organization.

THE DRAMA OF ABC

Introducing ABC into an organization has a dramatic impact. Perceptions about profitability—about which products, services, and customers are profitable and which are unprofitable—completely change. The understanding of where and why cost is incurred also changes.

You may suspect that many of your products, services, and customers are unprofitable. You may have seen case studies that show the extent to which ABC reveals miscosted and unprofitable cost objects. But none of this really prepares you for the truth about your own company.

Once you're over the shock, what do you do with this radically new picture of your organization?

The first step is to grasp the implications of the ABC information. Which products, services, and customers are unprofitable? Why are they unprofitable? What changes (such as revising product mix or increasing prices) are required to correct the problems? Is your market focus wrong? Are your processes too costly? What opportunities are there for cost reduction?

The second step is to create an action plan for improvement. This plan lays out the specific actions needed to improve your competitive position.

As an example, let's look at the impact of ABC at one company. It's a dramatic story, but one that has been repeated in many organizations.

The Printed Circuit Board Division[5]

At the time we moved into the marketplace, we had none of the skills and experience of our competitors. Our performance was poor, and we were losing money. Fifty percent of our products were generating less than three percent of our revenues. However, we didn't have accurate cost information, so we didn't know how unprofitable these products were.

General Manager of the Division

The story began when the printed circuit board (PCB) division of a large high-technology company received permission to sell to outside customers. Previously, the division had sold only to other parts of its parent company.

Venturing into the marketplace created major challenges for the division. How was it to set prices for the printed circuit boards? (Products had previously been priced according to the parent company's transfer price rules.) Which products would provide the most profit potential? Which customers should be the target of sales efforts?

The division was certainly not short of choices. It manufactured more than 4,000 different types of printed circuit boards. These boards varied in number of layers, density and placement of circuitry, fineness of the metal lines, and size and placement of the holes.

The division produced boards that covered all segments of the printed circuit board market. These segments covered a wide range of products, from simple low-technology boards to complex high-technology boards.

The Conventional Cost System

The division's cost system reported two types of cost. Material cost consisted of sheets of copper, fiberglass laminate, and metals (such as gold and nickel) used in plating. Material costs were traced to boards via the bill of materials. All other manufacturing costs (overhead plus direct labor) were assigned to boards using machine hours. Nonmanufacturing costs were expensed.

FIGURE 3-9

The Pareto Effect

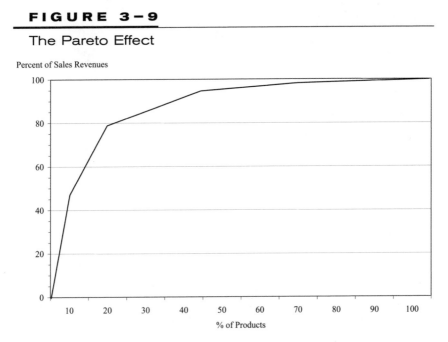

Percent of Sales Revenues

% of Products

Pareto's rule (20 percent of what you do accounts for 80 percent of what you care about) is alive and well in this company. The large numbers of products with low sales value owe a lot to inaccurate cost information.

Few at the division would have staked their reputation on the accuracy of the product costs reported by this system. It was felt that a single activity driver (machine hours) could not cope with the complexity and range of activities in the production process. Also, excluding nonmanufacturing costs—about 40 percent of total cost—was believed to be a critical omission.

A review of the relationship between products and sales revenues provided a startling premonition of what would be learned from ABC (Figure 3–9): 60 percent of the products accounted for only 6 percent of the plant's revenues. It seemed likely that the effort to sustain these low-value products greatly exceeded the revenues earned.

ABC's Impact

It took two years to complete the ABC system, but its design was radically different from that of the cost system it replaced (Figure 3–10).

FIGURE 3–10

Activity Drivers

Number of work orders

Number of customer orders

Number of part numbers

Square feet per circuit board

Number of layers

Number of sheets

Number of times pressed

Number of holes drilled

Number of sides

Image perimeter

Number of tests

Examples of activity drivers used by the ABC system employed at the printed circuit board division of a large high technology company.

The results were quite startling, too.

Products The old cost system painted a picture of comfortable profitability. There wasn't a single product with a profit margin of less than 26 percent.

The picture portrayed by ABC couldn't have been more different. Fully 25 percent of the products were unprofitable when only manufacturing costs were included. Over 75 percent were unprofitable when all costs, including the nonmanufacturing costs, were included. Figure 3–11 shows what this picture looks like for a representative product line.

How could such a radical shift in cost and profitability occur?

Let's examine one of the products that looked quite different under the two systems (Figure 3–12).

The manufacturing cost of board XYZ under ABC is 542 percent higher than the old standard cost ($4.30 versus $0.67). The total cost is a whopping 2,930 percent more than the old cost.

Why such big increases in cost?

The old cost system used machine hours to assign costs to the boards. This resulted in a "peanut butter" spread of overhead across different products regardless of variations in volume and use of nonmachine activities.

FIGURE 3-11

New Perceptions of Product Profitability

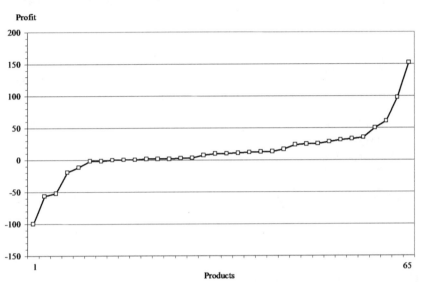

The printed circuit board division had thought that all products were profitable by a comfortable margin. But a close look at the product line, using ABC as the navigational aid, showed that over a quarter of the products were unprofitable (based on manufacturing costs), and over a half of them were no better than breakeven. When nonmanufacturing costs were included, a full 75 percent were unprofitable.

The fact was, board XYZ required extra nonmachine activities and special handling. For example, the board required hand taping and untaping of the gold borders, hand pinning and unpinning of each image during routing, extra baking of the edges, and hand sanding of the edges. All this special handling required additional support overhead. None of these "extras" were picked up by machine hours.

On the nonmanufacturing side, the cost of accepting and launching an order for board XYZ was estimated by ABC to be $800. With only 50 units manufactured, the ordering cost per unit was $16.

None of the real costs of the board were known under the old cost system. So, at a selling price of $1 per board, the division was happy with the profit margin of 33 percent reported by the old cost system. In reality, the margin was about a negative 2,000 percent—not a cause for happiness, but rather a cause for action.

FIGURE 3–12

The Cost of Low-Volume, Specialty Products Increases
by Orders of Magnitude

	Printed Circuit Board #XYZ			
	Price ($)	Cost ($)	Margin ($)	Margin (%)
Conventional standard cost	1.00	0.67	0.33	33
ABC manufacturing cost	1.00	4.30	(3.30)	(330)
ABC total product cost	1.00	20.30	(19.30)	(1,930)

ABC radically changes perceptions of cost and profitability for low-volume, specialty products such as this one.

Customers An ABC analysis of customer profitability was a real shocker.

Several key customers were found to be extremely unprofitable. These were customers that had previously appeared profitable under the old cost system. As a result, they had been targeted with additional sales effort.

Let's look at a typical customer. This customer bought 22 different boards from the division, all of them reported as profitable by the old system. Six of these products were also reported as profitable by ABC, but the remaining 16 were losing money.

Figure 3–13 shows the bottom line. Although the first few products were profitable, the addition of losing products brought down the cumulative profit earned from this customer. By the time all the money-losers were included, the division was losing nearly $45,000. This represented 30 percent of the revenues earned from the customer.

Management Buy-in How did management respond to such shocking information?

Production, engineering, and general management bought in readily. But marketing initially rejected the results.

A profitability analysis of key customers was presented at a meeting that included representatives of marketing. The marketing staff rejected the ABC costs and walked out of the meeting.

FIGURE 3-13

ABC Reveals the True Profitability of Customers

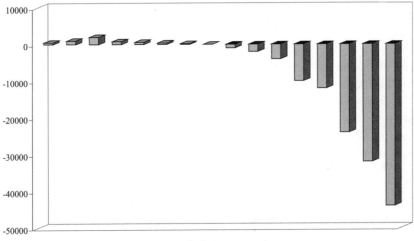

ABC shows a loss of about $45,000 on this customer. This stunning revelation contrasts with a previous picture of solid profitability. The question: Why was marketing spending so much time with this customer?

Such resistance was not surprising. Marketing had put a lot of effort into those customers, and it was natural that the department felt let down. The ABC information was correct, but it showed that the marketers' efforts had been misdirected.

Further discussions turned the situation around. Marketing eventually accepted the validity of the ABC methodology and the ABC information. From that point on, the marketing department was in the vanguard of the changes that ensued.

Plan for Change   The division moved rapidly to take advantage of the knowledge gained from ABC. In particular, ABC was used to

- Develop a strategy for targeting products and customers. (Which market segments should the plant focus on? What was the profile of the desired type of customer? How could sales be guided to sell the right kind of products to the right customers?)

- Develop a strategy for improving product design and improving the production process. (How could products be designed to reduce cost? Which cost-reduction opportunities promised the greatest payoff? What arrangements for the supply of raw materials best served the needs of the plant? What performance measures were most appropriate?)

The lessons? Be prepared for dramatic results. Take active steps to ensure that everyone in the company buys into ABC and the actions that are implied. And, finally, prepare an action plan that ensures positive change.

How the division used ABC information to guide these decisions is an important part of the story. We'll return to this story in Chapter 9 to see how the division was transformed into a high performing and profitable competitor.

CONSISTENCY WITH THE BUSINESS PRACTICES OF LEADING ORGANIZATIONS

In Chapter 2 we examined the limitations of accounting information for management decision making. In this chapter, we've introduced ABC, a new way of creating business intelligence for leading organizations. How consistent is ABC with the business practices of these organizations?

Strategic Focus

ABC provides an important link between strategy and operations. It reveals the activities that are currently in place to execute strategy. A review of these activities helps identify activities that are not supporting strategy and allows work effort to be redirected to activities that contribute to strategic success.

Customer Value

ABC reports information about what matters to the customer—how well each activity contributes to meeting the customer's needs. Measures of performance in terms of quality, time, and cost, for example, are reported for each activity.

ABC reports this information when you need it. The printed circuit board division of a large high-technology company, for example, reports the cost of poor quality in each process on a shift-by-shift basis (three

DOES ABC APPLY TO SERVICE AND GOVERNMENT ORGANIZATIONS?

Many examples of ABC—like the printed circuit board division case—involve manufacturing organizations. Does ABC apply well in service organizations such as financial institutions, hospitals, and government agencies?

The concepts of resources, activities, and cost objects are universal to all organizations. A hospital, for example, has resources (the physical facilities and staff) that perform activities (such as nursing) and provide services (such as open heart surgery) to benefit customers (the patients).

Service organizations have all the ingredients needed to make ABC a success. They typically have a lot of overhead cost representing many different activities. They have large numbers of cost objects with a lot of diversity (many different types of services and customers). Most service organizations and government agencies also lack even rudimentary cost systems. Some are an untapped opportunity to improve financial performance and face the same intense competitive and financial pressures found in the manufacturing sector.

ABC has been applied successfully in many service organizations and government agencies. The service organizations include hospitals, physicians' clinics, telecommunications companies, call centers, insurance companies, software companies, banks, and credit unions. Government agencies in which ABC has been applied include transportation and social services agencies and military organizations such as the U.S. Marine Corps and the U.S. Army.

times per day). This information is used daily to set priorities for efforts to eliminate quality-related problems.

Process

ABC is built around a process view of the organization. Cost is reported by activity, and activities are organized by process.

This information directs improvement efforts and provides feedback on what the improvement has accomplished.

For example, the Oregon Cutting Systems Division of Blount was surprised by the amount of waste associated with a batch-processing activity. This waste was revealed by the ABC system. The batch-processing activity was a large process that required lengthy setup, and there was a great deal of parts movement to and from the process. This centralized approach was inconsistent with Oregon Cutting Systems's cellular manufacturing operation; the cost and time associated with the extra activities were excessive.

OREGON CUTTING SYSTEMS DIVISION

The Oregon Cutting Systems Division of Blount, Inc., is the world's leading manufacturer of cutting chain for chainsaws and chainsaw accessories. It sells its products to professional loggers, chainsaw manufacturers, and consumers in 112 countries on six continents. Formerly called Omark Industries, Oregon Cutting Systems is a U.S. pioneer in applying world-class manufacturing techniques.

Quality

ABC sends the right quality signals, signals that encourage continuous improvement. Direct measurements of activity performance—quality, time, and cost—focus the activity on what is important to customers.

Carefully chosen activity drivers correctly signal cost-reduction opportunities. For example, the activity driver "number of different part types" shows that products with many low-volume parts are costly. It also shows that redesigning products to use high-volume common components reduces cost.

Measurement

ABC information is relevant to a wide array of business decisions in all types of organizations. It is useful for strategic decisions such as pricing and product and customer mix, and also for operational decisions that need process-based cost information.

ABC reports *accurate* customer and product costs. It does so by using more and more types of activity drivers to assign costs to customers and products. It assigns nonmanufacturing cost in addition to manufacturing cost. The result is that ABC costs are often substantially more accurate than conventional costs.

Experience with organizations that have implemented ABC suggests that the cost of doing so can be modest. Importantly, successful implementations of ABC such as in the printed circuit board division have a positive return on investment.

Recent developments in ABC have reduced the cost of ABC implementations and increased its value. Time-based ABC systems—described in Chapter 6—promise lower costs for development and system maintenance and a higher return on investment. This is particularly important in complex environments such as distribution and financial services, where a costing system might otherwise be cost-prohibitive despite many hidden opportunities to increase profit.

SUMMARY

Even the best-run organization has problems and opportunities—rocks and clear channels—that are hidden from view. And there are always hungry competitors, asset strippers or conglomerates—the sharks—waiting to take advantage of those who run aground on the rocks.

ABC provides important information about problems and opportunities. It reports accurate cost information that leads to a better understanding of product and customer profitability. It also provides information about activities that is useful in directing and accelerating improvement efforts.

And, unlike conventional costing, ABC fits the information needs of the aspiring high-performance organization. It helps keep you off the rocks and out of the jaws of hungry sharks.

KEY TERMS

Activity.   A description of the work that goes on in the organization and consumes resources. Testing materials is an example of an activity.

Activity-based costing (ABC).   A method of measuring the cost and performance of activities and cost objects. It assigns costs to activities based on their use of resources, and assigns costs to cost objects based on their use of activities. ABC recognizes the causal relationship between cost drivers and activities.

Activity driver.   A factor that measures activity consumption by a cost object. If drilling holes is an activity performed on a board, the number of holes drilled could be an activity driver.

Attributes.   Labels attached to data in an activity-based cost system to signify the meaning of the data and to facilitate the reporting of information.
Batch activity.   An activity that is performed on a batch of a product. Inspecting the first piece of each batch is a batch activity.
Core activity.   An activity that directly supports the mission of the organization. Repairing a pothole in a road is an example of a core activity for a transportation department.
Cost driver.   An event or causal factor that influences the level and performance of activities and the resulting consumption of resources, elapsed time, and quality. For example, defective materials that lead to low product quality are a cost driver of procurement and production activities. An activity may have multiple cost drivers associated with it.
Cost object.   The reason for performing an activity. For example, products and customers are reasons for performing activities.
Customer activity.   An activity that provides value to external customers. Providing technical assistance is an example of a customer activity.
Enabling activity.   An enabling activity is one that supports a core (mission critical) activity. Preparing pay checks for workers in core activities is an example of an enabling activity. See also secondary activity.
Functional silos.   Vertical dimensions of an organizational hierarchy where functional considerations override organizational considerations.
Non-value-added activity.   An activity that is judged *not* to contribute to customer value. Also, an activity that can be eliminated without reducing the quantity or quality of output. An example is the activity of moving parts back and forth.
Performance measure.   An indicator of the work performed in an activity and the results achieved. An example is the average elapsed time to perform an activity.
Primary activity.   An activity that has an output that directly benefits external products, services, or customers. Providing a consulting service to a client is an example of a primary activity.
Product activity.   An activity that benefits all units of a type of product. Changing engineering specifications on a product is a product activity.
Resource dictionary.   A compendium of attributes of individual resources such as job positions, types of equipment, and other resource elements. Attributes include skills, capacity, activities performed, and other performance information.
Resource driver.   A measure of the cost of resources used by activities. It takes the cost of the resource and assigns it to the activities.
Secondary activity.   An activity that (1) has an output that benefits an

internal customer or (2) has only a general benefit and no measurable benefit to internal or external customers. Career counseling is an example of the first type of secondary activity. Public relations is an example of the second type of secondary activity. See also enabling activity.

Service activity.   An activity that benefits all units of a type of service. Designing a new retirement plan for a group of external customers is a service activity.

Unit activity.   An activity that is performed on a unit of a product or service. Attaching a resistor to a printed circuit board is an example of a unit activity.

REFERENCES

1 German cost systems with as many as a thousand cost centers have been documented. There are so many cost centers that each one may represent an activity. See, for example, Robert S. Kaplan, "Metabo GmbH & Co. KG," Case 9–189–146 (Boston: Harvard Business School, 1989).

2 The idea that there are different types of activities is not new. Authors that have discussed these concepts include P. M. Dunne and H. I. Wolk, "Marketing Cost Analysis: A Modularized Contribution Approach," *Journal of Marketing*, July 1977, pp. 83–94; W. J. E. Crissy and F. H. Mossman, "Matrix Models for Marketing Planning: An Update and Expansion," *MSU Business Topics*, Autumn 1977, pp. 17–26; and "Report on the Committee on Cost and Profitability Analyses for Marketing," *The Accounting Review Supplement*, 1972, pp. 575–615. R. Cooper was the first to identify unit, batch, product, and process activities as characteristics of manufacturing activity-based cost systems in "Cost Classification in Unit-Based and Activity-Based Manufacturing Cost Systems," *Journal of Cost Management*, Fall 1990, pp. 4–14. P. B. B. Turney and J. Reeve extended this analysis and included customer activities in "The Impact of Continuous Improvement on the Design of Activity-Based Cost Systems," Summer 1990, pp. 43–50.

3 See Chapter 6 for a discussion of time-based ABC.

4 Peter B. B. Turney, "Using Activity-Based Costing to Manage Profitability in the Energy Services Industry"(monograph), Electric Power Research Institute, Palo Alto, 1997.

5 This case study is based on research conducted by the author at the printed circuit board division of a large high-technology company. The name of the company is disguised.

PART THREE

What ABC Looks Like

This section answers the question: What does an ABC system look like? It describes how ABC systems are organized to supply information about an organization's activities, products, and customers.

If you're interested in using ABC to improve your organization's financial performance, Chapter 4 tells you

- *What* information about activities, products, and customers is available in an ABC system
- *Why* this information is useful for manufacturing, service, and government organizations

If you're interested in understanding *how* an ABC model works, Chapter 5 describes

- How cost is assigned to activities, products, and customers in standard and time-based ABC models
- How useful information is reported in the ABC model
- What ABC models in manufacturing, service, and government organizations look like

Chapter 6 describes some of the latest developments in ABC. Included are explanations and illustrations of

- Resource planning
- Activity-based budgeting
- Performance budgeting
- Decision simulation
- Time-based ABC

CHAPTER 4

The ABC Model

The power of activity-based costing (ABC) lies in its ability to clearly portray both cost information and nonfinancial information. This includes portrayal of the relationships between the two as well.

These capabilities are best described through an overall, two-dimensional model. This model is significantly different from those used in earlier ABC applications. Those earlier models were essentially one-dimensional and limited in their abilities to provide cost and process information about activities.

Even with their limitations, the earlier one-dimensional models were still far more enlightening than other tools in use at that time. Indeed, those first successes formed a solid foundation for the evolution of ABC. Thus, it's certainly worthwhile to begin any introduction with those earlier applications.

With an understanding of the one-dimensional foundation, discussion can then proceed to the current two-dimensional model. This second-generation model contains both cost information and nonfinancial information about activities and provides a more powerful management tool. It allows new applications of ABC and extends the reach of ABC to administrative processes, service organizations, and government organizations.

EARLY ACTIVITY-BASED COSTING

Early ABC systems were found mostly in manufacturing companies. They were used to improve the accuracy of reported product costs. They proved themselves in helping companies to determine better product mixes and to set prices based on both actual cost and customers' willingness to pay.

You've read of some early ABC successes in previous chapters. For example, you saw how small, yet significant, strategic gains could come quickly from an ABC analysis. You also saw how strategic insights from in-depth ABC studies could be so significant as to suggest changes in business direction.

These and other successes set the course for early ABC systems. The primary objectives of these systems were

- To improve the accuracy of product costs by carefully changing the type and number of factors used to assign cost
- To analyze the profitability of products, developing new insights into the causes of unprofitability and courses of corrective action

The Use of Early Systems

The initial objective of ABC in most plants in the late 1980s was strategic product costing. But that's *not* how most plants ended up using ABC information.

In plants at Honeywell, Nortel, General Motors, and other companies, ABC was intended for strategic product costing. In most cases, however, it was eventually put to other uses. These included

- *Additional strategic uses*, such as profitability analyses of customers, markets, and distribution channels
- *Internal improvement uses*, such as activity management, waste identification, prioritizing cost-reduction opportunities, and simulating the costs of alternative product designs

This broadened usage was a direct result of the wealth of information that companies found in their ABC databases. In addition to more accurate product costs, there was information about the work that was going on, the resources required to perform this work, and the reasons why the work was being performed.

Recognizing the value of this information, managers scoured ABC for insights into how to improve their production processes. Where was the greatest opportunity to eliminate waste? What specific changes in product design would lead to the greatest improvement in competitiveness for that product?

This search yielded useful information to support improvement efforts. But it also provided an equal amount of frustration and confusion. It was difficult to use ABC for *internal improvement* because it was designed for a different purpose: *product costing*. It was also difficult to take ABC outside of manufacturing to service and government organizations, where structural and strategic differences required a different type of ABC model.

The Limitations of Early Systems

The primary limitation of early systems was the absence of direct information about activities. This basically was a result of how overhead cost was dealt with.

Overhead cost was divided into broad cost pools. Each cost pool corresponded to a group of activities that were consumed by products in approximately the same way. The activities themselves, however, were not defined individually. As a result, cost was *not* traced to each activity. It was also impossible for the system to include operational data about the performance of activities.

This situation can be explored further with the aid of Figure 4–1. This figure illustrates an early system used at the John Deere Component Works (JDCW) to cost screw-machine parts.

The system in Figure 4–1 divides overhead cost into seven broad cost pools. Each cost pool contains the costs of a group of activities that are consumed by products in roughly the same way. Also, each cost pool is assigned to products using a unique factor that approximates the consumption of cost.

For example, look at the overhead cost pool for activities associated with production orders. Overhead consumption is assigned to the screw-machine parts using "number of production orders." Each individual screw-machine part consumes cost from the pool based on the *cost per production order* multiplied by the *number of times the part was ordered*.

For John Deere, this ABC system met the strategic goal of significantly improving the accuracy of reported costs. Products that were heavy consumers of activities were assigned more cost than products that were light consumers. For example, a frequently scheduled part received more cost than one that was scheduled only once per year.

An Early ABC System

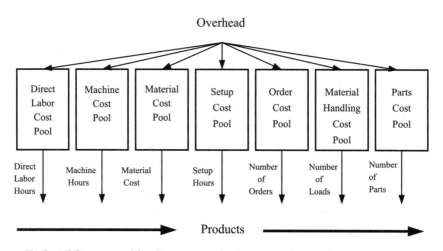

Early ABC systems, like this one at John Deere, broke overhead cost into a number of cost pools and used innovative ways of assigning cost to products. The result was a significant increase in the accuracy of reported product costs and important strategic insights.

More accurate product costs provided a *definite strategic advantage* for John Deere. At the time, JDCW was emerging from a sheltered role as a captive division and becoming a competitive entity that sold products to other companies. To do this successfully, JDCW needed accurate cost information to guide the choice of products to sell externally and to help set prices. ABC filled this need.[1]

Despite its clear advantages in supporting strategic decisions about product mix and price, the JDCW system was of limited help in supporting internal improvement. The system did not reveal the cost of individual activities, nor did it provide operational data about the performance of those activities.

Early ABC systems such as the one at John Deere could not be used to answer key operational questions. For example, how long did it take to perform the key activities? What was the quality associated with these activities? What factors increased the time and effort required to perform the key activities? The activity information required to answer these questions existed *outside* those early ABC systems.

TWO-DIMENSIONAL ACTIVITY-BASED COSTING

The desire for operational information about activities led to the appearance of a process-based ABC model. This was designed to supply information for internal as well as external improvement purposes. It is represented by the ABC cross in Figure 4–2.[2]

The ABC cross has two main views. The first is the *cost assignment view*. This is the vertical part of the model shown in Figure 4–2. It reflects an organization's need to assign costs to activities and cost objects (including customers as well as products and services) in order to analyze critical decisions. These decisions include pricing external and internal products and services, product mix, sourcing, product design decisions, and setting priorities for improvement efforts.

FIGURE 4–2

The ABC Cross

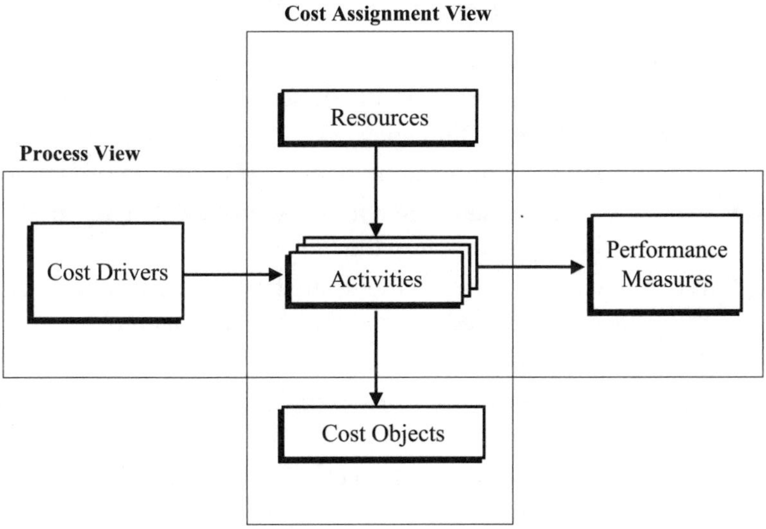

Activity-based costing has come a long way in a short period of time. Once thought of as just a better way of costing products, ABC now has more points of focus and additional uses. Cost information and nonfinancial information work together to yield strategic and operational insights.

The second part of the ABC model is the *process view*. This is the horizontal part of the model in Figure 4–2.

The process view reflects an organization's need for a *new* category of information: information about factors that influence the performance of activities (cost drivers) and performance measures that show how well the work is being done. Organizations use this information to improve performance and the value received by their internal and external customers.

Let's take a closer look at the cost assignment and process views, beginning with the cost assignment view.

The ABC Cost Assignment View

The cost assignment view provides information about resources, activities, and cost objects. The underlying assumption is that cost objects create the need for activities, and activities create the need for resources.

Let's examine this underlying assumption further with an example. Assume that a valve manufacturer receives an order for a specific type of valve. The order is the cost object. This cost object—filling the order—might require the following kinds of activities:

- Required materials are identified, ordered, received, and stocked.
- Production is scheduled, and material is requisitioned and moved to the production area.
- Tapping and machining equipment is set up before production.
- The materials are melted in a foundry, molds are made, and the molten metal is poured into the molds.
- When the metal cools, the molds are broken and removed, and the parts are machined, tapped, finished, and assembled.
- The first piece of each production run is inspected for defects.
- Parts are moved from one process to another upon completion of each process step.
- The completed valves are inspected, packed, and shipped to the customer.
- The customer is invoiced, and payment is received and processed.

The cost object—the order for valves—creates a demand for activities. These activities, in turn, create a demand for resources. The *flow of cost*, however, is in the opposite direction. This is shown by the downward arrows in Figure 4–2. Notice that the flow of cost is from the resources to the activities and then from the activities to the cost objects.

To explore this flow further, consider salaries and other costs for the valve inspection activity. The amount of salaries assigned is determined by the number of people performing this activity, the proportion of their time spent on the activity, and their salary level. Other costs are assigned in some logical way reflecting their use by the activity. The total cost of the inspection activity is then assigned to the valves based on the frequency of inspection and the effort expended to complete the inspection of each type of valve.

This cost information, provided by a modern ABC system, is quite different from the information provided by early ABC systems. You still get markedly more accurate product costs. But you also get high-quality information about activities and cost objects.

Information about Activities

Unlike earlier systems, second-generation systems identify the significant activities and attach costs to them. Knowing the cost of activities makes it easier to understand why resources are used. Moreover, the information provided makes it much easier to address such questions as

- Which activities require the most resources?
- What types of resources are required by these activities?
- Where are the opportunities for cost reduction?

It was difficult to answer such questions with early ABC systems because they focused on accurate product costs rather than on improved information about activities.

Information about Customers

Modern ABC systems have more points of focus. For example, they've added the customer as a cost object. This makes sense, since customers' needs for support often vary. Also, customer-support activities *are costly* in many companies.

In one plant, for example, careful study revealed that several key customers were actually unprofitable. This certainly came as a shock to marketing. Key customers are supposed to be profitable; that's why they're *key*.

But in this case, the fact was that marketing had been misled. The conventional cost system had shown that these key customers were profitable. Consequently, marketing had put a lot of effort into building up these customers.

Without ABC, marketing wouldn't have discovered the high cost of supporting these key customers. It would also have been blissfully unaware of the strategic implications of this knowledge—the need to redirect marketing resources to develop a profitable customer base.

Information about Nonmanufacturing Activities

The addition of customer focus takes costing into new parts of the organization. Customer-support activities, for example, invariably take place outside the manufacturing plant—in marketing, order entry, and customer service. In contrast, early ABC systems resided exclusively within the walls of the plant. Their focus was exclusively on manufacturing activities.

It makes better business sense to focus just as carefully on nonmanufacturing activities as on manufacturing activities. To verify this, look at the income statement for your company. Add up the nonmanufacturing costs. Then compute them as a percentage of total manufacturing and nonmanufacturing costs.

You may be shocked at the significance of these costs. Nonmanufacturing costs representing 50 percent or more of the cost of running a company are not uncommon. But these are the very costs that are completely ignored by cost systems that focus exclusively on the plant.

Deluxe Corporation's ABC model focused exclusively on nonmanufacturing activities. These were primarily "cost-to-serve" customer activities, such as order entry and order processing, and administrative activities, such as managing human resources, that supported the cost-to-serve activities. They accounted for over $400 million of cost and were critical to customer profitability.

The Extension to Service and Government Organizations

Early ABC systems were found almost exclusively in manufacturing companies. Today, however, ABC systems are found in service organizations such as financial and health-care institutions and in government agencies and the military.

Figure 4–3 shows examples of activities in a bank, such as processing a deposit and making a commercial loan. These activities relate to cost objects such as bank customers, accounts, and loans.

FIGURE 4–3

Bank Activities

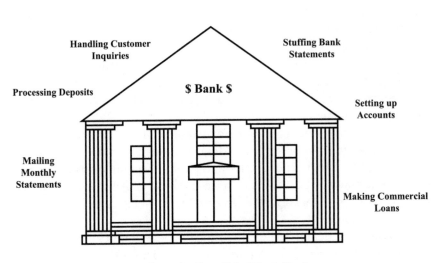

Banks have activities just as manufacturing companies do. They look different, but these activities perform work, consume resources, and serve cost
objects (such as accounts or loans) just as manufacturing activities do.

Such examples reinforce the value of ABC systems in a wide variety of
organizations. These systems provide detailed *business intelligence* about
the work going on in the organization and the reasons for performing that
work. This business intelligence facilitates calculation of the cost impact
of various strategic and operational decisions. These include decisions
about the strategic direction of the organization, the design of products
and services, and the identification of cost-reduction opportunities.

In summary, the cost assignment view allows management to obtain
answers to the following kinds of questions:

- What are the high-cost activities?
- What are the opportunities for improving product and service
  design to reduce cost?
- What are the opportunities for shifting the focus toward more
  profitable products, services, or customers?

The Process View of ABC

The horizontal part of the ABC model contains the process view (see Figure 4–2). It provides information about the work done in an activity and the relationship of this work to other activities.

To expand on this, a process is a series of activities that are linked in order to achieve a specific goal. Each activity is a customer of another activity and, in turn, has its own customers. In short, all activities are part of a *customer chain*, working together to provide value to the outside customer (Figure 4–4).[3]

At the valve manufacturer, for example, metal is melted in the foundry. Then it's forwarded to molding. Molding pours the molten metal into the molds, allows them to cool, and passes them on to an activity that breaks and removes the molds to release the parts. All these activities—and many more—work together to provide finished valves to the company's customers.

On a more detailed level, the process view of ABC includes information about cost drivers and performance measures for each activity or process in the customer chain. These cost drivers and performance measures are primarily *nonfinancial*. They are useful in interpreting and improving activity—and process—performance.

Cost Drivers

Cost drivers are factors that determine the workload and effort required to perform an activity. They include factors relating to the performance of prior activities in the chain as well as factors internal to the activity.

FIGURE 4–4

The Linked Chain of Activities

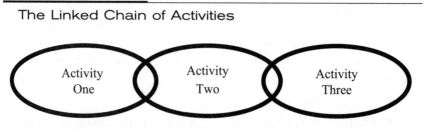

Each activity is a customer of another activity and, in turn, has its own customers. Together, activities form a *chain of customers*, all working together to provide value to the outside customer.

Cost drivers tell you *why* an activity (or chain of activities) is performed. Specifically, activities are performed in response to prior events. Scheduling a batch of parts, for example, is a response to a customer order or the scrapping of inventory—the *why*. In turn, scheduling the parts requires setting up equipment—the *effort*.

Cost drivers also tell *how much effort* must be expended to carry out the work. A defect in the part or data received from a prior activity, for example, can increase the effort required. A requisition containing the wrong part number requires correction prior to completing a purchase order. An engineering drawing that doesn't reflect the current process causes additional effort during machine setup.

Cost drivers are useful because they reveal opportunities for improvement. For example, a large bank sent orders for checks to the check supplier in a format that was incompatible with the supplier's system, with the result that the supplier could not process the orders electronically. A system change eliminated the need to reenter the orders and allowed the supplier to redeploy 40 data entry staff members.

Performance Measures

Performance measures describe the work done in an activity and the results achieved. They tell *how well* an activity is performed. They communicate how the activity is meeting the needs of its internal or external customers. They include measurements of the *efficiency* of the activity, the *time* required to complete the activity, and the *quality* of the work done.

The efficiency aspect is judged by first determining the activity's output volume. This is then compared to the resources needed to sustain that activity and its output level. For example, the number of molds processed in a month is computed for a molding activity. This measure of output is then divided into the resources required by that activity during the month. The result is a cost per mold, say $20, which may be compared with internal or external standards of efficiency.

ABC measures of the cost of outputs can be used to benchmark performance in similar processes. For example, a state department of transportation computed the cost of processing payments to construction companies in each of several regions of the state. This comparison revealed best practices and opportunities to reduce cost.

Still another dimension of performance is the time required to complete the activity. For example, in one Nortel plant, assembling Norstar telephone terminal systems takes about two hours from the time when parts arrive in production to the time when assembly is complete.

Such measures of elapsed time are indirect measures of cost, quality, and customer service. The longer it takes to perform an activity, the greater the resources required. These additional resources include the salaries of the staff members doing the work and the cost of the equipment used to carry out the work. Also, the longer the work takes, the more likely it is that it will have to be redone to correct mistakes or defects. Conversely, the shorter the elapsed time, the quicker the activity's response to changes in customer demand.

The short elapsed production time in Nortel's telephone terminal plant is indicative of low cost and *world-class* quality. Additionally, customer service from the plant is excellent. This is because the production mix can be shifted from one variation to another at short notice in response to a changing customer order mix.

A third aspect of performance is quality. For example, what percentage of the molded parts need to be reworked, and what percentage are scrapped? The higher these percentages, the lower the quality of the activity, the higher its overall cost, and the greater the detrimental influence on the next activity in the process. The value received by the customer may eventually be diminished as well.

Performance measures focus attention on the important aspects of activity performance and stimulate efforts to improve.

To recap, the ABC process view provides *operational business intelligence* about the work going on in an organization. This includes information about the external factors determining how often the activity is performed and the effort required to carry it out. Operational intelligence also includes information about the performance of an activity, such as its efficiency, the time it takes to perform it, and the quality with which it's carried out.

This operational information allows management to obtain answers to questions such as

- What events trigger the performance of the activity?
- What factors negatively affect the performance of the activity?
- How efficiently, how fast, and with what quality is the work carried out?

Moreover, the ABC process view brings the world of operations directly into the heart of the cost system. Cost information and nonfinancial information join forces to provide a *total view* of the work done, thus facilitating management of activities and improvement of performance.

The power of combined cost information and nonfinancial information can be illustrated by the process of selecting areas for improvement based on potential returns. For example, at the printed circuit board division (PCB), the number of defects in each activity was computed daily for each of the three shifts. This provided important information about the quality of each activity to the operators of the activity. The ABC system, however, allowed the division to go one step further—*to compute the cost of the defects*. This additional step riveted attention on the highest-cost defects, allowing operators to focus their attention on the corrective actions with the greatest payoff.

The importance of this benefit cannot be emphasized enough. While there were many quality improvement opportunities in the plant, there weren't sufficient resources to tackle them all at once. ABC information allowed PCB to set priorities and focus on the important opportunities first.

A Linked-Chain Example

A process is a chain of activities that work together to perform a specific objective. Activities in a process share common cost drivers and performance measures (Figure 4–5).

FIGURE 4 – 5

The Interdependency of Activities in a Process

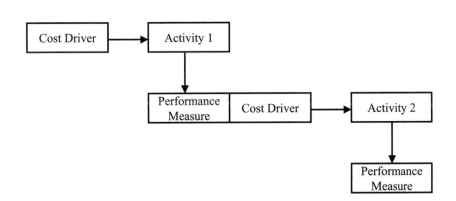

The work of each activity affects the performance of the next activity in the process. Performance measures for one activity, therefore, become cost drivers for the next activity.

This is true of the product and tooling development process of Dayton Technologies. There are three activities in this process: designing new products, designing new tools, and manufacturing new tools (Figure 4–6).

FIGURE 4–6

A Product Development Process at Dayton Technologies

Designing new products
  Cost drivers
  • Number of customer specifications
  • Classification of products
  Performance measures
  • Number of tangible shapes
  • Number of changes in shapes
  • Average design time
Designing new tools
  Cost drivers
  • Number of new shapes
  • Number of changes in shape
  • Classification of products
  • Volume of production
  Performance measures
  • Number of changes in specifications
  • Number of new drawings
  • Average design time
Manufacturing new tools
  Cost drivers
  • Number of new drawings
  • Classification of products
  • Number of changes in specifications
  Performance measures
  • Number of tools
  • Number of changes in tools
  • Elapsed tooling manufacturing time

These three activities work together to develop products and related tooling to meet customer specifications. The performance of each activity is linked by common cost drivers and performance measures.

DAYTON TECHNOLOGIES

Dayton Technologies, a division of Deceuninck Plastics Industries, manufactures vinyl parts for windows in its plant in Ohio. It specializes in the design and manufacture of custom window systems. Its ABC model provides examples for several chapters of the book.

As shown in Figure 4–6, "designing new products" has two cost drivers. The number of new customer specifications determines the volume of work. The classification of products determines the effort required to complete the designs. For example, more complex products are more difficult to design and require more effort. This second cost driver is common to all three activities in the process.

There are three performance measures for the activity "designing new products." The number of tangible shapes is a measure of activity output. The number of changes in shape (a quality measure) and the average design time measure how well the work is done.

"Designing new tools" has four cost drivers: the number of new shapes, the number of changes in shape, the number of product classifications, and the anticipated volume of production (volume influences the engineered life of the tooling). Note that the first two cost drivers are performance measures from the prior activity (its performance affects the downstream activity).

Performance measures for the activity "designing new tools" include the number of changes in specifications, the number of new drawings, and the average design time. These performance measures are cost drivers for the next activity in the chain—manufacturing the tools.

This example shows how each activity depends on the performance of its suppliers and the impact it has on its customers. Cost drivers and performance measures help you understand—and manage—these interdependencies.

S U M M A R Y

There are two dimensions to modern activity-based costing. The cost assignment view provides information about the work that is going on in a company as well as information about the products and customers benefiting from the work. The process view provides information about *why* work is performed, what factors determine the *effort* required to perform it, and *how well* the work is carried out. All of this facilitates the management of activities as a *chain of customers* collectively dedicated to meeting the needs of the external customer.

The real power of two-dimensional ABC is that judgments can be based on the combination of cost information and nonfinancial information. It directs product and customer strategy toward profitable opportunities. And it guides the improvement of a company's ability to design and build products and serve customers in its chosen markets.

KEY TERMS[4]

Activity.   A unit of work performed within an organization.

Cost assignment view.   The part of ABC in which cost is assigned to activities and the cost of activities is assigned to cost objects.

Cost driver.   An event or causal factor that influences the level and performance of activities and the resulting consumption of resources, elapsed time, and quality. For example, defective materials that lead to low product quality are a cost driver of procurement and production activities. An activity may have multiple cost drivers associated with it.

Cost object.   The reason for performing an activity. Cost objects include products, services, customers, projects, and contracts.

Performance measure.   An indicator of the work performed in an activity and the results achieved. It is a measure of how well an activity meets the needs of its customers. Performance measures may be financial or nonfinancial.

Process.   A series of activities that are linked to perform a specific objective.

Process view.   The part of ABC that provides operational information about activities.

Resources.   Economic elements applied or used in the performance of activities.

REFERENCES

1 R. S. Kaplan, "John Deere Component Works," No. 9-187-107/8 (Boston: Harvard Business School, 1986).

2 Figure 4–2 and later developments of this figure are based on joint work with Norm Raffish. It was first published by CAM-I in the Glossary of ABC and

ABM as the Two-Dimensional Diagram. It was later named the ABC Cross by the author.

3 Richard J. Schonberger, *Building a Chain of Customers: Linking Business Functions to Create the World Class Company* (New York: Free Press, 1990).

4 Some of the definitions in this section are adapted from Peter B. B. Turney and Norm Raffish, *A Glossary of Activity-Based Management* (Dallas: Computer Aided Manufacturing International, 1991).

CHAPTER 5

The ABC Building Blocks

This chapter takes you on a tour of the mechanics of activity-based costing (ABC). You'll learn all about the different types of activity-based information. You'll learn about the wealth of useful information residing in an ABC database. And, if you plan to design an ABC system, you'll learn what information to include in that system.

In this tour, you'll follow the flow of information through the activity. You'll discover that the activity exists at the intersection of the cost and process views of ABC. You'll also discover that much of the information in ABC either resides in or flows through the activities (Figure 5–1).

To help you grasp the key concepts as quickly as possible, the tour is presented in two parts. The first part follows the vertical flow of cost information through the activity. The second part follows the horizontal flow of nonfinancial information through the activity.

THE COST ASSIGNMENT VIEW

The cost assignment view is where an *economic picture* of the organization is created. Here you apply the improved methods of ABC to yield accurate and useful information for key business decisions.

The following items are the basic building blocks of the *ABC cost assignment view*:

- Resources
- Activities

FIGURE 5–1

The ABC Cross

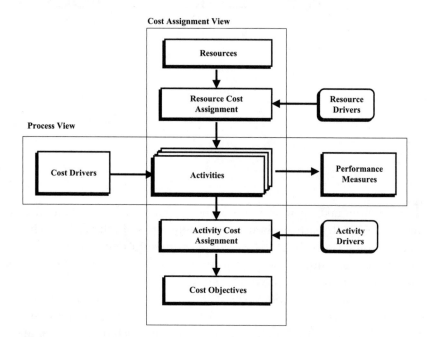

Activity-based costing comprises several building blocks. The building blocks in the vertical dimension work together to assign costs from resources to activities and from the activities to the cost objects. The building blocks in the horizontal dimension supply information about the performance of activities.

- Activity centers
- Resource drivers
- Activity cost pools
- Cost elements
- Activity drivers
- Cost objects

Let's first take a quick look at these building blocks and their general relationships. Then, with that overview in mind, we can take a more detailed look at these various building blocks. Figure 5–2 shows how these building blocks fit together.

Resources are economic elements directed toward the performance of activities. They are the sources of cost.

FIGURE 5-2

The Building Blocks of the Cost Assignment View

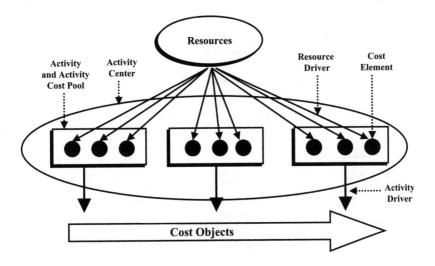

ABC uses several technical terms to describe the process of cost assignment. This diagram shows the relationship of each of these terms to the cost assignment process.

Resources in a manufacturing company include direct labor and materials, production support (such as the salary cost of material procurement staff), indirect costs of production (such as the power cost of heating the plant), and costs outside of production (such as advertising). Resources found in both manufacturing and service companies include the salaries of professionals and office support staff, office space, and costs of information systems.

Resources flow to *activities*, which are processes or procedures that cause work. In a customer service department, for example, activities can include processing customer orders, solving product problems, and processing customer returns (see Figure 5–3).

Typically, related activities are enclosed in an *activity center*. The activity center is a cluster of activities (usually clustered by function or process). In Figure 5–3, for example, the activity center contains all customer-support activities.

Various factors, referred to as *resource drivers*, are used to assign costs to activities. These factors are chosen to approximate the use of resources by the activities. In Figure 5–3, customer service cost is traced to three

FIGURE 5–3

The Building Blocks for the Cost of a Customer Service Department

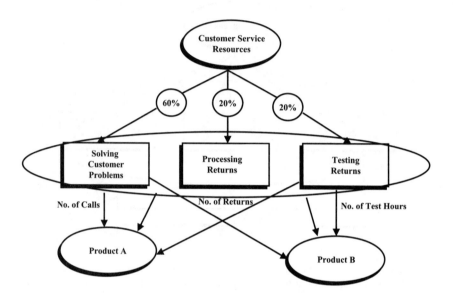

Resources are assigned to three activities based on actual measurements or estimates of effort. Cost is assigned to the products using three *activity drivers*.

activities.* The percentages shown (60 percent, 20 percent, and 20 percent) are based on actual measurements or estimates of the effort expended on each activity. An example of this would be ten people in the department, with six solving customer problems full time while the other four split their time between processing and testing returns.

Each type of resource traced to an activity (e.g., the salary cost of processing returns) becomes a *cost element* in an *activity cost pool*. The activity cost pool is the total cost associated with an activity.

Each activity cost pool is traced to the cost objects via an *activity driver*. The activity driver is a measure of the use of the activity by the cost objects. It is used to assign resources from the activities to the cost objects.

---

* It's assumed that the cost of the resources used in the customer service department has already been determined.

To relate this back to Figure 5–3, each activity has a unique activity driver to trace its cost to the products. Solving customer problems, for example, is traced to products based on the number of phone calls. This makes sense because the product that creates the most customer problems is likely to generate the most phone calls.

The *cost object* is the final point to which cost is traced. A cost object is the reason why work is performed in the company. It may be a product or a customer. Engineering, producing, marketing, selling, and distributing a product requires a number of activities. Supporting a customer also comprises a number of activities. The cost traced to each product or customer reflects the cost of the activities used by that cost object.

This vertical flow of information in ABC defines the economics of the company and the organization of work within it. It also provides the basic building blocks for creating accurate and useful cost information about the strategy and operations of the company.

Resources

ABC operates with measurements of the cost of resources. For example, how much have we paid in salaries so far this year? How much depreciation have we had? How much have we accrued in taxes? How did all this compare with the budget (what we should have spent)?

A primary source of cost information is the general ledger. The key is to assign the costs in the general ledger accounts to activities in a way that reflects how the resources are used to perform the work. If a piece of equipment is used in a road maintenance activity, for example, its cost should be assigned to this activity.

Activities

Activities are units of work. As such, they are part of the real organization of the company, not abstractions of an accounting system. Activities include processing a deposit to an account, maintaining a tank, issuing a driver's license, issuing invoices, and maintaining employee data. They are the centerpiece of ABC, and they must be defined before the assignment of cost.

Activities are either core or enabling. Core activities directly benefit the products, services, and customers of the organization. For example, designing a retirement plan for a customer is a core activity of a financial services company. An enabling activity is one that supports core activities. Preparing paychecks for the workers who are designing the retirement plan is an enabling activity.

Core activities vary from one organization to another because of each organization's type of business, technology, systems, process design, and other factors. For example, the activities "tapping parts" and "grinding parts" are found in a low-technology manufacturer. In contrast, the activity "attaching parts to circuit boards" is found in a high-technology manufacturer.

Enabling activities are more likely to be common across organizations. For example, preparing financial reports, processing new hires, and paying vendors are activities found in a wide variety of organizations. Differences in enabling activities may relate to differences in processes, technology, or management practices. For example, a manufacturing company that has adopted modern quality control practices may no longer inspect incoming parts.

Activities are listed in the *activity dictionary*. This is a master list of all the activities in the ABC model. It includes a standard definition of each activity, which includes the activity's description and a list of the tasks associated with it (Figure 5–4).

Resource Drivers

Resource drivers are the links between the resources and the activities. They take costs from the general ledger and assign them to the activities.

Let's say we have two significant resources associated with the inspection department: $100,000 in salaries and benefits and $20,000 for supplies. Salaries and benefits are assigned to each activity based on an actual measurement or estimate of the effort devoted to each activity. This measurement of effort is the *resource driver* for salaries and benefits.

For example, the effort may be determined by a count of the people assigned to an activity and by measurement or estimate of the time each person spends on that activity. If two out of ten people in the department are found to spend 50 percent of their time on inspection of customer complaints, then 10 percent (i.e., 2/10 multiplied by 50 percent) of salary and benefit cost (i.e., 10 percent of $100,000 = $10,000) is traced to this activity.

These measurements (which are usually quite reliable) are ordinarily obtained from time collection systems or interviews with the managers of the departments. (Interviewing and other data-gathering tools are described in Chapter 13.)

FIGURE 5-4

Activity Dictionary

Process: Order Capture   **Subprocess: Order Creation**

ID	Activity Name	Definition	Tasks	Source
75	Create Order— Electronic	Convert customer pricing requirements into precise manufacturing specifications.		SGA
73	Create Order— Mail	Convert customer requirements into precise manufacturing specifications.	➤ Open mail. ➤ Determine customer channel. ➤ Verify billing and shipping information. ➤ Determine product or service needs. ➤ Contact customer, if necessary, to clarify information. ➤ Input information into system. ➤ Release order for fulfillment.	SGA
373	Create Order— Teleservice	Convert customer requirements into precise manufacturing specifications.	➤ Determine customer channel. ➤ Verify customer information. ➤ Verify billing and shipping information. ➤ Determine product or service needs. ➤ Contact customer, if necessary, to clarify information. ➤ Input information into system. ➤ Release order for fulfillment.	SGA

(continued on following page)

(continued)

ID	Activity Name	Definition	Tasks	Source
74	Create Order— VRU	Convert customer requirements into precise manufacturing specifications.	➤ Create an order in the system through customer use of the voice-response unit (VRU) without the direct involvement of a Deluxe employee.	SGA
429	Develop/ Maintain Customer Order System Infra-structure	The development and maintenance of customer order system includes all expense items (labor and nonlabor) that are required to ensure the operation of the system on an ongoing basis and any potential expensable upgrades. The depreciation of the capitalized portion of the software is included as part of this activity.		SGA

An activity dictionary is a master listing of the activities in the ABC model along with a description of each activity. This example is of activities in the order capture process at Deluxe Corporation.[1]

Resource drivers can also be specified as cost per minute of time of the activity. For example, the cost of filling a pothole could be $10 per minute. This cost would be derived by dividing the cost of the resource by an estimate of the productivity of the resource. Cost per minute of time estimates are used with time equations (see later in this chapter).

Some resources can be directly assigned without resorting to estimates. In the case of supplies, for example, departmental records may show that $15,000 in supplies is used in first-piece inspection and $5,000 is used to resolve customer complaints. The resource driver in this case is the direct measurement of the use of supplies by the activities.

The part of each resource that is assigned to an activity becomes a *cost element* of that activity. In this example, $10,000 of salary cost and $5,000 of supplies (as determined above) are cost elements of responding to customer complaints.

FIGURE 5 – 5

The Bill of Costs

GL		Year to Date	
Account		**Resources**	**Actual%**
6311	Salaries	$4,000	44
6312	Benefits	1,200	13
7566	Postage	775	9
7642	Telephone	1,600	18
7756	Miscellaneous	1,500	16
	Total cost pool	$9,075	100%

Activity: Placing nonproduction purchase orders

Bill of Costs:

The bill of costs reveals the resources used by an activity. This is useful information for managing activities, because any changes in activity performance should be reflected by changes in resource requirements.

Cost elements are important if you wish to know which specific resources are consumed by an activity. To gain this knowledge, you need to create a list of an activity's cost elements. Such a list is shown in Figure 5–5 and is called a *bill of costs*.

Knowledge of cost elements helps in managing resources. In most cases, improving the efficiency of an activity does not automatically translate into cost reduction. The resources may be idle, but they remain committed to the activity unless steps are taken to remove them. The value of cost elements is that they clearly indicate which resources need to be removed or redeployed.

The total of all cost elements for an activity is the *cost pool*. The overall total in the cost pool is a guide to the significance of an activity as a resource user. This allows cost pools to guide the setting of priorities in improvement programs. Not all cost-reduction opportunities are equal. The activities with the largest cost pools provide the greatest potential for cost reduction.

Activity Centers

Just as your company has an organization chart to show its structure, so too must ABC organize activities in a meaningful way. There may be literally hundreds of activities in the database, and you can easily become lost without some method of organization.

The most common approach is to group activities into activity centers. An activity center is a collection of related activities, such as those in a particular department. A credit department activity center in a cellular telephone company, for example, includes the activities of checking credit and collecting overdue accounts.

Figure 5–6 shows the activities in an inspection activity center. This center directly parallels the inspection department in scope, but it contains information about the activities that would not be found in any conventional departmental report.

This information includes the cost of each activity, the resources used by each activity, and operational information about activity performance. It may also show the flow of work from one activity to another.

The purpose of the activity center is to facilitate the management of functions or processes. It does this by supplying pertinent information about all the activities in a particular function or process. It contains in one place the strategic and operational information relating to the center's activities. This information is used to help answer the following types of questions about the work of the center:

FIGURE 5–6

The Activity Center

Inspecting Department

Inspecting incoming material
Inspecting incoming components
Inspecting the first piece of each batch
Inspecting customer complaints

Activities are grouped in activity centers. Illustrated here are four activities in the inspection department. An activity-center report to the manager of this department contains a wealth of information about the work done.

- What work is performed in the activity center?
- Which activities consume most of the resources of this department or process?
- Which activities contain *waste* and are candidates for improvement?
- How does each activity meet the needs of its customer (i.e., the next activity in the process)?
- What is the overall performance of the department or the process?

It's common, *but not necessary,* for activity centers to parallel the company organization chart. In the next chapter you'll learn how to obtain useful information about processes from your ABC model.

Cost Objects

The cost object resides at the bottom of the cost assignment view of ABC. However, it is the starting point from which the work required by the company is defined—the activities required to produce the products and support the customers targeted by the company.

The Value of Cost Objects

Tracing costs to cost objects provides several important items of strategic information:

- It helps *define* how valuable cost objects are to the company that provides them, where value is computed as

  Profit = revenue − activity-based cost

- It helps *measure* the value received by the customer, where value is computed as

  Customer realization − customer sacrifice

  In this equation, customer realization is the sum of the product features, quality, and service received by the customer. Customer sacrifice is the ABC associated with this realization (the cost to serve) plus additional costs incurred by the customer (such as the time spent learning how to use the product).

- It *yields insights* about how the value of cost objects might be increased by reducing the cost of those cost objects. These insights come from information about the cost of each activity used by a cost object.

The Hierarchy of Cost Objects

Most companies have hierarchies of cost objects, one for products and one for customers (see Figure 5–7). Each hierarchy represents opportunities to review value at differing levels of detail (where the bottom represents the greatest amount of detail).

Part Numbers and Ingredients The most detailed cost object in the product hierarchy is the part number or ingredient. Tracing cost to this level of detail reveals varying patterns of cost if parts differ in design or volume.

Part-number costing provides economic intelligence to guide various decisions. These include choices about whether parts should be man-

FIGURE 5-7

The Hierarchy of Cost Objects

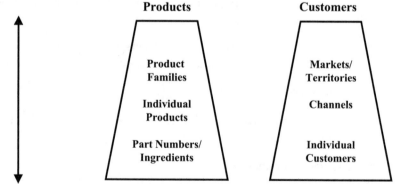

Less Detail

Products   Customers

Product Families   Markets/ Territories

Individual Products   Channels

Part Numbers/ Ingredients   Individual Customers

More Detail

Cost objects vary in type and detail depending on the purpose of activity-based costing and the nature of the organization. For example, if you are interested in broad strategic issues, reports of market profitability will be important. If you wish to determine the sourcing for a part, you need costs at the part number level.

ufactured internally or by an outside supplier and choices between product and process design alternatives.

One plant, for example, put in an ABC system to improve its ability
to make sourcing decisions. When it compared the new costs with its standard costs, it found that only 15 percent of its parts were sufficiently well
costed under the old cost system to make meaningful sourcing decisions.
And this plant was struggling to stay in business as products were incorrectly moved to outside suppliers.

In another example, the Oscilloscopes Group of Tektronix used ABC
to highlight cost differences between high-volume and low-volume parts.
The cost of high-volume parts was lower per part used because the cost
of the activities required to sustain the part was shared across a larger volume. These activities included purchasing, receiving, storing, and part-
number maintenance. Knowing that high-volume parts cost less
encouraged Tektronix product designers to use parts that were common
to multiple products.[2]

However, there is a downside to costing at the part-number level.
That downside is the potential impact on the cost and complexity of the
ABC system. This is because each individual cost object—each part number in this case—requires unique activity driver data that reflects its use
of activities.

At Stockham Valve and Fittings, for example, 80,000 part numbers
were costed using an ABC system with 58 activity drivers. This required
millions of pieces of data to connect activities to cost objects.

This was not an insurmountable problem for Stockham Valve. The
data for all but one of the activity drivers resided in its computer system
and were downloaded to the ABC system. All that was required was an
information systems specialist who planned and facilitated the down-
load.

STOCKHAM VALVE AND FITTINGS

Stockham Valve and Fittings is one of the largest full-line producers of bronze and iron valves and fittings in the United States.
Stockham's vertically integrated production process extends from the foundries where the
metal is melted to final finishing.
Its ABC system provides numerous examples for this and later
chapters.

Products   Part numbers and ingredients make up products, and this is the next level up the product hierarchy. Products are the individual items that are sold to customers. *Product families* are groups of products that are related by design, process, or market.

You saw in earlier chapters how conventional cost systems often significantly *miscost* products. Focusing the ABC system at the product level corrects these gross inaccuracies. It provides strategic intelligence about your ability to manufacture products or deliver services and to sell them at profit-generating prices.

Customers   Customer costing makes it possible to assess the profitability of individual customers or groups of customers. It often reveals levels of profitability that vary significantly from customer to customer, market to market, region to region, and distribution channel to distribution channel.

Customer costing is the calculation of the total cost of serving customers. This cost includes two components; one is the cost of the products purchased by the customer, and the other is the cost of the support activities received by the customer.

Figure 5–8 shows a profitability report for a particular customer for one month. The customer bought three products, for a total cost of $4,850. The customer placed ten orders during the month, received customer support over the phone, and had one visit from a field engineer, for a total support cost of $850. Unfortunately, the customer was not profitable because the revenues earned were insufficient to cover the total cost of products and support.

The ability to assess customer profitability has proved valuable to a number of companies. This was the case at the Kanthal division of Kanthal-Hoganas, a Swedish manufacturer of electrical resistance heating elements.

Kanthal's study of its customers revealed that, while 30 percent of the customers were very profitable, 70 percent were unprofitable or breakeven. The least profitable 10 percent of the customers collectively lost an amount equal to the entire reported profits of the company.

Armed with this knowledge, Kanthal shifted marketing resources from unprofitable to profitable customers. Over the year following the company's ABC study, sales increased by 20 percent while employment decreased by 1 percent. Profits increased by 45 percent.[3]

Groups of customers can also be combined to provide pictures of profitability for market segments, regions, and distribution channels. This analysis is useful when resource requirements and profitability vary from one customer group to another.

FIGURE 5–8

Activity-Based Customer Profitability Report

Customer: Bryant Manufacturing, Inc.

Product	Sales	Cost	Profit
A	$2,500	$2,160	$340
B	1,750	1,575	175
C	1,300	2,160	340
Total	$5,550	$4,850	$700

Customer Activity	Quantity	Cost per Unit of Driver	Cost	Profit
Ordering	10	$50	$500	
Customer support	2	75	150	
Field engineering	4	50	200	$850
Customer profit				$150

Think what you can do with information about customer profitability. It can help you pick and choose which customers you prefer to serve and the level of support that is necessary. It may show that price adjustments are appropriate. And it may show opportunities to improve the value you provide your customers.

For example, one company completed an activity-based analysis of the cost of distributing products through six different channels. This study revealed that the cost and profitability varied significantly from one channel to another. Marketing and administrative expenses varied from a high of 23 percent of sales to a low of 10 percent of sales. Profit margins varied from a high of 22 percent to a low of −19 percent.

The knowledge of channel profitability prompted a series of competitive actions. Marketing efforts were transferred to the more profitable channels, prices were adjusted, and discount structures were changed.[4]

Cost Objects in Service Organizations

Service organizations have specific services that they provide to their customers. A bank may offer checking accounts, mortgage loans, and financial advice to its customers. An insurance company may provide different types of insurance, retirement plans, and other services to its customers.

These services—and the customers who receive them—are the cost objects for the ABC model.

Cost Objects in Government Organizations

Government organizations also have cost objects, but they may not be as readily apparent as those in manufacturing or service organizations. For example, a state department of transportation has several activities relating to maintaining roads. These include treating cracks, filling potholes, joint repair, and hand patching. The objects of these activities are the state's highways. So the cost objects are the interstate, primary, and secondary highways and roads that benefit from these activities.

Activity Drivers

Activity drivers are methods for assigning the costs of activities to cost objects. They measure how often activities are performed on each type of product or customer or the time required to perform them.

An example of a transaction-based *activity driver* is the number of production runs by part number. This *cost assignment measure* reflects the use of batch-level activities, such as production scheduling or setting up a machine, by each batch of parts.

A transaction-based activity driver will provide accurate results under certain conditions. The activity driver "number of production runs" will accurately assign the cost of production scheduling *if* the time taken to schedule production is the same for each production run (see Figure 5–9).

A time-based activity driver provides a more accurate result when the time per transaction varies. For example, if certain types of product require more time to schedule, it will be better to use "time spent scheduling each product type" as the driver. This will accurately assign more cost to those product types that require more scheduling effort.

The objective is to pick the right number and type of activity drivers—and to match them carefully to the activities. Enough drivers of the right type are needed to report accurate costs. Too many may be costly, however, and may create a system that's too complex to understand and costly to maintain.

Activity drivers are a far cry from the arcane allocation procedures of conventional cost accounting systems. They are linkages between the products and the activities that represent opportunities for improvement in product or process design.

FIGURE 5-9

How ABC Can Report Accurate Product Costs Using Transaction Drivers

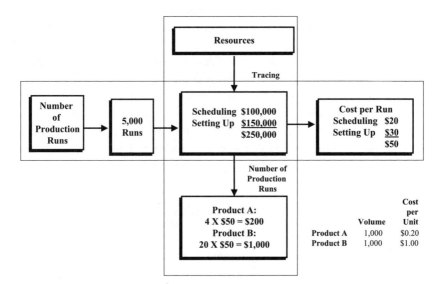

In this example, batches of product B are run five times as often as batches of product A, so batches of product B are scheduled and set up five times as often. The setup time is identical for each product. In these circumstances, the activity driver "number of production runs" correctly assigns five times more scheduling and setup cost to product B than to product A.

A design engineer at Hewlett-Packard's Roseville Network Division, for example, is likely to design a circuit board with fewer manual part insertions and more machine insertions. This occurs because ABC shows that the cost of a machine insertion is less than the cost of a manual insertion.[5]

John Deere Component Works decided to move the heat-treating facility in-line with the screw-machine process to eliminate the cost of moving parts one mile back and forth. This move was prompted by ABC data that revealed the high cost per move.[6]

To summarize, the cost assignment view shows the flow of cost from the resources to the activities, and from the activities to the cost objects. Resource drivers assign cost from resources to activities, and activity drivers assign cost from activities to cost objects. The result is useful and accurate cost information to guide business improvement.

TIME EQUATIONS

Until recently, it was difficult to build an ABC model in complex and diverse environments. Building an ABC model with many product and customer variations was costly and time-consuming and could overwhelm the capabilities of ABC software. This problem can be solved using time equations.

Time equations combine time measurements from individual activities to create a single driver. For example, the activities required in a distribution center may vary depending on the customer's requirements or product characteristics. All products will be picked from the shelf, but some will require special packaging because of their hazardous nature, and oversize products will need special handling. The activity equation for one product might look like this (units in minutes):

Pick time = 0.5 + 8.5 (if special packaging required for hazardous materials) + 10.0 (if special handling required for oversize products)

This equation shows the total time required for the specific cost object (specific product and customer). If the product is hazardous and oversize, it will require a processing time of 19 minutes. This time is multiplied by the cost per minute of the resource used to do the work to compute the activity cost assigned to the product.

The value of the time equation is its ability to assign the cost of activities economically to multiple cost objects. This particular equation requires only one activity (supplying product) rather than three activities (picking, handling, and shipping). It therefore accommodates a complex activity environment *without* requiring a complex ABC model.

Another advantage is that time equations use the data contained in a corporate database to cost businesses with hundreds of thousands (even millions) of cost objects. Time equations have been used successfully in distribution, financial services, and other organizations with vast amounts of complexity and diversity. They allow these organizations to benefit from the insights derived from ABC in a cost-effective manner.[7]

THE PROCESS VIEW

The second dimension of ABC provides information about the work done in the activity. Much of this information is nonfinancial. It encompasses information about factors affecting the workload of activities and information about how well the activity is being executed.

The key terms in the process view are

- Cost driver
- Performance measure

Cost driver is a causal factor that helps determine the workload of an activity. The number of active parts, for example, is a cost driver of the vendor management activity. The more different parts there are to procure, the more vendors there will be and the greater the work establishing and maintaining relations with these vendors.

Working to reduce the negative effects of cost drivers can yield important gains in efficiency. Reducing the number of different parts, for example, reduces the demand for part-related activities. Costs come down as resources are freed up, so production becomes easier and faster.

Performance measures define how well an activity meets the needs of its internal or external customers. Internal customers receive the output of an activity. Typically, an internal customer is the next activity in the manufacturing or business process. External customers are the individuals or companies that purchase the company's goods and services.

Performance measures differ from one activity to another and from one company to another. These differences reflect different customers and requirements.

The number of customer complaints, for example, is an appropriate performance measure for customer service activities. This number should be small if customer service is an important goal.

The number of modifications to products after the commencement of production is a measure of the success of engineering activities. This number should also be small if "getting it right the first time" is an important goal of design engineering.

Performance measures can be monitored over time, compared with performance goals, or compared with the performance of comparable activities inside or outside the company. This latter comparison is called *benchmarking*. Such comparisons are used to gauge how well the activity is being performed and to identify areas where improvement is needed.

For example, "first-pass yield" is a measure of quality performance. Let's say last month's performance is calculated as 92 percent. This is an improvement over the same period last year, when first-pass yield was 85 percent. However, a similar activity in a sister plant is achieving 95 percent, and a competitor's plant used as a benchmark is achieving 98 percent. Clearly the activity has a long way to go before it is matching the "best practices" in the industry.

As we saw in Chapter 4, performance measures for one activity can become cost drivers for the next activity in the process. The frequency of "out-of-specification" machining, for example, is a measure of the quality of work in the machining activity. It's a cost driver for *finishing*, which is the next activity to work on the parts.

A MANUFACTURING ILLUSTRATION

Figure 5–10 illustrates how two-dimensional ABC works. The total resource pool of $6,000,000 is the total budget for the procurement department. Of this cost, $450,000 is traced directly to the purchasing activity. (The resource drivers include estimates of effort expended on the activity and a specific measurement of the use of supplies.) The cost of the pur-

FIGURE 5 – 1 0

FIGURE 5 – 1 0

An Illustration of Two-Dimensional
Activity-Based Costing

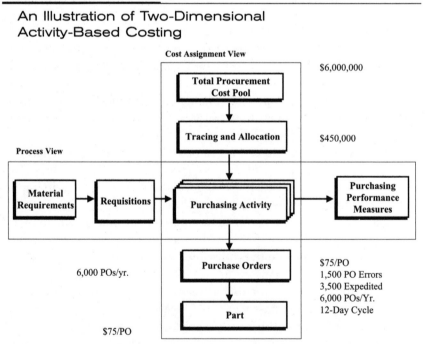

Preparing purchase orders occurs in both manufacturing and service organizations. ABC provides information for *managing* the activity's performance, *understanding* what it costs, and *quantifying* its impact on the cost of obtaining parts.

chasing activity is traced to part numbers via the number of purchase orders per part number (the activity driver).

The number of purchase orders measures the output of the activity (the number of times the activity was performed). Other performance measures include the number of errors made, the number of purchase orders expedited, and the elapsed time required to complete a purchase order. A volume of 6,000 purchase orders and an activity cost of $450,000 yields a cost per purchase order of $75.

In this example, the activity driver and the performance measure of output are the one and the same. This matching of activity driver and performance measure is common in ABC, but there are exceptions.

For example, if the number of purchase orders per part number is not captured by the company's information system, an alternative activity driver (such as the number of different parts) is required. Alternatively, if the effort required to complete a purchase order varies systematically from one type of part to another, a different activity driver (such as a direct measurement of the effort involved) may be necessary.

On the input side, the activity must cope with a volume of incoming requisitions of 8,000. A requisition *is not* a cost driver of the purchasing activity. Rather, it is the paperwork, or "trigger," that initiates the work.

The volume of requisitions is determined by two cost drivers—the number of customer orders and the number of scrap tickets. Customer orders and scrap tickets are factors that trigger the preparation of a purchase requisition (and the need to complete a purchase order).

Figure 5–10 shows the demand for the purchasing activity coming from purchases of parts. The level of work, however, is determined by the cost drivers—end product demand (the number of customer orders) and the quality of the parts and their processing (the number of scrap tickets). An improvement in the quality of a machining activity, for example, reduces the number of scrap tickets and, as a result, reduces the number of requisitions and the demand for purchasing replacement parts.

Performance is monitored by several measures. The cost per purchase order averages $75. The frequency of errors is one in four (1,500 out of 6,000 per year). Over half the purchase orders were expedited rather than being completed in the normal processing cycle. It took an average of 12 days to complete the processing of a purchase order.

Performance is judged by comparison with past performance and comparison with similar activities elsewhere. The graph in Figure 5–11 reveals a pattern of improvement. But it also reveals a large performance gap that needs to be closed before "best practices" are equaled.

FIGURE 5 — 1 1

Performance Measurement

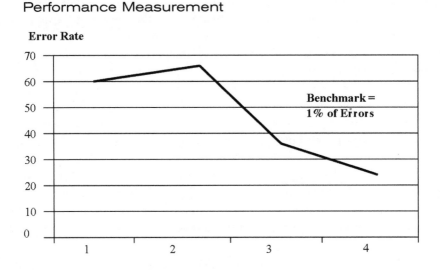

The quality of work in this purchasing activity has improved. But it's still a long way from matching the benchmark activity.

A SERVICE ILLUSTRATION

Two-dimensional ABC also applies to service organizations. Consider the example of a telecommunications company that performs credit checks on new customers.

Credit checking is one of several activities in the credit department. The cost of department resources is divided between these activities based on headcount and percent of effort devoted to each activity (this is the resource driver). The cost of the credit-checking activity is assigned to new customers (the cost object) using "number of new account activations" as the activity driver.

The two primary cost drivers are "number of sales prequalifications" and "percentage of prequalifications performed outside of office hours." The first cost driver recognizes that sales activity creates the need to complete credit checks.

The second cost driver reflects a policy that credit checks outside of regular office hours be performed by a service bureau. This affects cost because a service bureau credit check is more costly than one done in the credit department.

Two performance measures are tracked for this activity. The "number of new account activations" keeps track of the volume of work done. The "percent of new accounts that suffer credit problems" monitors the quality of the work done.

A GOVERNMENT ILLUSTRATION

ABC is the ideal tool for federal, state, and local government agencies that are looking to address budget pressures and develop performance measures. Here is an example of two-dimensional ABC in a housing authority. This agency is responsible for administering federal [Housing and Urban Development (HUD)] housing programs in a major metropolitan area. Its responsibilities include providing housing vouchers to low-income people. See Figure 5–12.

The activity "issuing housing vouchers" requires people to do the work, office space in which to fill out paperwork and meet with clients, computer equipment for updating records and communicating, and sup-

FIGURE 5—12

A Government Illustration of ABC

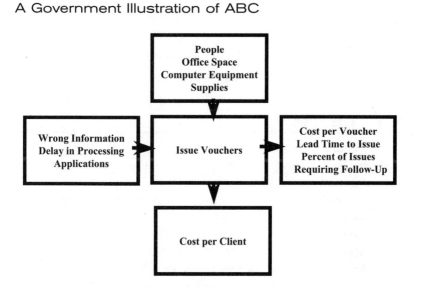

This example is from a housing authority that provides housing vouchers to low-income people.

plies such as forms. Cost drivers that increase work effort, lengthen time, and reduce quality include incorrect information about clients and delays in processing applications. These factors affect the key performance measures—the cost of issuing a voucher, the lead time required, and the quality achieved. The cost object is the client, and the cost of issuing a voucher is the activity cost associated with serving the client.

SUMMARY

The building blocks of ABC provide cost and operational information about the work going on in the company. They provide answers to questions about this work and reveal opportunities for improvement. Here's a summary of these building blocks and their uses:

Building Blocks	Purpose
1. Resources	Resource management
2. Activities	Activity management
3. Activity center	Process management
4. Resource driver	Resource management
5. Activity cost pool	Prioritizing cost reduction
6. Activity cost element	Resource management
7. Activity driver	Activity management
8. Cost object	Strategic management
9. Cost driver	Cost reduction
10. Performance measures	Performance assessment

KEY TERMS

Activity.   A unit of work performed within an organization.

Activity center.   A report of pertinent information about the activities in a function or process.

Activity cost pool.   The total cost assigned to an activity. The sum of all the cost elements assigned to an activity.

Activity dictionary.   A listing of the activities, including a description of each activity and the tasks associated with that activity.

Activity driver.   A factor used to assign cost from an activity to a cost object. A measure of the frequency and intensity of use of an activity by a cost object. If performing customer engineering work for a customer is an activity, the number of engineering hours could be the activity driver.

Cost driver. An event or causal factor that influences the level and performance of activities and the resulting consumption of resources, elapsed time, and quality. For example, defective materials that lead to low product quality are a cost driver of procurement and production activities. An activity may have multiple cost drivers associated with it.

Cost element. The amount paid for a resource and assigned to an activity. Part of an activity cost pool.

Cost object. The reason for performing an activity. Cost objects include products, services, customers, projects, and contracts.

Performance measure. An indicator of the work performed in an activity and the results achieved. A measure of how well an activity meets the needs of its customers.

Resource driver. A measure of the cost of resources used by activities. It takes the cost of the resource and assigns it to the activities.

Resource. An economic element applied or used in the performance of activities.

Time equation. A compound equation combining time estimates from several activities into a single activity driver.

REFERENCES

1 Peter B. B. Turney, "Deluxe (B)," UVA-G–0549 (Charlottesville: Darden Graduate School of Business, University of Virginia, 1999).

2 Peter B. B. Turney and Bruce Anderson, "Accounting for Continuous Improvement," *Sloan Management Review*, Winter 1989, pp. 37–48.

3 Robert S. Kaplan, "Kanthal (A) and (B)," 9–190–002/3 (Boston: Harvard Business School, 1990).

4 Robin Cooper, "Winchell Lighting, Inc, Introduction, (A) and (B)," 9–187–073/4/5 (Boston: Harvard Business School, 1987).

5 Robin Cooper and Peter B. B. Turney, "Hewlett-Packard: The Roseville Network Division," 9–188–117 (Boston: Harvard Business School, 1989).

6 Robert S. Kaplan, "John Deere Component Works (A) and (B)," 9–187–107 (Boston: Harvard Business School, 1987).

7 Robert S. Kaplan and Steven R. Anderson, *Drive Growth with Customer Profitability Management* (Boston: Harvard Business School, 2003).

CHAPTER 6

Resource Planning and Time-Based ABC

Most ABC models are historical. They look backwards and create a picture of the immediate past. As we have learned, these historical models are useful in revealing high-cost processes, unprofitable products and customers, costly supplier relationships, and poorly designed products. Historical ABC analyses serve as a guide to future action, and prompt actions to reduce cost and improve profitability.

What are the limitations of historical ABC? First of all, we won't know what things cost until *after* the period is over. Second, they are not dynamic in that they cannot easily be modified to show what things will cost if circumstances change. Third, ABC is difficult to perform in complex, high-transaction environments.

These limitations are removed by two new developments. One is resource planning. Resource planning modifies the way ABC works to allow the asking of "what if?" questions and the simulation of results under different scenarios. The second development is time-based ABC, which improves the accuracy of cost information and reduces the cost of model development and maintenance.

RESOURCE PLANNING

Resource planning ABC models answers a lot of useful questions. These include

- If the output of an activity increases, what will the impact on resource requirements be?
- If we adjust resource deployment to meet the demands of the new plan, what will our new financial budget be?
- If the efficiency of the activity increases—for example, through the elimination of non-value-added steps—what will the impact on the cost of work and the use of resources be?
- If we add resources allowing increased output, what will the net revenue impact be?

The key to resource planning is to recognize the difference between resources required and resources available. Resources required are those that, given current levels of productivity, are needed to complete the planned output. Resources available are those that management has deployed to do the work.

What is the significance of this difference? In conventional ABC, the cost of the resources available is assigned to activities *regardless of whether or not they are used*. The result is that 100 percent of cost is assigned to activities.

In resource planning ABC, only the costs of the resources required are assigned to activities. This means that the cost of activities is limited to the cost of performing the activity. Additional resources made available by management, but not used to do the work, represent excess capacity. Excess capacity can be positive (resources currently unemployed) or negative (there aren't enough resources to do the planned work). In terms of ABC, this can be expressed as follows:

$$\text{Cost of resources available} = \text{cost of resources required} + \text{cost of unused capacity}^1$$

Resource planning models built using this equation are different from historical ABC models. They are different because they rely on physical measurements of resource productivity and capacity. The flow of cost is also different in resource planning ABC models. Let's take a closer look (see Figure 6–1).

Resource planning starts with the number of planned cost objects. For example, assume that the forecast number of service installations is 1,000. Also assume that it takes, on average, five purchase orders to order the needed parts. This means that 5,000 purchase orders must be processed to meet the plan.

FIGURE 6-1

Resource Planning

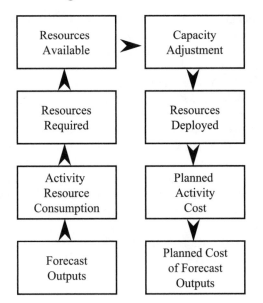

The first part of resource planning is figuring out the resources you need to do the forecast work. This is not a costing exercise. Rather, it is an exercise in determining physical requirements and comparing this amount with the resources currently available to do the work. The second step is capacity planning and costing.

What is the impact of 5,000 purchase orders on the work involved and the resources required? To determine this, you need to know the time or amount of each resource required to process each purchase order. For example, if it takes a half hour to process one purchase order, then 2,500 hours will be required to process 5,000 purchase orders.

Inevitably this simple calculation is more complex in real-world situations. We need to measure the productivity of the resource. We need to estimate the practical capacity available in the activity—in this case, the number of purchase orders that can be processed under normal circumstances and reasonable assumptions. We also need to recognize that resources may also perform other activities, resulting in different outputs.

Once we have completed this computation of physical resource requirements, we are ready to move to the next step. This is planning

BUSINESS INTELLIGENCE ABOUT RESOURCES

The cost dimension of ABC has three components: resources, activities, and cost objects. Historically, most of the emphasis in ABC has been placed on activities and cost objects. Resources has been a repository for cost information from the general ledger. This information has been reorganized by resource type rather than general ledger line item, but it has still been a staging point for getting cost to the activities.

This all changes with resource planning. The resources compo-nent of ABC is now a repository of human resource information as well as key data on equipment, technology, and facilities. It is a dictionary of skills, capacity, productivity, and activity capability. When combined with information from human capital management, equipment management, and other systems, it becomes a powerful database of organizational capability and capacity management information.

capacity, determining the cost of required resources, and assigning this cost to planned output.

Planning capacity is the decision about what resources to deploy to do the planned work. How many resources do we have available today? Given the planned requirements, does this mean that we have unused resources or that we have too few resources on hand? If we have unused resources, can we reduce their quantity or redeploy them to other productive uses? If we have too few resources on hand, can we find properly trained resources to fill the gap? If we can't, how do we manage demand?

Activity-Based Budgeting

Resource planning has probably got your imagination running wild with the possibilities it opens up. Imagine the finance director of a large state government agency. One of her responsibilities is to prepare the annual plan and budget and submit it to the governor for scrutiny. Once it has survived the governor's scrutiny, she will probably have to appear before a legislative committee for further grilling.

Do you think this process is either easy or enjoyable? Certainly not! Preparing the budget with traditional accounting tools is mostly a shot in the dark. It is susceptible to the opinions and biases of the management team. In fact, you could characterize budgeting as "the process of determining the increase or decrease from last year's budget based on relative political power."

And then it gets worse. When the finance director appears before the governor and the legislative committee, she will be asked tough questions about why she proposes an increase in spending, and how it relates to required service levels. They may even ask how well the department is performing! This is difficult because there are few credible facts that she can present in support of her budget proposal.

It is different with resource planning. A budget built from an underlying resource planning model is fact-based rather than opinion-based. It is more accurate and easier to defend.

Many organizations use resource planning to prepare an activity-based budget. For example, a retailer in the U.K. prepares an activity-based budget for its distribution activities.[2] Caterpillar, Inc., has used activity-based budgeting for several years.[3] Dayton Technologies designed its ABC system specifically to support activity-based budgeting.

Navistar successfully implemented activity-based budgeting in 1999. This effort leveraged an existing ABC model and was designed to allow operational managers to

- View the impact of changes in the product mix on resources and activities
- Forecast the potential impact of future growth and new products
- Focus the annual budget cycle on activities and processes
- Manage capacity constraints by resource and activity

In addition to these planned benefits, activity-based budgeting helped Navistar identify and track its continuous improvement programs. Navistar also experienced a significant reduction in the effort required to evaluate the impact of various mix and volume scenarios.[4]

Government organizations find resource planning a cost-effective engine for performance budgeting. Performance budgeting is mandated by the U.S. Government Performance and Result Act (GPRA). It is an integrated system of strategic planning, performance measurement, and budgeting.[5]

Resource planning helps organizations develop outcome-based spending plans in as little as half the time required to develop traditional budgets. The ease of preparation is in contrast to historical difficulties with zero-based budgeting (ZBB) and performance planning budgeting systems (PPBS).

Decision Simulation

Resource planning ABC models are forward looking. Rather than measuring the past, they predict future costs based on certain assumptions. This makes them ideal for answering "what if?" questions and simulating the cost impact of different decision scenarios.

Take the case of a state department of revenue. One of the department's responsibilities was collecting taxes from delinquent taxpayers. The department had two different activities to collect taxes, varying in cost and method of collection.

Like most state departments at the time, the department had a very tight budget. A close look at the two activities and their success rates showed that the revenues collected exceeded the activity cost of collection. It was likely that an *increase* in the budget for collections would provide a positive return. But which method would offer the largest return and the best chance of obtaining new budget funds?

The department used resource planning to determine the net revenue impact of additional funding of the collection activities. The analysis showed that while both methods were cost-effective, method 2 returned the larger amount of net revenues. Method 2 was significantly more productive in collecting taxes from taxpayers who owed more than $10,000 in taxes (Figure 6–2).

The simulation was sufficiently compelling to justify additional budget funding for the collection activities. It was dubbed the "activity-based revenue" method by the staff of the department.

Decision simulations using resource planning have many applications, including the following:

- Understanding the cost and capacity impact of process improvements
- Identifying which resources should be redeployed from process improvement
- Examining alternative ways of using capacity
- Estimating the cost impact of new initiatives or mandates
- Managing the velocity of cost changes to minimize the increase in resource requirements when demand increases and to increase the reduction in resource requirements when demand diminishes

FIGURE 6-2

Activity-Based Revenue

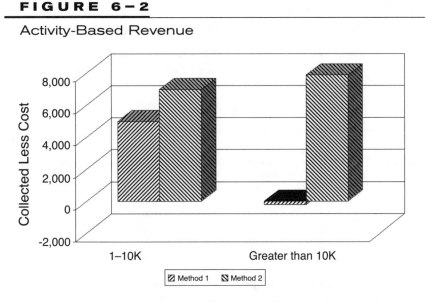

Net tax revenues collected using method 2 exceed those collected using method 1. Method 2 is particularly cost-effective for collecting from taxpayers who owe more than $10,000.

TIME-BASED ABC

Combining resource planning with activity time measurements creates a variation on ABC known as time-based ABC. This approach is a significant breakthrough for the field of ABC. The *Economist* dubbed this approach "Son of ABC."[6] Here is how it works.

A warehouse employs 20 people at a monthly cost of $4,000 per person. This gives a total budgeted cost for people of $80,000. (A summary of this example is found in Figure 6–3.)

Each warehouse employee is at work for a total of 10,560 minutes during a typical month. The time available to do work is less than this amount because of breaks, holidays, staff meetings, and the like. The available time is generally 75 percent of the total time, so each person has 7,920 minutes available to do work in each month. Multiplying this by 20 employees provides the practical capacity of the warehouse—158,400 minutes. This is the time available to perform activities.

Will the time available to do the work be sufficient, given the likely demand for product from the warehouse? Will it be insufficient? We can

FIGURE 6-3

Warehouse Example of Time-Based ABC

People	Monthly Cost ($4,000 per Person)	Time per Person (in minutes)	Available Time per Person (75%)	Practical Capacity (in minutes)
20	$80,000	10,560	7,920	158,400

Cost per Minute (monthly cost divided by practical capacity) = $0.50

Activity	Unit Time	Cost per Unit (unit time × cost per minute)	Monthly Quantity	Demand (in minutes)
Pick	15	$7.50	8,000	120,000
Special pack	10	$5.00	2,000	20,000
Air shipment	5	$2.50	1,000	5,000

Resources required = 145,000

Capacity Use (resources required divided by practical capacity) = 92%

answer this question if we know the activities, the time it takes to do the work each time there is a customer order, and the total volume of work for each activity.

For example, the pick activity takes 15 minutes for each order. If there are 8,000 orders in a month, the total time to pick product will be 120,000 minutes. A review of Figure 6–3 shows the same calculation for the special pack and ship-by-air activities. Based on the forecast demand, the total minutes required are 145,000. This represents 92 percent of the available minutes during a month.

How do we interpret the capacity utilization of 92 percent? If each person in the warehouse provides 5 percent of the available capacity, then 92 percent represents 18.4 people. Thus, 1.6 people are unemployed at the forecast level of demand.

What are the planning implications of this information? Possibly one person should be transferred to another department in the company. Possibly two people could be transferred and the remaining staff asked to work a little overtime. Alternatively, the forecast for the following month could be higher—in which case it might make sense to maintain current staffing levels.

What if the time-based ABC model shows that there are insufficient resources available to complete the required work? Options could include increasing staffing, working overtime, or improving the efficiency of the work. This latter option involves changes in the process that reduce the time needed to process each order.

In addition to its predictive capabilities, time-based ABC also increases the accuracy of ABC models. In a standard ABC model, all costs are associated with activities and cost objects, regardless of whether or not the resources they represent are fully utilized. In contrast, time-based ABC attaches to activities and cost objects only the cost of resources used. The cost of unused minutes is the cost of unused capacity. This approach is more accurate and avoids the risk of the "death spiral" scenario described in Chapter 2.

In practice, there may be another reason why time-based ABC models are more accurate. This is because time-based ABC models can accommodate differences in customer demand in a cost-effective manner.

In the warehouse example in Figure 6–3, for example, the unit cost of picking a product is $7.50. The unit costs of special packing and shipping by air are $5.00 and $2.50, respectively. Customer A orders a product that requires no special handling and is shipped via ground. The cost of processing customer A's order is $7.50. Customer B orders a product that is environmentally hazardous and requires special handling. It is also shipped via air. The total cost of customer B's order is $15.00. (Each customer has its own equation showing the time it takes to meet that customer's requirements. Time equations are covered in Chapter 5.)

A standard ABC model can produce the same result by identifying each activity separately. The time-based ABC model, however, uses a single activity—processing orders—and provides the same accurate result using a time equation to model each customer's demands. The data for the time equations are found in the company's ERP system, allowing automation of the measurement approach. The time-based ABC solution is therefore more cost-effective than the standard ABC approach.

In practice, it is likely that a standard ABC model will not include each individual activity in the warehouse. Rather, it will include only the higher-level activity "process orders." This is because the increase in the number of activities increases the cost of building and maintaining the model. In practice, therefore, time-based ABC models are likely to be more accurate than the standard ABC models they replace.

The ability to accommodate varying customer demands in a cost-effective manner opens up a new opportunity for ABC: large-scale customer profitability systems. For the first time, ABC can measure the cost and profitability of customers when there are millions of customers and high levels of process complexity and customer diversity.

For example, each month Charles Schwab reports the profit from each of 8,000,000 customers. A large communications company reports profit for more than 20,000,000 customers. Percival Foods reports the profit on 500,000 customers.[7]

The Percival Foods model is a good example of how much complexity can be handled by modern ABC systems. In a typical month, the Percival ABC model processes transactions for 400,000 orders, 600,000 shipments, and 800,000 invoice history transaction lines. The model includes 9,000 general ledger lines and about 350 activities.

ABC for customer profitability is covered in depth in Chapter 10.

SUMMARY

Resource planning turns ABC into a predictive tool. It forecasts resource capacity based on planned outputs and a standard process. It serves as both a planning tool and a decision analysis tool. It is the basis for preparing fact-based budgets as well as business cases for differing scenarios.

Time-based ABC is a cost-effective method of implementing resource planning. It uses time equations to simplify and automate the ABC model. It is used to build ABC models in complex, diverse environments. It is particularly effective in building customer profitability models where millions of customers vary in their demands.

KEY TERMS

Activity-based budgeting (ABB).   Preparation of cost budgets using resource planning to estimate workload and resource requirements.

Decision simulation.   Analysis of the cost and profit impact of alternative decision scenarios using resource planning.

Performance budgeting.   An integrated system of strategic planning, performance measurement. and budgeting. Mandated by the U.S. Government Performance and Results Act (GPRA), it uses resource planning to formulate the budget.

Practical capacity.   A realistic estimate of the amount of time available to do work, after deducting breaks, sick leave, staff meetings, and other nonproductive uses of time.

Carmel Clay Public Library
Thursday February 25 2016 02:45PM
www.carmel.lib.in.us
Phone: (317) 844-3361
Telephone Renewal: (317) 814-3936

Barcode: 31690011821189
Title: The Supreme Court [videorecord...
Type: DVD
Due date: 3/3/2016,23:59

Barcode: 31690018763533
Title: Remix strategy : the three law...
Type: BOOK
Due date: 3/17/2016,23:59

Barcode: 31690010797786
Title: Common cents : how to succeed ...
Type: BOOK
Due date: 3/17/2016,23:59

Total items checked out: 3

Visit our website to view
your account details and
material due dates.

Resources available.   Resources currently deployed to the process and available to meet customer needs.

Resource planning.   An activity-based model that predicts resource requirements based on forecast levels of demand.

Resources required.   Resources required to process the forecast outputs.

Theoretical capacity.   Total time available to do work before deducting nonproductive time.

Time-based ABC.   A method of implementing ABC and resource planning using time equations. It may be more accurate than standard ABC models and costs less to build and maintain.

Time equations.   Compound equations combining time estimates from several activities into a single activity driver.

R E F E R E N C E S

1 Robert S. Kaplan and Robin Cooper, *Cost and Effect* (Boston: Harvard Business School Press, 1998).

2 J. Innes and F. Mitchell, *Activity-Based Costing: A Review with Case Studies* (London: The Chartered Institute of Management Accountants, 1990).

3 C. J. McNair, "Interdependence and Control: Traditional vs. Activity-Based Costing Responsibility Accounting," *Journal of Cost Management*, Summer 1990, pp. 15–25.

4 Heather Kos and William S. McKinney, "Walking the Talk: Implementing Real Activity-Based Budgeting" (Beaverton: ABC Technologies, 1999).

5 Information on performance budgeting and the Government Performance and Results Act (GPRA) can be found at http://www.dod.mil/comptroller/icenter/budget/perfbudg.htm.

6 "Easier than ABC: Will 'activity-based-costing' make a comeback?," *Economist,* October 25, 2003.

7 See Chapter 10 for a description of Percival Food's ABC system.

PART FOUR

Activity-Based Management

Part 4 reveals how ABC information is used to achieve the *ABC performance breakthrough*. You'll learn the secrets of activity-based management (ABM) and the "tools of the trade." You'll also learn about organizations that use ABM to improve their financial performance and customer profitability.

ABM uses ABC information to help meet two important goals. First, it helps improve the *value* received by the customer. Second, it helps improve the *profits* earned—or cost-effectiveness achieved—from providing this value.

Chapter 7 answers the question, "What is activity-based management?" You learn

- How to improve the performance of activities
- How *not* to cut cost the *old-fashioned accounting way*
- How to permanently reduce cost the *activity-based way*

Chapter 8 showcases the tools of activity-based management. You learn to

- Use strategic analysis to find profitable opportunities
- Apply value analysis to processes
- Perform cost analysis to identify cost-reduction opportunities
- Use storyboarding to document, measure, analyze, and improve process performance

- Use life-cycle costing to make decisions about products based on their lifetime costs of ownership and use
- Use target costing to design products to meet a predetermined cost

Chapter 9 shows how ABM helped a company move from *worst-in-class* to *best-in-class* performance in just two to three years. This case study is a lesson in the ways in which ABM can help improve a company's competitive position and financial results.

Chapter 10 focuses on customer profitability—a major emphasis of modern ABC systems. The Deluxe Corporation and Percival Foods cases illustrate how to uncover profit drivers and improve customer and company profitability.

This section of *Common Cents* brings to life the concept of *business intelligence* using ABC. Putting ABC information in the hands of decision makers increases their power to improve financial performance.

CHAPTER 7

Activity-Based Improvement

To achieve continuous improvement, you must be informed. You need accurate and timely information about the work that is being done (the activities) and the objects of that work (the products and the customers). That is what activity-based costing (ABC) is all about.

But gaining good-quality information is only half the battle. The real key to success is putting ABC information to work to *identify appropriate strategies, improve product design,* and *remove waste* from operating activities.

In striving for these goals, you'll find numerous ways to improve your ability to meet customer needs profitably. Take the case of Stockham Valve and Fittings. Stockham used ABC to

- Match parts to the lowest-cost processes
- Pick new parts patterns to reduce subsequent manufacturing cost
- Initiate equipment modifications to reduce cost
- Increase the price of products that were priced below ABC cost
- Drop unprofitable products from marketing's price sheet and the production schedule

...and Stockham Valve and Fittings has barely started to tap the potential of ABC!

Using ABC to improve a business is called *activity-based management*, or simply ABM. ABM is management analysis that brings the full benefits of ABC to your company. It guides efforts to adapt business strategies to better meet competitive pressures, as well as to improve business operations.

An increasing number of organizations now practice ABM. General Motors, Hewlett-Packard, Siemens, Navistar, Tektronix, Black & Decker, General Electric, Deluxe Corporation, Standard Insurance, the U.S. Army, the U.S. Marine Corps, the South Dakota Department of Transportation, and a host of other organizations, large and small, have put ABC systems in place at various locations. All are managing activities as the route to business improvement.

In this chapter you'll learn how you too can use ABM for business improvement. The keys to this include the following:

- How ABM uses ABC information
- What ABM is
- How to improve the performance of activities
- How *not* to reduce cost the *old-fashioned accounting way*
- How to permanently reduce cost the *activity-based way*

THE LINK TO ABC

Activity-based management and ABC are made for each other. ABC supplies the information needed to manage activities for business improvement. ABM uses this information in various analyses designed to yield this improvement.

Figure 7–1 shows this interrelationship. ABC is in the center, at the heart of activity-based management. Activity-based management encircles ABC, drawing its power from the ABC database.

Basically, ABM consists of several analysis tools that use ABC information. These include value analysis, storyboarding, and strategic analysis. All of them will be covered in the next chapter. For now, however, let's focus on the more basic element—*how activity-based management works*.

ACTIVITY-BASED MANAGEMENT

Activity-based management aims directly at two goals that are common to all organizations. The first goal is to improve the value received by

FIGURE 7-1

ABC and Activity-Based Management (ABM) Are Closely Interlinked

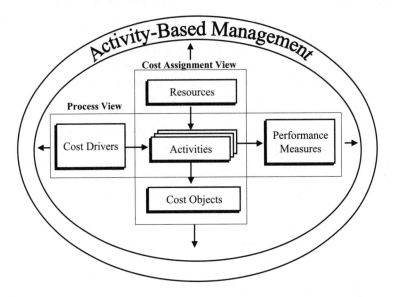

ABM focuses on business improvement, and ABC supplies the information needed for analysis.

customers. The second is to improve profits by providing this value (or in the case of not-for-profit organizations, improving the cost-effectiveness of the value to clients). These goals are reached by focusing on the management of activities.

This starts with a simple understanding: Customers or clients have very simple wants. They want products and services that fit a specific need. They want quality. They want service. They want an affordable price. They want to be delighted. *And they want it now!*

Meeting customer wants is one thing. Meeting them profitably is quite another.

It's not enough to tell stockholders that your products have the highest quality in the industry, or that customers consistently rate you highest in customer satisfaction. You must also provide an adequate return on stockholder investment.

If you are a government agency, it's not enough to show that you provide the highest quality of service. Your stakeholders—particularly

WHAT IS CUSTOMER VALUE?

Customer value involves what customers get (the realization) and what they give up to get it (the sacrifice). Subtract sacrifice from realization and you have customer value.

Realization comes in a bundle. Included in the bundle are the features of the product or service. For a car, features include interior space; engine size; type of transmission; front-, rear-, or all-wheel drive; and so on. For a checking account, features include electronic bill paying, access to automatic teller machines, and 24-hour verification of your account balance.

But realization goes well beyond features. Whether they are buying cars or checking services, customers value good quality and service. In some cases, quality is the primary purchase consideration. In all cases, quality affects the cost of using the product or service.

Customers also buy future costs when they buy a product or service. Future costs are incurred to use and service a car. Fees are incurred for services associated with a checking account. Some products (such as nuclear fuel) also have disposal costs.

There's no realization without sacrifice. Many products and services require time and effort, both in the initial purchase and in learning how to use them. It takes time, for example, to master a new software program.[1]

the executive and legislature that provide the agency's funding—expect an efficient delivery of service.

There's really no conflict here. In the long run, your profitability or efficiency is important to your customers. This is because your customers want you around for the long haul (which you won't be if you're unprofitable or high cost).

To support this, ABM adheres to the belief that managing activities is the route to profitably or cost-effectively improving customer value. Each activity contributes in its own way to this overall goal. Each makes a measurable contribution to its customers—be it quality, timeliness, reliable delivery, or low cost.

It's important to realize, too, that managing activities *is not* a custodial task. Rather, it's a process of relentless and continuous improvement of all aspects of your business.

THE RULES OF ACTIVITY-BASED MANAGEMENT

Rule 1 Deploy resources to the activities that yield the maximum strategic benefit.

Rule 2 Improve what matters to the customer.

This involves an ongoing search for opportunities to improve. That search, in turn, involves a careful and methodical study of activities. What activities should be performed? And how should these activities be carried out?

Let's address those questions by looking at some examples of improving strategic position and capability.

Improving Strategic Position

Activities are determined by strategic choices. A successful business deploys resources to those activities that yield the highest strategic benefit.

Example: A hospital makes a strategic decision to be a certified trauma center. This deliberate choice determines the activities and resources needed. A trauma center requires a different set of medical activities—and resources—than would a cancer treatment center or other types of medical services.

What is needed: The hospital must analyze ABC information about the link between its strategy and the activities and resources needed to put the strategy into place. These analyses can guide strategic decisions prior to implementation, as well as help evaluate the ongoing effectiveness of these decisions.

As another example, Armistead Insurance Company used ABC to refine the strategy of a computer data services unit. This unit performed data analysis for fast-food franchisers. Unfortunately, the operation was unprofitable, and the existing cost system provided few insights into why this was so.

ABC showed that Armistead's customers differed in cost and profitability. Small customers were found to be unprofitable because of the high cost of acquiring and installing a new system for each of them. As a result, Armistead raised prices on small franchisers and started a program to reduce the cost of acquiring new customers.[2]

Improving Strategic Capability

The key to implementing any strategy successfully is to improve what matters to your customer. This is not a new idea. The economist Ludwig von Mises, for example, wrote about it 70 years ago. But it's never been more important than it is now.

What really does matter to your customer? That's going to vary from business to business, and from activity to activity within the business.

Example: Ford Motor Company says, "Quality Is Job One." What Ford means is that good quality is the most important consideration for its customers.

What is needed: Ford needs to analyze information about quality. What does *quality* mean to its customers? Is it low number of faults on delivery or doors closing with a satisfying clunk? If it's number of faults on delivery, what's the defect rate? What has been the trend for this key performance measure? Which activities were responsible for the defects? How much cost is associated with this *poor quality*?

ABC can supply much of this information. It points out the cost of poor quality by measuring the costs of detection and correction activities. Information on cost drivers and performance measures reveals opportunities for improvement and helps monitor progress. The impact of poor quality on product cost is revealed in each product's bill of activities. (This last piece of information is important because quality can vary significantly from product to product.)

Dayton Technologies is a case in point. It was widely believed at Dayton that scrap was free. For one thing, very little material was lost. Scrapped extrusions were ground into powder and fed back to the extruders as raw material. For another, the existing cost system "confirmed" that scrap cost nothing—only good extrusions carried cost.

Implementing an ABC system brought Dayton Technologies face to face with the reality of scrap. The company found that it was expensive to run extruders just to produce scrap (including the cost of extra capacity). There were also many costly activities associated with detecting and correcting quality problems (such as inspecting, checking line work, and handling returns from customers). And grinding up rejected extrusions required additional equipment and resources.

Dayton's ABC system also revealed the impact of quality differences from one product to another. Reviewing the bill of activities revealed the cost of poor quality for each product and identified candidates for quality improvement.

IMPROVING PERFORMANCE

There are three steps to improving activity performance. First, analyze activities to identify opportunities for improvement. Second, look for factors that cause waste (the cost drivers). Third, measure the things—time, quality, and so on—that an activity should be doing well if it's contributing to the organization's success and the profitable servicing of customers.

THE STEPS TO IMPROVEMENT

Step 1   Analyze activities.
Step 2   Dig for drivers.
Step 3   Measure what matters.

Analyze Activities

Understanding why work is done and how well it's done is the key to eliminating waste. This can also strengthen strategic position, as many organizations can testify. Here are some analysis guidelines to follow.

Identify Nonessential Activities
If an activity *is not* essential, it's reasonable to ask, "Why do we do it?" If we ask *why*, it's an easy step to the next question, "How do we get rid of it?"

Activities with value fall into one of two categories. In the first, an activity has value if it's essential to the customer. Polishing a precision optic, for example, has value because the customer wants outstanding optical performance.

In the second, an activity has value if it's essential to the functioning of the organization. Preparing financial statements, for example, is not of immediate concern to customers. But it does satisfy an organizational need. (You must prepare financial statements to satisfy stockholders, bankers, regulators, and other stakeholders.)

All other activities are non-value-added. These are activities that are judged nonessential, and they are candidates for elimination.

Expediting products is an example of a non-value-added activity. Customers don't care whether products are expedited. They just want to receive the product by a certain time. So expediting really doesn't add

HOW TO ANALYZE ACTIVITIES

Step 1 Identify nonessential   **Step 3** Compare activities to
activities.   the best practices.

Step 2 Analyze significant   **Step 4** Examine the links
activities.   between activities.

value for the customer. It can be eliminated, without customers even noticing, if order and manufacturing lead times are reduced. This, in turn, permits reduced batch sizes and increased flexibility.

Analyze Significant Activities

A typical business can have two to three hundred activities. There simply isn't the time (or the resources) to analyze all of them at once.

The key, then, is to focus on significant activities—the ones that are important to customers or to operating the business. Moreover, these are the activities that provide the greatest opportunities for improvement.

In fact, I've yet to visit an organization that didn't fit Pareto's rule: *80 percent of what you care about is determined by 20 percent of what you do.*

You can easily test this for yourself. Pick a department in your organization. Then rank its activities in descending order of cost. You'll likely find that 20 percent of the activities cause 80 percent of the cost—and those are the activities that are worth analyzing.

Compare Activities to the Best Practices

An activity should bear comparison to a similar activity in another company or another part of the organization. Just because an activity is value-added doesn't mean that it's efficient or that its work is of good quality.

Comparing an activity to a benchmark of good practice helps determine the scope for improvement. Xerox, for example, has an extensive benchmarking program. Activities are rated on such factors as quality, lead times, flexibility, cost, and customer satisfaction. Each activity is rated against an identified best practice. In the case of distribution, for example, the best practice was that of the mail-order distributor L.L. Bean.[3]

As another example, you may determine that "taking customer orders" is an essential activity. You find that it's being done manually. The best practice, however, uses Internet order taking, which costs less per transaction, has a lower error rate, and provides faster service. Clearly there's room for improvement over manual order taking.

Examine the Links between Activities

Activities work together in a chain to meet common goals. The links in this chain must be constructed to minimize time and duplication of work.

The product design process illustrates what can be accomplished here.

In the traditional approach, design activities are performed serially. Product designers prepare the product specifications without consulting production. When the design is finished, production tries to manufacture the product (often with difficulty). Not surprisingly, this approach is repetitive, time-consuming, and costly.

Concurrent engineering is a better way to go. In this approach, activities are performed concurrently. Product design, manufacturing, marketing, and procurement work together toward a common goal. There's less repetition and duplication, and better-quality products get to the customer faster.

Studying product or transaction flows can also reveal delay and repetition. *Ideally*, work should proceed in an uninterrupted, continuous flow. Each activity should process a transaction only once.

For example, a study of Pacific Bell's customer payment center found that 25 percent of the center's work was devoted to processing 0.1 percent of the payments. More than a third of all payments were processed twice, and some were processed several times.

To improve on this, a new work flow was proposed to change the way payments were processed. Individual work cells were proposed for each type of payment processing. The emphasis was on processing each payment once in a continuous flow. It was estimated that these changes would reduce resource requirements by 25 percent.[4]

Dig for Drivers

Identifying nonessential and poor-performing activities is the first step in improvement. The second step is to look for things that require you to perform nonessential activities or to perform below par. These things are the cost drivers.

For example, let's say you identified "moving the product" as nonessential. The customer doesn't care about the product's being moved from one process to another because that activity doesn't affect what's received. So "moving the product" is a non-value-added activity.

But how do you eliminate the activity? You can't, as long as there's distance between the two processes. Failure to move the product would result in piles of inventory at the end of the first process and no work for the second process.

The distance between the two processes (or the plant layout) is the moving activity's cost driver. If you reorganize the plant to place the two processes next to each other, the cost driver is eliminated. It's no longer necessary to move the products over a distance.

Understanding and managing cost drivers is crucial to improvement. Simply understanding that waste exists doesn't automatically result in removal of that waste. Only when the causes of waste (the cost drivers) are addressed can it be removed.

Measure What Matters

Activity and cost-driver analysis is periodic. But activity performance goes on day in and day out. How do you ensure that ongoing efforts will successfully (and collectively) focus on what matters to the organization?

The answer is to develop a performance measurement system that fosters improvement in the right areas. Such a measurement system has three elements.[5]

Determine the Mission
The first step is to determine what matters to the company. Generally this results in a strategic plan—a statement of mission and the key objectives that are considered important to achieving the mission.

Zytec Corporation, for example, wrote a mission statement that focused on the following six objectives:

1. Improve total quality commitment.
2. Reduce total cycle time.
3. Improve Zytec's service to customers.
4. Improve profitability and financial stability.
5. Improve housekeeping and safety.
6. Increase employee involvement.

These objectives defined what was important to the success of the company as a whole. They articulated a vision of how the company should focus its improvement efforts.[6]

HOW TO MEASURE PERFORMANCE

Step 1 Determine the mission.
Step 2 Communicate the objectives.
Step 3 Develop the measures.

Partly as a result of this approach to performance measurement, Zytec's improvement program was extremely successful. Major improvements were seen in all areas of the mission statement.

Communicate the Objectives

After specifying what matters, the next step is communicating the strategic plan to the people in the organization. This is done with a *strategy map*, a clearly understandable cause-and-effect diagram of the strategy. Through the strategy map, each person understands the importance of the company's mission and how each objective relates to his or her activity. With this understanding comes the possibility of a collective focus on a common goal.[7]

Develop the Measures

The final step is to develop a scorecard of goals and performance measures for each area of activity. These measures signify how each activity contributes to the overall mission. They also coordinate and motivate the efforts of the activity, and they provide facts about the performance of the activity that direct improvement efforts.

Zytec did this by identifying annual improvement targets for all activities associated with each of the six objectives. For example, the automatic insertion activity identified its total quality commitment as "improve yields by 2 percent." It set its cycle-time target as "reduce average cycle times by 5 percent."

As another example, the Oscilloscope Group at Tektronix found ABC to be a fertile source of performance measures. Cost drivers were plotted against the cost of related activities over time. The organization planned to prepare large charts showing these relationships and to display them in the activity area. The idea was to draw people's attention to the relationship between the cost driver's quantity and the resources dedicated to the activities.

FIGURE 7-2

Cost Driver Chart from Tektronix's Oscilloscope Group

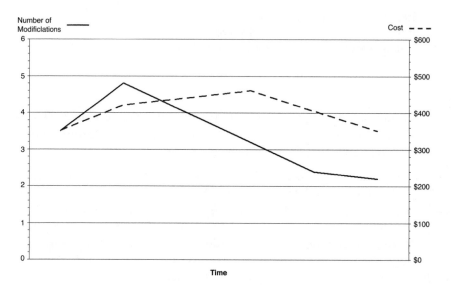

This chart plots the cost assigned to activities, such as maintaining bills of materials, against the cost driver "number of modifications." This stimulated extensive discussion of how to respond to a significant drop in the number of engineering modifications to products.*

Figure 7–2 shows such a chart for the cost driver "number of modifications." The number of modifications was a count of engineering changes made to products. It was believed that this affected several activities, including engineering and bill-of-materials maintenance.

While the graphs were being prepared, there was a significant drop in the number of modifications. There was also a reduction in the resources used, but the effect was neither immediate nor proportionate to the drop in modifications.

Before any resources could be redeployed, a number of questions had to be addressed. Should there be "surge capacity" for a new product introduction? (There usually were many modifications associated with a new product.) What was the impact of the engineers learning to handle modifications with less time and fewer resources? How should the company

*The numbers shown are not the actual Tektronix numbers.

deal with the concern of some engineers that the analysis might result in layoffs?

Despite these questions, it was believed that the measurement exercise was worthwhile. The graphs stimulated a lot of discussion about managing activities and use of resources. This resulted in positive changes, which is the goal of ABC.[8]

REDUCING COST THE OLD-FASHIONED ACCOUNTING WAY

ABM is quite different from old-fashioned management accounting. Management accounting focuses on meeting cost targets. Standard costs and traditional expense budgets define the goal, and the analysis focuses on controlling variances (the difference between actual and budget). The emphasis is on "managing by the numbers" while paying little attention to the underlying activities or the customers who benefit.

Attempting to cut costs without restructuring the work is putting the cart before the horse and is doomed to failure. Many companies attest to cutting costs the old-fashioned accounting way, but few achieve lasting savings. In some cases, costs have actually gone up, while employees complain about stress and increased workloads.

In contrast, the heart of ABM is the activity. Cost management focuses on the performance of each activity and its use of resources. Managing activities better—*not some abstract measure of cost*—is the key to permanent cost reduction.

REDUCING COST THE ACTIVITY-BASED WAY

Reducing cost is *only one* of several focal points of ABM. This is the first major difference between ABM and the old-fashioned accounting way. Improving quality, flexibility, and service—the importance of which vary from one business to another—is also central to ABM.

The second major difference is the way costs are reduced. Cost reduction is best achieved by changing the way activities are used or performed (managing the activities first), then redeploying the resources freed by the improvement.

The following five guidelines show how to reduce cost the activity-based way:

HOW TO REDUCE COSTS PERMANENTLY

Rule 1 Reduce the time and effort required to perform activities.
Rule 2 Eliminate unnecessary activities.
Rule 3 Select low-cost activities.
Rule 4 Share activities wherever possible.
Rule 5 Redeploy unused resources.

1. Reduce the Time and Effort Required to Perform Activities

A key element of improvement is reducing the time and effort needed to perform activities. This reduction can come from process or product improvement.

For example, the time needed to set up a machine can be reduced by improved training, eliminating conflicts in employee assignments, and placing tools and dies in convenient locations. Practicing the setup routine can create the manufacturing version of a Grand Prix pit-stop team. Reductions of 90 percent in setup time are not unusual.

Reductions in setup time can also come from changes in product design. Engineers at Dayton Technologies, for example, changed the specifications for the vinyl weatherizing material used in extruded window frames. This eliminated the need to add a weather-resistant coating to the frame. As a result, setup time was reduced because a simpler die could be used and a second extruder wasn't required.

Reductions in time and effort may come not from the activity in question, but from the preceding activity. For example, the defect rate of parts received by a machining activity is a cost driver for that activity. Improving quality in the preceding activity reduces the quantity of this cost driver and the effort required by machining.

In another case, a retail distributor used ABC to highlight "breaking up packages" as a high-cost activity. This cost was reduced by asking suppliers to reduce the size of the packages and to design packages for easier break-up.[9]

2. Eliminate Unnecessary Activities

Some activities are candidates for elimination because they aren't valued by customers and aren't essential to running the organization. It's possible,

DOES IMPROVED QUALITY REDUCE COST?

It used to be a common belief that improved quality meant higher cost. This seemed reasonable. Doesn't improved quality mean more inspectors, more rework, more costly warranties, and the like?

How wrong we were. It's *poor* quality that costs money (and loses customers). Poor quality is doing the job more than once. It's wasting materials. It's having costly systems to keep track of defective parts. It's paying the salaries of hordes of inspectors. It's incurring the cost of warranties and customer returns. And it's suffering the anger of disgruntled customers.

Improving quality is a sure way to reduce cost. Do it right the first time. Work on reducing cost drivers that cause errors (such as frequent schedule changes, excessive process variability, or poor product design).

Paradoxically, reducing cost the activity-based way almost always improves quality. Eliminating unnecessary work, for example, reduces opportunities to "get it wrong" and tightens the linkages between activities.

Activity-based management fits well with any quality improvement program. It encourages the actions that improve quality, and it directs attention to the quality improvements with the greatest cost-reduction potential.

for example, to eliminate material-handling activities through changes to the processes or products.

There are a variety of possibilities here. Steps can be taken to ensure that all incoming materials and parts are fit for use. The parts can be delivered directly to the shop floor as needed. Changes can be requested in the vendor's production process to improve quality and increase responsiveness. And parts that cause quality problems can be redesigned to eliminate those problems.

Once these changes have been made, it's *no longer necessary* to inspect parts when they're delivered or to place the parts on the shelf in the stockroom. Eliminating these activities reduces overall cost and the cost of products that no longer use those activities.

Stockham Valve and Fittings, for example, used ABC to identify process changes that would eliminate scrap, rework, and other activities associated with poor quality. The design of the core box was changed on one particularly costly product. The improved quality was enough to reduce the product's cost by 20 percent.

Stockham also used ABC to identify a group of products that had potential for cost reduction. Among the changes made was an improvement in the tooling on one product. This single change eliminated several manufacturing operations and the related setup, moving, and scheduling activities.

Prior to this, the product's ABC cost had exceeded its selling price. Now it's competitive again.

3. Select Low-Cost Activities

Designers of products and processes often have choices among competing activities. This offers a means of reducing cost by picking the lowest-cost activity.

A designer of an electronics product, for example, may be able to specify the type of activity required for inserting components into circuit boards. Components such as resistors, diodes, and integrated circuits (ICs) may be inserted either manually or automatically. Depending on the design of the component, several different automatic activities can be used to insert components, including axial, radial, and IC insertion and surface mount devices.

Each of these activities has a different set of resources associated with it. Manual insertion is predominantly a direct labor activity. Automatic insertion, however, requires equipment, software, setup for each batch of circuit boards that receives components, and additional process engineering and training. The resources required for each type of automatic insertion or placement also differ.

Because each of these activities has a different cost, the designer's selection has an important impact on costs. At Hewlett-Packard's Roseville Network Division, for example, the ABC system showed that manual insertion cost about three times more than automatic insertion.[10]

Process designers face similar choices. For example, a part designed for machine insertion might also be inserted manually. A process designer may choose to have the part inserted manually because a drop in the batch size makes it uneconomical to program and set up an insertion machine.

Stockham Valve and Fittings used ABC to identify parts that could be run at lower cost on different equipment. One product, for example, was sold for $9.68 per unit, but had an ABC cost of $12.63. Despite this loss, the product could not be dropped (it was a complementary product sold to a key customer). Its price couldn't be increased, either.

The solution was to shift production to an automated machine that was more suited to the design and volume of the product. This shift reduced the number of operations required. It also reduced the need for batch activities, such as scheduling and moving, and reduced the cost to $9.86 per unit. While this represented a small loss on the product, the customer was now profitable overall.

4. Share Activities Wherever Possible

If a customer has unique needs, it's necessary to perform activities that are specific to that customer. However, if customers have common needs, it's wasteful not to service those needs with the same activities.

For example, product designers can use common parts in new product designs. A common part is one that's used in several products to perform the same function (such as a gasket used in several car models). The only parts that need to be unique are those that add product-differentiating functions valued by customers.

The activities associated with common parts—such as part number maintenance, scheduling, and vendor relations—are shared by all products that use them. Sharing parts increases the volume of parts served each time an activity is carried out, thus reducing the cost per part.

This insight was recognized by the Oscilloscope Group of Tektronix. This group introduced an ABC system that used "number of different parts" as an activity driver. This driver then assigned the cost of procurement activities to the parts.

The result was an increase in the reported cost of unique (and therefore low-volume) parts and a reduction in the cost of common parts. The engineers responded over a three-year period by redesigning portable oscilloscopes to reduce their part counts from 3,500 to 2,500.[11]

Process designers can also cut costs by combining products into work cells. This is possible when products have similar designs (members of a product family) and when the manufacturing process is sufficiently flexible to handle any differences. Cost is reduced because the products in the cell share activities such as supervision, testing, training, scheduling, material handling, storage, and documentation.

5. Redeploy Unused Resources

In the final analysis, cost can be reduced only if resources are redeployed. Reducing the workload of an activity does not, *by itself*, reduce the equipment or the number of people dedicated to that activity. There must be a conscious management decision to deal with the freed resources. This can be done by growing the business to take up the slack, redeploying the resources to other activities, or removing the resources from the company.

ABC can be used to calculate the type and amount of unused or underused resources. Resource plans based on this information then become the basis for redeployment.

S U M M A R Y

Activity-based management (ABM) uses ABC information to help meet two important goals. The first is to improve the value received by customers. The second is to improve the profits earned (or to be more cost-effective) in providing this value.

ABM helps improve both strategic position and strategic capability. It helps improve strategic position by showing how resources can be deployed for maximum strategic gain. It helps improve strategic capability by guiding improvements in the factors (such as quality, service, and low cost) that are most important to customers.

There are three steps to improving activity performance. The first step is to analyze activities in order to find opportunities for improvement. The second step is to look for factors that cause waste (the cost drivers), then look for ways to remove them. The third step is to encourage and reinforce the right kind of improvement by measuring the important elements of performance.

ABM is quite different from old-fashioned accounting approaches to improvement. Accounting focuses on meeting cost targets. Costs are cut by eliminating staff and other resources without reference to the underlying work.

In contrast, ABM focuses on restructuring the work to *achieve lasting cost reductions*. This involves the following steps:

- Reduce the time and effort required to perform activities.
- Eliminate unnecessary activities.
- Select the lowest-cost activity to perform work.

- Share activities wherever possible.
- Redeploy resources made available by improvement efforts.

These efforts are as likely to improve quality as they are to reduce cost. ABM and quality management go hand in hand in any improvement program.

KEY TERMS

Activity analysis.   The evaluation of activity performance in the search for improvement opportunities.

Activity-based management (ABM).   A discipline that focuses on the management of activities as the route to improving the value received by customers and the profit achieved by providing this value (or its cost-effective delivery).   This discipline includes cost-driver analysis, activity analysis, and performance analysis. ABM draws on activity-based costing as a major source of information.

Benchmark.   An activity that is a *best practice* and by which a similar activity will be judged. Benchmarks are used to help identify opportunities for improving the performance of comparable activities. The source of a benchmark may be internal (such as another department in the same company) or external (such as a competitor).

Cost driver.   An event or causal factor that influences the level and performance of activities and the resulting consumption of resources, elapsed time, and quality. For example, defective materials that lead to low product quality are a cost driver for procurement and production activities. An activity may have multiple cost drivers associated with it.

Customer value.   The difference between customer realization and sacrifice. Realization is what is received by the customer. It includes product features, quality, and service, and also the cost to use, maintain, and dispose of the product. Sacrifice is what is given up by the customer. It includes the amount paid for the product plus the time spent acquiring the product and learning how to use it. To maximize customer value, it is necessary to maximize the difference between realization and sacrifice.

Scorecard.   A list of goals and associated performance measures for an area of activity such as a division, department, or process.

Strategy map.   A visual cause-and-effect representation of an organization's strategy. Used to communicate strategy effectively, it helps guide the development of scorecards.

REFERENCES

1 This discussion of customer value is based on definitions found in M. Stahl and G. Bound (eds.), *Competing Globally through Customer Value: The Management of Strategic Suprasystems* (Westport, CT: Greenwood Publishing, 1991).

2 J. L. Colley, Jr., R. A. Gary IV, J. C. Reid, and R. C. Simpson III, "Data Services, Inc. (B)," UVA-OM–582 (Charlottesville: University of Virginia).

3 *Competitive Benchmarking: What It Is and What It Can Do For You* (Stamford, CT: Xerox Corporate Quality Office, 1984).

4 H. Thomas Johnson, Gail J. Fults, and Paul Jackson, "Activity Management and Performance Measurement in a Service Organization," in Peter B. B. Turney (ed.), *Performance Excellence in Manufacturing and Service Organizations* (Sarasota, FL: American Accounting Association, 1990).

5 Howard M. Armitage and Anthony A. Atkinson, "The Choice of Productivity Measures in Organizations," in Robert S. Kaplan (ed.), *Measures for Manufacturing Excellence* (Boston: Harvard Business School Press, 1990).

6 Robin Cooper and Peter B. B. Turney, "Zytec Corporation (B)," 190–066 (Boston: Harvard Business School, 1989).

7 For an example of strategy maps and scorecards in a government organization, see Peter B. B. Turney, "The South Dakota Department of Transportation: The Fast Road to Better Performance," Cost Technology, Inc., 2003.

8 For an extensive discussion of performance measurement issues, see Robert W. Hall, H. Thomas Johnson, and Peter B. B. Turney, *Measuring Up: Charting Pathways to Manufacturing Excellence* (Homewood, IL: Dow-Jones Irwin, 1990).

9 J. Innes and F. Mitchell, *Activity-Based Costing: A Review with Case Studies* (London: The Chartered Institute of Management Accountants, 1990).

10 Robin Cooper and Peter B. B. Turney, "Hewlett-Packard: The Roseville Network Division," 189–117 (Boston: Harvard Business School, 1989).

11 Robin Cooper and Peter B. B. Turney, "Tektronix: The Portable Instrument Division," 188–142, 143, 144 (Boston: Harvard Business School, 1988).

CHAPTER 8

The Tools of Activity-Based Management

Now you understand what activity-based management (ABM) is all about. It helps improve your ability to profitably deliver value to your customers. It relies on managing activities better to achieve this improvement. It differs markedly from old-fashioned accounting approaches to improvement. And it draws heavily on information in the ABC system.

Now the question is, how do you do it?

To answer that, let's look at the following "tools of the trade" for ABM:

- Strategic analysis
- Value analysis
- Cost analysis
- Storyboarding
- Life-cycle costing
- Target costing

Some of these tools of the trade have been practiced for a number of years. General Electric, for example, has practiced value analysis for at least a quarter of a century. Others have come about more recently. All of these tools, however, benefit from ABC analysis. All of them can make contributions to increasing the competitiveness of your organization.

STRATEGIC ANALYSIS

The strategic value of ABC is easily recognized. When ABC reveals that 80 percent of your products are unprofitable (as is typical of many ABC studies), the implications for pricing policy and product mix are loud and clear.

But strategic analysis using ABC information goes far beyond pricing and product mix considerations. It includes customer value analysis, competitive studies, sourcing, and product strategy analysis. Let's look at each of these in turn.

Pricing

ABC is invaluable for pricing decisions. Some organizations—including defense contractors—base their prices exclusively on cost. Others use cost in combination with competitive factors to set price.

For example, the Oscilloscope Group of Tektronix used ABC to help win a military contract. This was a strategically important contract that Tektronix did not wish to lose.

The Oscilloscope Group believed that Tektronix would win the contract if it had the lowest price. It was important, however, to ensure that the bid did not fall below cost.

ABC provided the baseline for setting the price. A bid was made that was low enough to win the contract, yet exceeded the contract's ABC cost.

ABC may reveal many hidden opportunities to adjust prices. One company, for example, found that most of its low-volume specialty products were losing money, often by orders of magnitude. Some products were obvious candidates for the axe, but others were important to the company's customers. Was there any opportunity for increasing prices on any of those products?

The answer was yes. The price was increased on a select number of products. In several cases, the customer response was one of inevitability: "We're surprised you haven't done it before."

The company's competitors also followed the new prices without hesitation. It's possible that these competitors recognized that the old prices failed to reflect true cost.

In some cases, the customers weren't willing to pay the higher price. Even this was an important opportunity. Clearly the company was unable to provide value to these customers at a price it could afford. These customers could be served with other products or lost to competitors. Most importantly, however, there were opportunities to reduce the cost of these products via continuous process improvement and product redesign.

In some cases, ABC may reveal opportunities for repricing, but the market does not allow unilateral price changes. A local warehouse, for example, implemented ABC—the only warehouse in the area to do this. The ABC system revealed a systematic pattern of underpricing and overpricing services, yet the warehouse didn't have the market clout to change industry prices.

The solution? The warehouse intensified its marketing efforts on services that were currently overpriced, and reduced its emphasis on underpriced services. This produced a significant increase in profitability. And as a nice bonus, that increased profitability was invisible to the competition.

Customer Value Analysis

The central goal of ABM is to improve the profitable delivery of value to your customers. To do this, customer value analysis focuses directly on the activities and activity-based cost of the customer.

The Oscilloscope Group of Tektronix, for example, analyzed differences in profitability between different types of customers. It was found that small customers were generally unprofitable or had been ignored by the sales force.

The ABC information showed *why* the small customers were unprofitable. It was the high cost of marketing and distributing products to these customers.

One reason for the high cost was that the cost of marketing and distribution activities exceeded nonmaterial manufacturing costs. A second reason was the expense associated with the dominant channel of distribution.

Oscilloscopes were distributed using a direct sales force. These sales engineers were well qualified (and therefore well paid). They also required an expensive infrastructure to support them.

The relatively high cost of distribution was less of a burden with large accounts. Large customers had sufficient volume to cover the cost. They also typically bought high-priced, top-of-the-line products with high profit margins. Small customers, however, didn't purchase enough product to justify the time and cost of the sales engineers. Small customers also preferred the lower-margin, low-end products.

The solution? A new distribution channel, *Tek Direct*, was introduced. This channel emphasized telemarketing with a focus on selling low-priced oscilloscopes to small accounts.

Not only did this new approach substantially lower the cost of serving small accounts, it opened a potentially huge market that had previously been neglected. This consisted of customers who were not directly targeted using the traditional high-cost distribution channel. This market was estimated to number in the hundreds of thousands of customers.

Competitive Studies

Strategic analysis can be used to *understand competitors' profitability* as well as your own. The knowledge gained can be used to make selective price changes, to change marketing emphasis, to pinpoint required reductions in cost, to enter new markets, or to counter unfair competitive actions.

The Oscilloscope Group of Tektronix, for example, used ABC to study the manufacturing and distribution costs of products sold by competitors. ABC provided the insights needed to determine the activities likely to be involved in building and distributing these competing products.

Costs were estimated from the activity information and from cost data in annual reports. The Oscilloscope Group did reverse engineering ABC style!

The analysis helped Tektronix understand its position vis-à-vis the competition. The knowledge gained from the analysis was used to assess the relative price of Tektronix products, the potential for market-share gains, and the need for reductions in the cost of distribution activities.

Sourcing

Deciding who does what is strategic for any company. Which parts do you manufacture, and which do you source from outside suppliers? Which services do you provide internally, and which do you contract to a third party?

A manufacturer of plumbing fixtures, for example, completed an ABC study that showed major swings in cost from one process to another and one product to another. Among other things, the study revealed that costs assigned to the auto polishing activity increased by $1 million, while inner-assembly cost decreased by $300,000. Also, the cost of some low-volume parts increased by thousands of percent.

The company used ABC information to review its sourcing policy. Based on the insights provided by ABC, low-volume parts and high-cost activities were sourced to outside vendors. This was a completely new—*and profitable*—approach for a vertically integrated company that had traditionally done everything in-house.[1]

How important is ABC information in reviewing outsourcing decisions? The South Dakota Department of Transportation was approached by a vendor offering to manufacture road signs. In the absence of ABC, the department did not know the internal cost of manufacturing road signs and was unable to determine the lowest-cost alternative. This experience was a key factor in the Department of Transportation's adoption of ABC.

Product Strategy Analysis

ABC vividly portrays differing patterns of profitability among products. Analyzing these patterns may show, for example, that products fall into quadrants that differ by profit and volume (Figure 8–1). Each quadrant will require a different product strategy.

FIGURE 8–1

Product Strategy

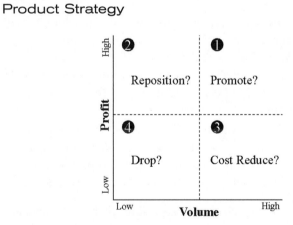

ABC may show that products fall into distinct categories of profitability and volume. These insights are useful because each category requires a different strategy.

This type of analysis was done by a retailer with hundreds of stores in the United Kingdom. The retailer first placed each product into the appropriate quadrant based on the results of ABC. Then strategies for each of the four product types were evaluated.

Quadrant 1 products were candidates for extra promotion and more prominent display. Quadrant 2 products received additional advertising, improved shelf location, and price reductions to boost volume. Quadrant 3 products were studied for cost-reduction opportunities. Quadrant 4 products were reviewed for possible elimination from the line.[2]

In summary, strategic analysis helps you deploy resources to those activities that yield the highest benefit. It helps you choose the best way to profitably serve your customers.

VALUE ANALYSIS

Value analysis is the intensive study of a business process with a view to improving the process and reducing cost. Its goal is to ensure that you perform the right activities in the right way.

Value analysis works with the following information:

1. *Activities.* Value analysis focuses on the activities in the process—what they are, what resources they consume, their cost drivers, and how they work together. Most of this information is found in the ABC system.

2. *Activity analysis.* Value analysis uses knowledge about activities gained during activity analysis. This is information that describes *why* and *how well* the work is done. It includes the designation of activities as value-added or non-value-added, whether they are significant, and how well they stack up against benchmark performance.

3. *Cost drivers.* The cost drivers—*those factors that cause work*—are the key to putting value analysis to work. Reducing the impact of negative cost drivers is the key to eliminating nonessential activities and removing waste from essential activities.

As an example, General Electric applied value analysis to an electro-mechanical assembly department and obtained dramatic results. This department assembled large products in small volumes.[3]

General Electric had previously implemented world-class manufacturing concepts in this department. This included just-in-time inventory flow. However, the efforts had failed to improve performance significantly. Value analysis was viewed as the missing catalyst for improvement.

To understand how value analysis was applied, let's take a closer look at the activities in the department. Figure 8–2 shows a partial list of those activities. Also shown is the equivalent number of people working in each activity (such as 3.9 people accumulating material).

Each activity in Figure 8–2 is designated as value-added, gray, or waste. Value-added activities are important to the customer, while non-value-added activities are not. The customer *wants* an assembled product, so assembly is classified value-added. Waiting for material, however, is clearly of no benefit to the customer, so it's non-value-added.

A third category—*gray*—is used for activities that are of no value to customers, but that may be essential to the functioning of the department. Assigning work and communicating with employees fall into this category.

Value analysis was focused on the significant activities in the department. These were the five activities with the most waste, making them candidates for the greatest improvement. These activities are shown in Figure 8–3 along with their cost drivers.

As the next step, the cost drivers were divided into those that were internal to the department and those that were external. Internal drivers were factors that could be changed by the department without outside

FIGURE 8–2

Activity Distribution Closely Interlinked

Activity	Equivalent People	Value Added	Gray	Waste
Assemble	10.7	10.7		
Accumulate material	3.9			3.9
Expedite material	2.1			2.1
Wait for material	1.2			1.2
.				
.				
Assigning work	1.2		1.2	
Employee communication	0.3			0.3
Total	31.5	10.7	4.7	16.1
Percent		34%	15%	51%

This is a partial listing of the activities in an electromechanical assembly department at General Electric. Each activity is classified according to whether it is valued by the customers of the department.

FIGURE 8-3

Highest-Waste Activities

Activity	Accumulate Material (Floor)	Expedite Material	Move Material	Rework	Test/Verify	Total
Equivalent people	3.9	2.1	2.1	1.9	1.8	11.8
Internal drivers	Stock layout	Scrap	Material flow	Assembly errors	Interpretation of design	
	Stocking procedures	Stock errors	Handling equipment	Large batches	Training	
	Material flow	Ordering errors		Damage	Quality problems	
		MRP lead times		Methods/procedures		
External drivers		Engineering change notices		Engineering change notices		
		Schedule changes		Supplier quality		
		Supplier/delivery & quality				
	Volume of part numbers		Labor classification	Quality of design	Design	
					Regulations	

This value analysis focused on the five activities with the most waste. Improvement (and cost reduction) was made by eliminating the negative effects of key cost drivers.

involvement. The activity "accumulating material," for example, was affected by the way stock was laid out, by the procedures in the stockroom, and by the flow of material in assembly.

External drivers also caused work, but were largely determined outside the department. "Accumulating material," for example, was affected by the number of different parts—the more parts, the more difficult and time-consuming the work.

The project team identified stockroom layout and material flow in assembly as the department's key cost drivers. The team then attacked these drivers to achieve performance improvement.

The results of the value analysis effort were dramatic. Productivity was improved by over 20 percent. Inventory levels and the time required to move a product through the process were cut in half. Also, quality improved as the number of defects fell.

More importantly, customer satisfaction increased with improved quality. Customers were also pleased with the improvement in on-time delivery and the drop in order lead times.

Value analysis has been applied in many different business settings, with similar positive results. General Electric has used it to improve performance in small departments as well as in businesses with thousands of employees. Value analysis has also been used successfully in a beverage company, a telephone company, and a bank.

In all cases, the purpose of value analysis was to *improve the ability to profitably serve customers*. In General Electric's heavy mechanical and electrical assembly business, for example, value analysis was followed by an increase in market share, a rise to number one in the market, and a significant return on investment.

COST ANALYSIS

ABC supports cost-reduction efforts in two ways. First, it helps organizations find the opportunities with the greatest cost-reduction potential. ABC is a navigational aid that helps quantify the size of the hidden "rocks"—and pick the biggest ones as cost-reduction targets. We'll look at *goal seeking* and *Pareto analysis* as ways of doing this.

Second, you can use ABC to simulate the impact of cost-reduction actions. *Cost-reduction analysis* helps build commitment in advance and subsequently confirms positive results.

Goal Seeking

One way to identify cost-reduction targets is *goal seeking*. Goal seeking starts with the *bill of activities*. This is a listing of the activities and activity drivers associated with a product or service. The idea is to use the information in the bill of activities to identify cost-reduction opportunities for improving the competitiveness of the product or service.

Oregon Cutting Systems used goal seeking as a way to identify products with lower-than-acceptable profit margins and improve those products' profitability. For example, Figure 8–4 shows the summary activity costs by process for a component of the chain used in chain saws. This component was the high-cost part in a low-margin product.

The activity cost summary report reveals the sources of highest cost for the component. For example, batch processing activities account for about a third of the cost of the part. What is the reason for the high cost of these activities?

Batch processing is a central production activity to which parts are moved from the product cells. The activities in this process are shown in

FIGURE 8-4

Goal Seeking (1)

Oregon Cutting Systems			
Component, Part #AB343			
Summary of Activity Costs by Process			
Activity	**Level**	**Driver**	**Unit Cost**
Procuring parts	Batch	# times requisitioned	$4.29
Initiating production			6.35
Batch processing			12.41
Individual processing			8.19
Planning production	Product	# of part #s	3.79
Changing specifications	Product	# of ECNs	2.98
Total			$38.01

Goal seeking analyzes activity costs to find opportunities to improve a product's competitiveness. This report shows the main groupings of activities needed to make this component at Oregon Cutting Systems. Notice that *batch-processing* is the most costly activity.

Figure 8–5. The process is first set up to produce each batch of parts. The pans containing parts are then dipped into a chrome bath. After the batch process, the parts are inspected for defects, then transported back to the product cells.

There are three non-value-added activities in Figure 8–5 that are candidates for improvement: setting up, inspecting, and transporting. Which one would you improve for the greatest cost savings?

A review of the cost drivers for these activities revealed that plant layout was the most important factor. The plant was laid out in product cells, yet batch processing was a large central process serving several product cells. This layout required that parts be moved to and from the process, and the variety of work affected both quality and setup time.

The ideal solution was to replace the large central process with small processes dedicated to the individual product cells. This would eliminate the transporting activity entirely. The number of setups would be less because each small process would be dedicated to a product family. The time required for setup would probably go down as well, because of the similarity of the parts in each cell and the improved opportunity for learning.

FIGURE 8-5

Goal Seeking (2)

Oregon Cutting Systems Component, Part #AB343 Batch Processing Activities

Activity	Level	Driver	Value-Added	Non-Value-Added
Setting up	Batch	# of setups		$2.94
Processing parts	Unit/Batch	# of pans	$6.04	
Inspecting parts	Batch	# of setups		1.14
	Unit/Batch	# of pans		
Transporting parts	Unit/Batch	# of pans		2.29
Total			$6.04	$6.37

This detailed bill of activities reveals the activities and activity costs involved in batch processing. It shows three non-value-added activities, each a candidate for elimination or improvement.

In practice, installing small local processes requires a capital investment. If funds aren't available, cost reduction should focus instead on improving the existing process. This might include reducing the time required for setup or improving quality so that parts inspection can be eliminated.

Pareto Analysis

Another way to identify cost-reduction targets is to look for the activity drivers that account for most of the cost traced. Pareto analysis involves arranging activity drivers in descending order of the amount of cost assigned.

Figure 8–6 shows a Pareto analysis prepared at the Business Products Division of Nortel. Each bar in this figure represents the percentage of cost assigned by activity drivers of a common type. For example, 25 percent of the cost is assigned via material-type drivers. These include "number of receipts," "number of purchase orders," "number of material inspections," and "number of movements."

Based on this Pareto analysis, the division selected material-related activities as targets for cost reduction. Not only was this the second high-

FIGURE   8–6

Pareto Analysis at Nortel

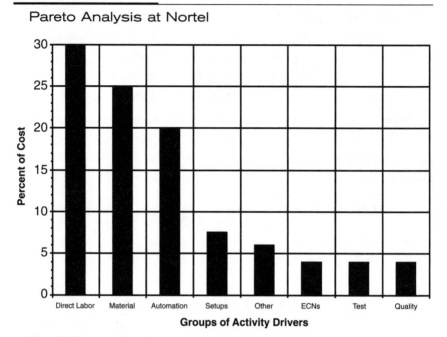

Nortel's Business Products Division grouped its activity drivers into common types such as material and quality. Each bar on this chart represents the cost assigned via each group of drivers. It shows that direct labor, material, and automation drivers account for most of the cost—and offer the major opportunities for improvement.

est area of cost, but in many cases the activity cost exceeded the components' material costs by orders of magnitude.

A look at the cost drivers associated with these activities shows why the cost was so high:

- The large *number of vendors* created high demand for vendor development and maintenance activities.
- The large *number of different part types* increased the demand for purchasing, receiving, inspection, stocking, and other such activities.
- *Procurement procedures* were cumbersome and involved numerous people. The purchasing department used a computerized shop-floor scheduling system to determine what needed to be

purchased. On-hand quantities in the stockroom were verified and phone calls placed to vendors. Purchase orders were prepared and mailed. Once the parts were received, they were inspected, counted, moved, stored, and paid for.

Cost-Reduction Analysis

ABC is an economic *and* performance model of a business or process. It provides building blocks for simulating the impact of changes in operating a business or process or the impact on the type of business conducted.

For example, the Business Products Division of Nortel used cost-reduction analysis to identify the *best way* to reduce the cost of material-related activities. The simulation focused on alternative ways of procuring "C" parts (low-cost and high-volume parts). There were thousands of these parts, and they accounted for the bulk of the activity.

The cost of each alternative was computed using the ABC model. The activity-driver quantities for each one were multiplied by the cost per unit of the activity drivers.

The analysis identified the lowest-cost alternative and totally changed the way C parts were procured. This alternative also eliminated two of the three cost drivers (the number of vendors and the procurement procedures themselves).

Under this alternative, all C parts were purchased from one supplier. A single purchase order was issued to cover the plant's needs for an entire year. The supplier was given a three-month production schedule and agreed to visit the plant once a week to replenish kanban bins on the shop floor.

The impact on cost—as computed by the ABC system—was substantial. Only one purchase order and 12 invoices were processed each year (versus thousands under the current system). In addition, several activities were entirely eliminated for the C parts, including receiving, counting, unloading, inspecting, moving, and stocking. Noncost improvements included increased flexibility, reduced lead times, and reduced likelihood of component obsolescence.

It's interesting to note that previous improvement efforts at the division—applications of traditional world-class manufacturing techniques—had turned up only small increments of improvement. It took ABC to point out where the greatest improvements could be found, and to focus efforts on successful waste elimination and simplification.

The ability to simulate the cost impact of improvement programs has benefits in addition to identifying the lowest-cost alternative. Improvement programs may now proceed on the basis of analysis rather than faith alone. Management commitment to improvement is easier to obtain, and the ability to communicate the results helps transfer the learning across the organization.

For example, one manufacturing plant was unable to persuade its parent company to allow it to drop some complex low-volume products. The plant knew that these products required excessive effort that was *not rewarded* by revenues (even though its conventional cost system indicated the opposite).

An ABC study confirmed the plant's intuitions—the products did cost a lot more than they generated in revenues. These results were presented to the parent company.

The parent company's first response was to dismiss the ABC product costs as invalid. But it did permit the plant to seek an outside supplier bid to manufacture the products.

The bid turned out to be higher than the ABC cost. This was enough to convince the parent that the ABC cost was indeed valid. Permission was granted to remove the products from the plant.

The lesson is clear: Cost-reduction analysis using ABC does not reduce cost. Cost can be reduced only if changes are made in performing activities and if the redundant resources are redeployed. Cost analysis does help identify cost-reduction opportunities, garner management support, communicate the learning associated with the improvement, and generally reinforce the entire improvement effort.

STORYBOARDING

Storyboarding is a detailed analysis of a process that is targeted for cost reduction and improvement. It includes working with representatives of the work area to build a model of the activities in the process, set performance measures, and identify cost drivers. It culminates in the development of action plans to reduce cost and improve the functioning of the process.

As developed by Cost Technology, Inc., storyboarding uses index cards, sticky dots, and other media to display the activity-based information on storyboards (special-purpose bulletin boards that are placed on a wall). The process combines the involvement of workers from the process with the analytical power of ABC (see Figure 8–7).

FIGURE 8-7

Storyboarding

Storyboarding combines the knowledge and involvement of the workers with ABC analytics. The result is a "high-tech, high-touch" process that yields immediate and measurable cost savings as well as buy-in and enthusiasm for the ABC initiative. Photograph is used with the permission of Cost Technology, Inc.

The heart of the storyboarding process is cost-driver analysis, leading to the selection of a handful of cost drivers that have the highest measurable impact on the process. These are the factors that—if the issues are resolved—promise the greatest cost reduction, lead-time reduction, and quality improvement. The process also shows the amount of time freed up for the people engaged in the process as a result of the resolution of these issues.

Action plans to effect these changes are developed and presented to management for approval. These action plans are usually compelling because they follow a clear analytical path that narrows the alternatives to the ones that *measurably* reduce the most cost. Storyboarding works in manufacturing, service, and government organizations in all parts of the value chain. It works in production, engineering, cost-to-serve, and administrative processes. It works just as well with employees in a research organization who hold doctorates as it does with non-English-speaking workers in a production department who have only a grade school education.

There are several options for applying storyboarding. It can be focused on a particular department and the activities that department performs. This is a great place to start the analysis. For example, a storyboarding analysis of a contracts and procurement process in a not-for-profit organization yielded significant cost savings opportunities. These cost savings, once implemented, convinced management to move to a large-scale ABC implementation.

Alternatively, the analysis can include multiple departments that share a common process, such as procurement or engineering. This cross-functional analysis yields cost reductions and improvements for an end-to-end process. For example, a cross-functional storyboarding analysis of the material supply process of a large military base yielded millions of dollars in savings and a streamlined reengineered process.

Finally, storyboarding the same process from different parts of the organization supports best practices analysis. For example, a food retailer storyboarded the warehouse function in each of its supermarkets. It brought the individual teams together to compare their processes and performance measures, and it identified best practices to implement companywide.

The bottom line with storyboarding is its ability to routinely uncover cost savings of 10 to 30 percent in just a couple of days. Storyboarding also leads to high levels of learning and buy-in for ABC. It is a great adjunct to any ABC implementation because it provides an immediate and measurable return on investment.[4]

LIFE-CYCLE COSTING

Life-cycle costing looks at products over their entire life cycle rather than just for one year. A product's life cycle encompasses initial research and development, proceeds through introduction and growth in the market, and ends with maturity, decline, and abandonment.

A life-cycle perspective yields insights into product cost and profitability that are not available from viewing a single year. A product that has just been introduced has a low volume. It's incurring start-up costs, and it may look uncompetitive in a one-year view. A product that's mature, however, may be reaping the rewards of hard work in previous years. So it appears highly profitable.

But it's misleading to use a single-period model to compare the cost of a new product with that of a mature product. It's possible that incorrect conclusions will be drawn from the relative cost and profitability of the two products.

Dayton Technologies illustrates why a life-cycle perspective is important. This company develops new window systems, designs the dies required to manufacture the vinyl components of the windows, and then manufactures the dies. All this work occurs over one to two years before any production occurs. The development effort requires as much in the way of resources as the production itself.

What is critical, however, is the strategic nature of window and die development. This is where the company commits itself to the customers it will serve, and the products it will provide, over the next few years.

Intelligent strategic decisions—and the commitment of scarce engineering resources—require a life-cycle perspective. Each customer has different requirements. Some customers, for example, may stick with the same window design for years and buy the product in high volumes. Other customers, however, may request constant changes to the design, buy in low volume, and phase out the product quickly.

Clearly the cost of serving these different types of customers over the product's life cycle is quite different. And unless the prices charged are different, the economics will be quite different, too.

Life-cycle costing also highlights the activities and resources needed to take a product from development to abandonment. Indeed, the analysis may show that the product is uncompetitive and that a reduction in life-cycle cost is in order. The life-cycle costing information pinpoints which activities can be improved and shows the impact of this improvement on product cost.

A major defense contractor, for example, used life-cycle costing to look for ways of reducing the cost of a large subassembly. The life cycle of this product included a transition phase during which production was moved to a lower-cost facility.

The study confirmed that moving production did reduce cost over the life cycle of the product. The transition itself required various activities and resources, but these costs were more than offset by lower production costs in the new facility.

The defense contractor also did an analysis of activities across the phases of the life cycle. This analysis identified activities with superior performance and common cost drivers. It was discovered, for example, that cost drivers relating to shortages and poor quality accounted for more than a fifth of total life-cycle cost.

How does life-cycle costing work? In its simplest form, it's the accumulation of a product's development and start-up costs and applying these costs to units over the product's life (Figure 8–8). This includes costs incurred prior to introduction, such as initial die manufacture, and anticipated costs during the product's life, such as replacement of the die.

In Figure 8–8, the product's development and start-up costs are $20,000. These costs are placed in a special life-cycle account. The total cost in this account is then divided by an estimate of production over the product's life. In this example, the estimated volume is 10,000 units, and the unit cost is $2.

FIGURE 8–8

The Mechanics of Life-Cycle Costing

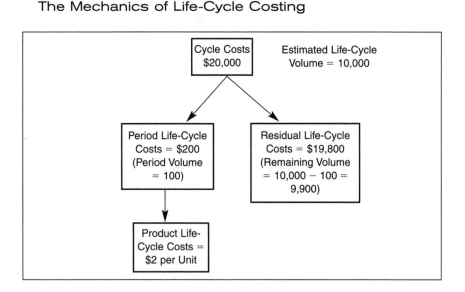

Life-cycle costing requires estimates of life-cycle costs and volume.

In the first year of production, 100 units of the product are made. A cost of $2 is added to the current period's cost of each unit to give the life-cycle cost.

The cost in future periods may need adjustment. For example, the estimate of life-cycle volume may be revised. Additional life-cycle costs may be incurred at levels other than those anticipated. Also, depreciation may need to be computed on a replacement-cost basis.

A key to the success of life-cycle costing is the accuracy of the estimates of product life and costs. Some companies have developed elaborate systems for estimating these data. Boeing and British Aerospace, for example, use sophisticated statistical models.

Life-cycle costing involves all functions of the company. Dayton Technologies includes marketing, engineering, and manufacturing in the estimating process. Marketing receives feedback on actual sales versus estimated sales. It initiates the sales estimates, so it is held responsible for significant differences.

CAN ABC BE USED BY DEFENSE CONTRACTORS?

Defense contractors face a dilemma. On the one hand, they face intense competitive pressures. Reductions in government defense spending are accompanied by dual sourcing of major weapons systems. A leader/follower arrangement ensures that the lowest-cost supplier gets the lion's share of the business.

On the other hand, in the past government procurement regulations have required contractors to use conventional cost systems and to base their prices on the costs reported by these systems. However, these systems inhibit the improvements that are necessary to win and maintain leadership positions on government contracts.

Can a defense contractor use ABC? The answer is a qualified yes. You can replace your existing cost system with ABC if you proceed cautiously and obtain the necessary approval. According to Jack Haedicke and David Feil at Hughes Aircraft, the key to obtaining such approval is to inform, educate, and involve:[5]

> *Inform.* Inform the Defense Contract Audit Agency (DCAA) of your plans. This avoids any possible misunderstanding of your reasons for implementing ABC.
>
> *Educate:* Educate your local audit staff about the purpose and

design of your ABC system. They may not be familiar with ABC, and education is necessary for proper communication. It's an ongoing task, starting with implementation planning and ending with the evaluation of the results.

Involve: Involve your local audit staff in the implementation process. This gives them an opportunity to provide input and to influence the direction of the project. It also ensures that they have ownership when the ABC system is complete.

Does a defense contractor need ABC? *The answer is a resounding yes.* Hughes Aircraft, for example, used ABC to determine what it should manufacture internally and what it should subcontract to achieve the lowest cost. Hughes has also used ABC to identify opportunities for process improvement and to identify the lowest-cost processes across the company. ABC supports more accurate estimates of contract costs. It's used by Hughes's engineering staff to "design to cost." And it supports improvement efforts all over the company.

TARGET COSTING

Operating managers often say that product design is their most important cost driver. They point to the number of process steps, product complexity, and parts types and volumes as factors beyond their control.

If product design is such an important cost driver, it makes sense to work on reducing its negative effects. This means making conscious decisions during the design process about the impact of design on cost.

Designing a product to meet a specific cost is called *target costing*. This is a device for linking engineering decisions to market requirements.

It involves setting the planned market price for a new product. Distribution costs and profits are then subtracted from this price to leave the required manufacturing cost. This cost is the target the engineers shoot for.

ABC makes target costing possible. It does this by providing the framework for estimating the impact of design decisions on cost.

Engineers at Hewlett-Packard, for example, use ABC to pick the least expensive activities for a product. They build up the cost of each alternative design using the activity-driver rates from the ABC system. Then they pick the design with the lowest cost (and the proper functionality).[6]

Engineers at some companies have even developed rules of thumb based on ABC. The Oscilloscope Group of Tektronix did this to prepare its *cost guidelines* for design. These guidelines summarized the relative cost of key design alternatives. The placement of a part using surface-mount technology, for example, cost 1.5 times its placement with machine insertion.

These guidelines were also a reminder to engineers of the impact of their decisions on cost. It was estimated, for example, that 80 to 90 percent of the cost of an instrument was frozen when it left engineering (Figure 8–9).

Tektronix also used target costing in its cathode-ray tube (CRT) division. This division supplies CRTs for use in analog oscilloscopes.

In one example, an internal Tektronix customer set a target transfer price for a new CRT. The CRT division would get the business if it could meet the target price.

The CRT engineers used ABC to examine the impact of several design alternatives on activities and resources. For example, a new design for a major component of the CRT—the CRT gun—was proposed. The new gun would require an additional production operation, but the improved quality would reduce the testing needed compared to that for

FIGURE 8–9

Cost Guidelines for Product Design

1. Cost of insertion and placement activities relative to machine insertion:

Placement (surface mount)	1.5X
Robot insertion	3.0X
Hand insertion (pre-solder)	6.0X
Hand insertion (post-solder)	10.0X

2. Purchasing and inspecting parts from a nonqualified vendor is three times more expensive than from a qualified vendor.
3. Engineering modifications cost $2,500 each.
4. Many costs vary with the number of part types rather than the volume of parts.
5. Ninety percent of nonmaterial manufacturing costs vary with the complexity of the instrument.
6. An automatic test on a circuit board costs $3.00 per board.
7. The cost of a product is 80–90% frozen when it leaves engineering.

Cost guidelines developed from ABC at the Oscilloscope Group of Tektronix highlight important cost information. These guidelines influence engineers in their design choices and remind them of the impact of their decisions on cost.

existing guns. Overall, ABC showed that the cost of the new gun would be less.

This design review continued until the CRT target cost was met. The business was won, and the new CRT is now in production.

SUMMARY

The tools of ABM are ways of applying ABC information to improve performance. They work in the following manner:

- *Strategic analysis* helps you deploy resources to those activities that yield the highest benefit. It helps you choose the best way to profitably serve your customers.
- *Value analysis* is the intense study of a business process with a view to improving the process and reducing its cost. Its goal is to ensure that you perform the right activities in the right way.
- *Cost analysis* supports cost-reduction efforts in two ways. First, it helps the organization find the opportunities with the greatest cost-reduction potential. Second, it helps build commitment to improvement in advance, and it communicates what has been learned from the improvement.
- *Storyboarding* is a detailed ABC analysis of key processes. It results in action plans to reduce cost and reengineer the process. It identifies the resources freed up by the action plans and reengineering effort, allowing them to be redeployed to more value-adding work.
- *Life-cycle costing* looks at cost over a product's life cycle rather than for just one year. It facilitates judgments about cost and profitability that just can't be made from a single-year perspective.
- *Target costing* is the use of ABC information to design products to meet a predetermined cost. It links engineering decisions to market requirements. It's also a reminder to engineers of the important role their decisions play in determining cost.

KEY TERMS

Cost analysis. Simulation of cost-reduction opportunities. Cost analysis helps you select the opportunities that yield the greatest improvement. It also helps build commitment to improvement actions and helps communicate the knowledge gained through the improvement.

Customer value analysis. Study of customer activities directed at finding ways to improve customer value and reduce the cost of delivering that value.

Goal seeking. The search for ways to improve the competitiveness of a product or service. The search starts with identification of high-cost activities in the bill of activities. It then proceeds through the causes of high cost and finishes with actions to reduce or eliminate the effect of these causes.

Life-cycle costing. Costing products over their entire life cycle rather than for a single accounting period. The product life cycle spans development, introduction, growth, maturity, decline, and abandonment. Life-cycle costing helps assess product profitability.

Pareto analysis. The arrangement of activities or activity drivers in descending order of cost. The activities or drivers accounting for the majority of the cost are targeted for cost reduction.

Storyboarding. A structured method of applying ABC analysis to processes. It is a team-based, visual approach to cost reduction, process improvement, process reengineering, and best practices development.

Strategic analysis. Analysis of products, services, and customers for strategic opportunities. Strategic analysis may point out opportunities for repricing, redirecting resources to more profitable opportunities, and changing product strategy.

Target costing. Setting cost targets for new products based on market price. The analysis starts with an estimate of the selling price and subtracts profits and distribution costs to arrive at the target cost. Engineers then use ABC to help design a product at this cost.

Value analysis. Intense study of a business process with the intent of improving the process and reducing cost. Its goal is to ensure that you perform the right activities in the right way.

REFERENCES

1 Michael O'Guin, "Focus the Factory with Activity-Based Costing," *Management Accounting*, February 1990, pp. 36–41.

2 J. Innes and F. Mitchell, *Activity-Based Costing: A Review with Case Studies* (London: The Chartered Institute of Management Accountants, 1990).

3 Thomas O'Brien, "Improving Performance through Activity Analysis," in Peter B. B. Turney (ed.), *Performance Excellence in Manufacturing and*

Service Organizations (Sarasota, FL: American Accounting Association, 1990).

4 Peter B. B. Turney, "Beyond TQM with Workforce Activity-Based Management," *Management Accounting,* September 1993, pp. 28–31.

5 Jack Haedicke and David Feil, "Hughes Aircraft Sets the Standard for ABC," *Management Accounting,* February 1990, pp. 29–33.

6 Robin Cooper and Peter B. B. Turney, "Hewlett-Packard: The Roseville Network Division," 188–177 (Boston: Harvard Business School, 1989).

CHAPTER 9

Building the World-Class Organization

Activity-based management (ABM) helps organizations become—*and continue to be*—world class. Being world class involves achieving high standards of business performance, profitably meeting customer needs, and continuously improving performance.

There's nothing "business as usual" at a world-class organization. The things that matter are different (they are the things that matter to the customer). The organization is managed differently (decision making is pushed to the lowest levels of the organization). And the organization uses different tools to improve business (such as the balanced scorecard and ABM).

ABM brings *information empowerment* to aspiring world-class companies. Putting activity-based costing (ABC) information in the hands of those doing the improvement increases their power to improve.

Analyzing ABC information, for example, helps reveal the causes and the extent of poor performance. It also helps focus efforts to improve quality or eliminate waste in areas where the payoff is the greatest.

This chapter shows how *information empowerment* worked in a printed circuit board (PCB) division of a large high-technology company. We saw in chapter 3 how this division's ABC analyses revealed a dramatic pattern of unprofitable products and customers. Now we'll see how the division put knowledge gained from ABC to work in creating a world-class company.[1]

The contribution of ABM at the PCB division was as important as ABC's new perceptions were dramatic. *This division became the benchmark facility in the printed circuit board industry—the world-class plant against which all others compared themselves.* Figure 9–1 shows the dramatic turn-around in financial results that accompanied this success.

ABM was a key reason for the turnaround. The division's general manager summed it up this way:

> We could not have achieved our success without ABC. It has helped us focus on what we do best and has accelerated our improvement efforts. Its influence extends to all corners of the plant and governs short- and long-term decisions alike. And you can see clearly the positive impact of ABC on the bottom line. All told, I would estimate that at least a third of our improvement is due to ABC.

FIGURE 9–1

The Financial Turnaround

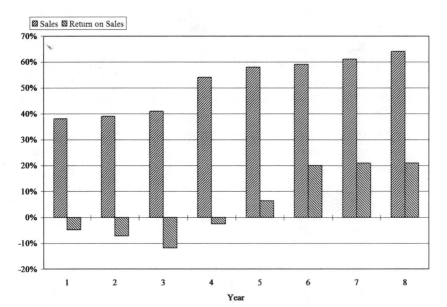

PCB's story begins in year 1, when a benchmarking study revealed that the plant was "worst in class" in its industry. ABC was introduced in year 4 and had an immediate impact on profitability. By year 6 the division was "best in class" in the industry and the most profitable PCB company in the world.

The case of the PCB division illustrates how ABM fosters world-class performance. It describes how the division used ABC for

- Strategic management
- Performance management
- Supply-chain management
- Investment management

STRATEGIC MANAGEMENT

Strategic management is the use of ABC and market information for two purposes:

1. To help set strategic priorities
2. To help implement the chosen strategy

The PCB division learned from its ABC study that many of its products and customers were unprofitable. But *which types* of products and customers were unprofitable? How should the division change its strategy as a result of this knowledge? And how should it implement the changes once they'd been identified?

Product Strategy

A close look at the ABC data showed that product profitability varied with technology, volume, and life cycle. With this information, management made the following decisions.

Technology Decision—Focus on High-Technology Products

ABC showed that product functionality had an enormous impact on the amount and type of production and support activities required. Boards varied in terms of number of layers, circuit density, and fineness of printed metal lines.

High-technology boards—ones with more layers, more density, and finer lines—were far more expensive to manufacture than low-technology ones. One high-technology board, for example, required more tools (film) from engineering, more materials and sequence scheduling, more expensive drills with shorter lives, and more inspections than a low-technology board of the same size.

But high-technology boards commanded a much higher price than low-technology ones. This made them more profitable. Boards with 10 layers or more carried an average profit margin of 46 percent, whereas two-sided boards earned a *negative* 49 percent margin (Figure 9–2).

Management decided on high-technology products as its strategic priority. These boards were well suited to the division's engineering and production capability, and they promised excellent profitability.

Volume Decision—Focus on Low-Volume Boards

The division also found that, in general, high-volume products were less costly (and more profitable) than low-volume products. This was because the cost per product unit of the activities associated with a product was lower when the costs were shared over a larger volume.

For example, the cost of creating a board-test program for use with automated testing equipment *did not* vary with volume. As a result, if two boards were of equivalent design, but of different volume, the test program development cost per unit for the higher-volume board would be less.

There was a similar effect for activities associated with taking a customer's order. These activities included order processing, order entry,

FIGURE 9-2

PCB's Market Choices

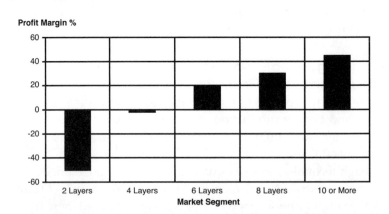

The PCB division participated in five distinct market segments. ABC helped the organization decide which segments to focus on by revealing wide disparities in profitability between segments.

credit checking, scheduling, and maintaining the database. The activity demand was generally the same for each order, but the volume per order varied. The cost per unit of high-volume orders, therefore, was much less than that of low-volume orders.

This created a dilemma for the division. Many low-volume boards were also high-technology boards. (Companies at the leading edge of their markets typically ordered in low volumes.) A strategic decision to drop low-volume boards would conflict with the decision to focus on high-technology boards.

It was clear that the division had to sell low-volume boards to complement its high-technology focus. But how could this be done profitably?

The first step was to institute a minimum-order charge.

This covered the cost of order- and batch-related activities. It also made customers conscious of the impact of their order size on the division's activities and costs. The minimum-order charge was a short-run solution, and it got the attention of customers.

The long-run solution was to reduce the cost of low-volume production. To do this, the division introduced computer-integrated manufacturing (CIM). This reduced the costs of order- and batch-related activities. For example, CIM allowed customers to use an electronic link to transmit engineering drawings directly to sales. This reduced the engineering cost and time associated with placing an order.

The division also acquired a production facility that specialized in high-volume, low-technology production. An ABC study showed that the costs of high-volume, low-technology boards dropped as much as one-third in this facility. The facility met the parent company's need to meet a minimum level of demand for these types of boards. It also freed up capacity in the main facility, which was then filled with high-margin, high-technology products.

Product Life-Cycle Decision—Acquire Products Early in Their Life Cycle; Dispose of Products Late in Their Life Cycle

A review of product profitability could not be done without reference to the product's life cycle. This was because cost (and profitability) varied considerably in the different phases of a circuit board's life cycle.

Figure 9–3 shows this life cycle. The circuit board is designed, and a few boards are produced for design verification during the prototype phase. This prototype production typically has short lead times and frequent engineering changes.

FIGURE 9-3

The Life Cycle of a Printed Circuit Board

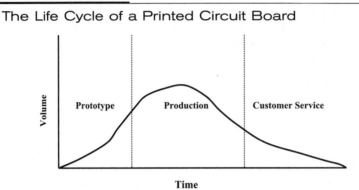

Boards go through three phases. The prototype phase is where the design is verified and, if necessary, revised. The production phase sees the tested product shipped to the customer in quantity. The customer service phase covers sales after the board has been discontinued.

The production phase is where actual customer orders are placed and filled. It's characterized by repetitive orders and infrequent design changes.

The third phase is customer service. This is a period of declining sales after the product has been phased out. Orders from customers to replace boards that have failed in the field typically are received infrequently, in low volumes, and over a number of years.

Figure 9–4 shows the costs of a typical board in each phase of its life cycle. The intense use of engineering and support activities and the low volume are reflected in the high cost during the prototype phase.

FIGURE 9-4

Variation in Product Cost over the Life Cycle

	Prototype	Production	Customer Service
Production activities	$378	$130	$534
Support activities	184	3	86
Total cost	$562	$133	$620
Volume	6	500,000	10

The cost of a board changes dramatically over its life. The most profitable life-cycle strategy was to seek business early in the product's life cycle and "hand off" customer service boards wherever possible.

The cost per unit plummets during the production phase. This reflects the stability of the product (its reduced need for activities) and the high volume over which costs are spread.

The customer service phase sees costs return to prototype levels as volume falls and demand for activities picks up. For example, boards in this phase commonly require additional engineering to accommodate changes in the production process.

A review of ABC information showed that boards were typically profitable during the prototype and production phases, but not during the customer service phase. On balance, boards acquired during the prototype phase were profitable over their entire life cycle. Boards acquired late in the production phase were unprofitable.

What was the appropriate response to this knowledge? The first response was to reemphasize the prototype business. The earlier in its life cycle that a product was contracted for, the more profitable it would be.

The second response was a three-part strategy to reduce product costs in the customer service phase. To do this:

- Customers were offered reduced prices for a single "last buy."
- PCB located suppliers specializing in low-volume production of obsolete parts. Customers, if they were willing, could take their service needs to these suppliers.
- Customer service orders were subcontracted to the specialized suppliers. This alternative was the most costly of the three, because additional activities were needed to order, schedule, track, and pay for the subcontract work.

In short, the PCB division used *life-cycle cost data* to help formulate a strategy to maximize profitability over the product's life cycle. The decision to acquire board contracts early in the board's life fit well with the plant's technical skills with prototype boards. Eliminating much of the customer service work was also done without abrogating commitments to customers.

Customer Strategy

A management review of the division's product strategy showed that the marketing emphasis should be on customers who needed high-technology, low-volume boards at the prototype stage. Were there any other customer characteristics that should be reviewed?

An analysis of ABC information on customers revealed two group-ings, each with a different profitability profile:

Group 1. These customers followed "good business practices." They maintained a long-term relationship with one supplier and obtained all of their board needs from this supplier.

Group 2. These customers had no loyalty to any one supplier. They moved their business from one supplier to another, constantly searching for the lowest price.

The PCB division decided to serve the first customer group, the ones fol-lowing "good business practices." This was done for two reasons. First, the division's strategy emphasized quality and customer service. It was easier to do this when there was a stable relationship with the customer.

Second, the ABC information made it quite clear that the cost of serving loyal customers was a lot less. There was less sales effort, less order processing effort, less engineering effort, less material handling effort, and less effort associated with higher quality.

The decision to seek customers with good business practices increased the division's profitability. It also fit well with the division's desire to focus its efforts on providing quality and service to a small group of customers on an ongoing basis.

Strategy Implementation

ABC information allows you to pick a strategy with confidence. You take your bearings from an accurate compass setting.

The next step is to follow your chosen course. This requires you to take steps to implement your chosen strategy, and ABC can help here, too.

The division used ABC to persuade sales to sell products that fit best with the chosen strategy. When a customer called in for a bid, the product was costed using ABC. This was done by building up the cost from the characteristics of the product, such as number of layers, number of holes, and the *activity-driver rates* in the ABC system.

Sales staff performance and compensation were tied to profitability based on ABC cost. This gave salespeople a strong incentive to pay atten-tion to the profit impact of their sales.

Sales staff response to this performance measurement and incentive program was immediate. In the first month after the introduction of the program, there were substantial changes in product mix. This quickly moved the division in the direction of its chosen strategy.

PERFORMANCE MANAGEMENT

Performance management applies activity-based management to meeting the goals of improved performance. This is aided enormously by the array of available ABC weapons, such as cost analysis and performance measurement, for waging war on waste.

Performance management at the PCB division focused on four areas. First, ABC was used to guide product design. Second, ABC helped prioritize cost-reduction opportunities. Third, ABC was used to guide total quality control (TQC). Fourth, ABC data were used to measure performance in the plant and monitor ongoing improvement.

Product Design

An important ABC application was guiding product designs to achieve lower cost. In doing this, the division was right in step with Hewlett-Packard and the Oscilloscope Group of Tektronix. What was unique about the division was the customer involvement in the cost-reduction efforts.

Figure 9–5 provides an example of ABC's cost-reduction power. It compares the design and cost of two circuit boards. Notice that there are three differences in the design of the two boards. However, these differences do not affect the functionality of the boards.

The differences between the boards in Figure 9–5 are minor adjustments in board size, hole sizes, and board thickness. Yet these minor design adjustments yielded a 15 percent cost reduction (as estimated by ABC).

The division went straight to the customer to achieve these design-based cost reductions. This was necessary because customers often did their own board design.

Involving the customer in this way soon became a competitive weapon for the PCB division. Customers clearly saw the impact on cost (and their purchase price) of making changes in their boards.

The changes increased the net value customers received from the division and encouraged them to send them more business. In some cases, entire product families were sourced at the division because of design and cost improvements made to a single product. Some customers moved their engineering database to the division, and turned over the design work or did the work jointly with the division.

The result was *customer entrenchment*. Cost reductions, single sourcing of product families, and joint engineering created a long-term incentive for customers to stay with the division. It was a powerful competitive

FIGURE 9−5

How Design Affects Product Cost

Trade-off	Design 1	Design 2
1. Size of board	36.72 sq. in.	38 sq. in.
Impact:	9 boards/flat	10 boards/flat
2. Size of holes	2% of holes > 0.021 in.	All holes < 0.021 in.
Impact:	Larger holes use lower-cost drill bits	
3. Thickness of board	0.022 in.	0.021 in.
Impact:	Thinner board uses 2 parts versus 3	
Cost:		
Production activities	$ 94	$ 80
Support activities	$ 10	$ 9
Total cost	$104	$ 89

Small changes in design can have a major impact on a product's cost. The three changes shown here affected the use of activities and resources enough to reduce cost by 15 percent with no sacrifice in board function.

weapon when played alongside the division's leadership in quality and customer service.

Improvement Prioritization

The trip to *world class* is not made in one nonstop journey. Rather, it consists of many small trips, each making a small (but important) contribution to improvement.

But which route gets you to your world-class destination the fastest?

There are many improvement opportunities in the typical company. Some return more improvement for the effort than others, and there usually aren't enough resources to travel all routes at once.

The PCB division used ABC to help it identify the improvement projects with the greatest cost impacts. This was a good use of ABC analysis because improvement projects can vary widely in their impact on activities and resources.

Figure 9–6 shows examples of four types of improvement projects and the associated cost savings. Some projects actually eliminated the

FIGURE 9–6

Examples of Improvement Projects

Eliminate Activities

1. Modify solder mask equipment to apply mask to both sides simultaneously
   Savings: $ 47,000

2. Move inspection equipment into work cell to eliminate handling activities
   Savings: $ 32,000

Substitute Lower-Cost Activities

1. Punching instead of routing high-volume parts   **Savings:** $ 16,000
2. Use long-life drill bits, reducing the need to change bits   **Savings:** $ 9,500

Reduce the Resources Required by Activities

1. Change layout of imaging area to reduce distances between the location of activities and supplies   **Savings:** $ 93,500
2. Bevel edges of material prior to issue to reduce incidences of rework caused by scratches   **Savings:** $ 71,000

Combined or Share Activities

1. Substitute standard for nonstandard materials, allowing sharing of many activities such as database maintenance and handling   **Savings:** $238,000

There are many opportunities for improvement. Each project has a different impact on activities and cost. But they all save money. The key is to pick the ones that offer the greatest savings—and this is where ABC is invaluable.

need to perform activities. Moving inspection equipment into a work cell, for example, eliminated the need to move the boards.

Other projects substituted lower-cost activities for higher-cost activities. An example is using punching rather than routing to remove boards from flats.

A third type of project reduced the resources needed to perform the activities. Changing the layout of the imaging area, for example, reduced the space and supplies required by imaging.

The fourth type of change allowed activities to be combined or shared in order to achieve cost savings. For example, using standard materials instead of nonstandard materials allowed products to share database, purchasing, scheduling, inspection, and handling activities.

Total Quality Control (TQC)

High quality was an important goal for the PCB division. As with most improvement goals, however, there were usually more quality improvement projects to be completed than the available resources could handle.

Quality improvement and cost reduction go hand in hand. Therefore, the cost-reduction potential of a quality improvement project is a good indicator of that project's potential.

The division applied ABC to TQC in two ways. First, the defects associated with each activity were costed for each of the three daily shifts.

A report on the *cost of poor quality* for each activity was prepared immediately after each work shift. A graph showed the trend in physical defects *and* cost. The report allowed each activity in the plant to focus immediately on the quality problems with the biggest cost impact.

Second, a *top 10 offenders* list was prepared daily (Figure 9–7). This reported the 10 products with the highest cost of poor quality on the previous day. It riveted attention on the products that were guiltiest, had the costliest sins of poor quality, and provided the greatest potential for redemption.

When a product unit on this list was scrapped, a report was prepared that showed both the cause of the problem (such as machine or operator error) and the cost. This report was sent to the person or activity most likely to be able to correct the problem.

This use of ABC made quality problems visible within a matter of hours, or even minutes. Under the previous system, it took weeks before

FIGURE 9–7

The Top 10 Offenders List

	Total Units	Rework Units	Scrap Cost	Total Cost	Cause
1	35	32	$1,201	$5,279	A7
2	390	387	$642	$2,874	L4
3	8	8	$1,007	$2,118	E1-3
4	23	21	$871	$2,109	56-9
5	12	5	$732	$1,650	A7
6	32	32	$687	$1,587	JE-6
7	25	25	$596	$1,298	GC-1
8	14	11	$298	$986	EI-3
9	10	10	$256	$754	H1
10	7	7	$228	$635	A6

The PCB division prepared a *top 10 offenders* Pareto report daily. This report identified the products with the highest *cost of poor quality*. These were the products that would benefit the most from corrective action.

quality problems were identified, and even then it wasn't possible to estimate each problem's cost.

These daily cost-of-quality reports could not have been prepared without linking ABC with computer-integrated manufacturing (CIM). For the PCB division, ABC plus CIM equaled *real-time* and *cost-effective* quality control.

Performance Measurement

ABC provides a boost to performance measurement. Performance measurement, in turn, reinforces the benefits of ABM.

Performance measurement wasn't initially a goal of the division's ABC system, but it was a natural development. As people became accustomed to thinking about activities, they developed their own measures of performance.

They typically chose measures that helped them manage their own activities better. These were measures that tracked customer-oriented goals such as quality and lead times.

The tooling department, for example, learned about the high cost of rework from ABC. Workers in that department used ABC to calculate and monitor two performance measures in physical and dollar terms:

1. The number of film packages reworked

2. The number of sheets reworked per package

Focusing on these two measures led to rapid and significant reductions in rework. This reduced tooling costs and freed resources for more productive work. It also had a "waterfall" effect as quality improvement cascaded across the organization.

Performance measurement helped make ABC a local tool at the division. ABC wasn't just a plaything of the finance department. It was the basis for *information empowerment* in all corners of the plant.

SUPPLY-CHAIN MANAGEMENT

Partnerships with suppliers are just as important as partnerships with customers. All activities have customers and suppliers. Some suppliers are outside the company and some are inside. Those outside suppliers are just as important as internal suppliers in determining levels of cost, quality, and customer service.

The PCB division's first application of ABC to supplier management was to model the activity cost of two very different supplier strategies. The first strategy was to buy each material from several different suppliers. The second was to buy materials from a single source.

The ABC analysis showed that single sourcing was by far the cheaper strategy. This was because activity use was less with one supplier.

For example, adding a second supplier for laminate (the basic raw material for printed circuit boards) involved

- Setting up and maintaining dual processing specifications
- Setting up and maintaining two bills of materials
- Managing dual safety stocks
- Receiving and warehousing two part numbers
- Inspecting incoming materials twice as often
- Dual troubleshooting of quality problems at each process step
- Analyzing process changes and additions twice

This list of additional effort doesn't include *indirect* effects. These indirect effects included increased obsolescence, increased human error due to confusion, and increased scrap.

The division used ABC to prepare some interesting rules of thumb about the cost of multiple suppliers. Figure 9–8 illustrates the full drama of these rules. For example, the cost of maintaining and managing a supplier averages $37,000 per year.

FIGURE 9–8

Rules of Thumb for the Cost of Maintaining
Multiple Suppliers

---

1. The average cost of adding a new supplier is over $800 if no engineering, manufacturing testing, or qualification is needed.
2. The cost of maintaining and managing a supplier averages $37,000 per year. This cost does not include additional testing and inspection for critical manufacturing processes.
3. The total cost of maintaining a back-up supplier "just in case" of a shortage, or in case the main supplier is lost, is over $180,000 per year.

If you don't believe multiple sourcing is costly, take a look at these dramatic rules of thumb. They were prepared by the PCB division with the help of ABC.

The news that single sourcing costs less was timely. It reinforced the belief that single sourcing was better for the organization's more immediate goals—better quality and service.

The division's second application of ABC to supplier management centered on creating a new relationship with the plant's laminate supplier. ABC was used to model a new supplier relationship that would dramatically reduce the cost and time for procuring laminate and would also improve laminate quality.

The current approach was shipment of bulk laminate sheets from the supplier's plant in one state to another supplier in another state. This second supplier cut and packaged the material to the division's specifications. The packaged material was then shipped to the division's plant, where it was unpacked, inspected, and stocked.

This approach had a negative impact on time and activities. The average lead time, from placing an order to receipt on the manufacturing floor, was eight weeks.

ABC showed why it took so long—there was a lot of work required at the division and the supplier plants. Activities such as maintaining, ordering, scheduling, receiving, unpacking, inspecting, warehousing, and releasing parts were needed for over two hundred different laminates. These were in addition to a similar list of activities for each supplier.

All that work represented a lot of non-value-added activity. Just look at the cost drivers.

The main cost driver was the supplier's location in a different state many miles from the division's plant. A secondary cost driver was the need to ship the laminate to a second supplier for cutting to size.

The key to eliminating the waste, and cutting cost, was to eliminate those two cost drivers. Arrangements were made with a supplier to build a plant to manufacture laminate adjacent to the division's plant. Laminate was then transferred in bulk through the adjoining walls of the two plants.

Part of the raw material section of the warehouse was converted into a cutting operation. (The space was no longer needed to store laminate.) The laminate was then cut to the proper shape as required, *just in time* for processing.

The impact on activities—and cost, quality, and lead times—was dramatic:

- Gone was a whole set of activities at both the division and the supplier. These included purchasing, scheduling, inspecting, packaging, moving, warehousing, shipping, and handling.

- Cutting the laminate cost less because parts were cut only when needed and in the right size and quantity.
- Shortening the supply pipeline reduced the resources needed for transporting and holding inventory.
- The PCB division now purchased only one type of laminate (bulk sheets). Activities associated with this single part, such as maintaining the part database, ordering, tracking, and scheduling, were now shared by the entire volume of laminate purchases.

ABC proved to be the perfect tool for a plant that was looking for ways to get closer to its suppliers. It was the impetus for moving to a single supply source for each type of material. And it was the inspiration behind relocating a major supplier to a spot adjacent to the division's plant.

The benefits in reduced cost, improved quality, and better customer service were real. It was the kind of *performance breakthrough* that ABM is all about.

INVESTMENT MANAGEMENT

The purpose of capital spending was to improve the ability to meet customer demand, improve quality, and reduce lead times. ABC played a major role in determining how these objectives could be met with limited funds.

To do this, ABC was applied in two ways. First, ABC was used to load the plant based on profitability and available capacity. This increased profitability and identified bottlenecks. Second, ABC was used to determine which bottlenecks should be removed (via capital spending).

This is how the plant was loaded:

1. The plant production schedule was prepared. Initially, this was the most profitable mix of products that could be produced.
2. The schedule's product mix and volume were translated into actual demands on each activity in the production process. This was done via the activity drivers in the ABC system. The number of holes to be drilled in the products, for example, determined the workload for the hole-drilling activity.
3. Each activity's required capacity was compared to available capacity. This identified bottlenecks.
4. Schedule adjustments were made to accommodate the bottlenecks.

This worked well in the short term. The plant was balanced to produce the most profitable mix.

In the long run, however, it was possible to eliminate bottlenecks through judicious capital investments. For example, it was difficult to get products through final inspection. The inventory piled up in front of this activity equaled three days of production.

Analysis showed that 35 percent of this inventory was eventually routed back to previous activities in the process for rework. An additional 6 percent of the boards were scrapped after final inspection.

It was clear that poor quality was the major cost driver as far as capacity was concerned. The key to eliminating bottlenecks was to improve quality and eliminate scrap and rework.

An ABC study showed that over $300,000 would be saved if poor quality were caught in the activities where the problems originated. The size of the savings was sufficient to justify a capital investment to solve the problems.

An investment was made in automated optical inspection equipment for the tooling activity. The investment ensured that quality problems originating in tooling would be caught and corrected in tooling. This eliminated a major cause of rework and scrap at the earliest point in the production process. Gone was an entire chain of poor quality, scrap, and associated activities and resources.

The result was elimination of the bottleneck in the final inspection activity. Capacity was now available for additional revenue-generating production, lead times were reduced, and on-time delivery was enhanced. On the cost side, there was a significant reduction in the need for such activities as inspection, rework, handling, and warranty servicing.

ABC was therefore an important investment management tool. It helped identify key bottlenecks that caused lost revenues. It also helped identify the causes of these bottlenecks and guided capital investments to the places where they would be of greatest benefit.

SUMMARY

ABM brings *information empowerment* to companies aspiring to world-class status. It puts ABC information in the hands of the people doing the improvement. And analysis of this information increases these people's power to improve.

The PCB division used ABM to

- *Set strategic priorities and help implement its chosen strategy.* ABC identified profitable products and customers and focused sales attention on those targets.
- *Manage performance to profitably meet its business goals.* ABC was used to improve product design, target the cost-reduction and quality improvement opportunities with the greatest payoffs, and encourage continuous improvement via activity-based performance measures.
- *Manage suppliers for a long-term relationship that emphasized quality, short lead times, and low cost.* ABC revealed the waste associated with multiple and remote suppliers. It helped the PCB division develop new strategies that emphasized close, ongoing relationships that yielded better service, improved quality, and a substantial drop in cost.
- *Direct investments to the areas that would yield the greatest improvements.* ABC revealed bottlenecks in the plant and identified which ones cost the most in lost profits. This knowledge helped direct investments to the areas where they would increase profits the most.

ABM was the single most important factor in transforming the PCB division from an unprofitable enterprise into the world's most profitable circuit board company. The division's success is a testimony to the ability of ABM to create improvements that go straight to the bottom line.

KEY TERMS

Investment management.   The use of ABC to manage capacity for maximum profitability and to direct capital spending to the most profitable improvement targets.

Performance management.   The use of ABC to improve financial performance. It includes searching for low-cost product designs, identifying cost-reduction opportunities, guiding efforts to improve quality, and measuring performance.

Real time.   The rapid reporting of data from an activity or process. It provides the ability to change the performance of the activity while the work continues.

Strategic management.   The use of activity-based analysis to set and implement strategic priorities.

Supplier management.   The use of ABC to identify waste (in terms of cost, time, and poor quality) in supplier relationships and to help build strong customer-supplier partnerships that can eliminate this waste.

REFERENCES

1 This case study is based on research conducted by the author at the printed circuit board division of a large high-technology company. The name of the company is disguised.

CHAPTER 10

Customer Profitability

The customer gets a lot of attention nowadays. And you might well say, "It's about time, too." Meeting the needs of the customer is central to the success of any business or government agency in today's competitive world.

There are many ways in which the modern organization can focus on the customer. Customer relationship management systems maintain customer information in an easy-to-use format. Management methods such as quality function deployment are designed to capture customer needs and translate them into customer-focused solutions.

So what is missing from the typical customer-centric management system? Most businesses do not know which customers are profitable and which are unprofitable. Sure, they know which are their largest customers (based on sales), and they know which customers have the highest gross margins (sales less direct costs of sales). But they don't know which customers are profitable—unless, that is, they have an activity-based costing (ABC) system that is designed to report customer profitability.

We have already seen the impact of ABC on reported customer profitability. The company described in Chapter 9, for example, used ABC to reveal hidden patterns of profitability (and unprofitability) in its customer base. It used this information to make changes in market strategies and customer emphasis and markedly improved company profitability.

ABC-based customer profitability systems are now entrenched in financial services, manufacturing, packaged goods, distribution, and other types of companies. Charles Schwab, Deluxe Corporation, Klein Steel, Procter & Gamble, and General Mills are just a few examples of companies that report customer profitability on a regular basis. They routinely make decisions on customer mix, features, price, service levels, and cost to serve using ABC information.

Companies today are trying to uncover profit drivers—actions that help to improve the bottom line (net margin) as opposed to gross margin. Customer profitability analysis helps identify high costs and additional activities associated with customers. These activities reduce the net margins for these customers. Sometimes, companies with very large customer bases may also group their customers into categories. Profitability analysis can be done for each category. Let's take a closer look at two companies—Deluxe Corporation and Percival Foods—and see how ABC helped them create *profitable* customer value.

DELUXE CORPORATION[1]

The Deluxe Corporation (Deluxe) is the world's largest printer of checks as well as a provider of electronic products and services to financial institutions and retail companies. Profitable and stable for most of its history, Deluxe faced new competitive pressures during the 1980s and 1990s.

Deregulation of the banking industry in the 1980s spurred consolidation of Deluxe's banking customers. In addition, electronic banking transactions such as credit cards and debit cards were reducing the use of checks. These changes were accompanied by increasing pressure by banks on Deluxe's prices.

The impact of these pressures could be seen in Deluxe's financial results. Return on sales dropped from 12 percent in 1989 to 2 percent in 1997. Return on equity dropped from 24 percent in 1989 to 7 percent in 1997.

Deluxe responded by adopting a business alignment model designed to focus the company on serving its customers profitably. ABC was a component of this model. The director of profitability commented on the purpose of ABC:

> For us, understanding customer profitability amid a maturing check market and an intensely competitive pricing environment was essential. At the same time, we viewed ABC as a means to improve relationships with our customers, by using ABC to identify costs along the supply chain and help our customers reduce their costs and improve their profitability.

In order to achieve this purpose, Deluxe identified some questions that ABC would have to answer:

- Who are our most profitable customers?
- Which practices should we adopt?
- What new products and services should we provide?
- How can we reengineer customer relationships to make them more efficient while lowering costs?
- What was our cost to serve, and how did that cost affect customer profitability?

Deluxe's existing cost system did not answer these questions. It was a traditional manufacturing cost accounting system. It did not measure customer profitability, and it excluded administrative, sales, marketing, and other customer-related activities.

A diagram of Deluxe's ABC model is found in Figure 10–1. It is a great example of a complex ABC model that reports essential business

FIGURE 10–1

Deluxe's Customer Profitability Model

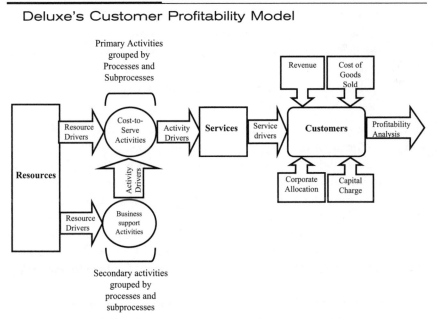

This model accounted for 18,000 customers, 8,700 employees, over $1 billion in sales, and over $400 million in selling, general, and administrative costs.

intelligence for a strategic purpose. The Deluxe model has the following features:

- It includes cost-to-serve activities, such as customer management and order processing.
- It includes business support activities, such as payroll and human resources.
- Activities are organized according to process and subprocess. For example, the activities "prepare customer presentations" and "negotiate contracts" are part of the demand cultivation subprocess. Demand cultivation is a subprocess within the customer management process.
- The assignment of support activities to cost-to-serve activities is based on the relative level of support for the cost-to-serve activities
- There are two kinds of cost objects: services (or channels) and customers. Services are different ways of selling checks to the customer, including via the Internet, over the telephone, and by mail. The cost of services is assigned to customers.
- The ABC model reports the DVA (Deluxe value added) of each customer. DVA is each customer's contribution to shareholder value. It is computed by deducting the cost of capital of the assets used by each customer from net customer profitability.
- Customers are grouped by market segments. Market segments include large banks, small banks, and savings and loan institutions.

Reports from the ABC model reveal important patterns of profitability and cost. The reports show that market segments varied quite significantly in profitability (Figure 10–2). One segment was unprofitable, and two were just above breakeven. Deluxe targeted market segment 3 for immediate corrective action because it was at breakeven and accounted for 37 percent of customer orders.

Why was segment 3 low in profitability? An ABC analysis revealed that a large number of customers were unprofitable or breakeven (Figure 10–3). Figure 10–3 shows the cumulative profitability of customers, starting with the most profitable customer on the left.

A careful look at Figure 10–3 reveals that one customer accounted for about 120 percent of the profits from that segment. About 20 percent of the customers accounted for about 500 percent of the profitability.

FIGURE 10-2

Deluxe Market Segment Profitability Report

DVA per Order by Segment

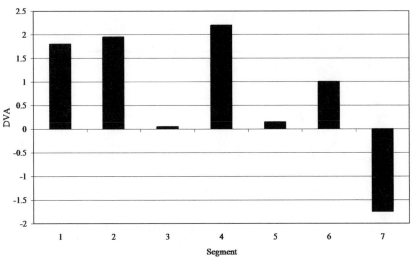

The profitability of Deluxe's market segments varied considerably. Note segment 3, which is low in profitability and represents 37 percent of customer orders.

About 70 percent of the customers were at breakeven, and the remaining 10 percent accounted for about minus 400 percent of the profits.

Understanding why customers varied in profitability required further analysis of the ABC information. The ABC model showed that customers varied in the level of service they received from Deluxe. Higher levels of services incurred more cost.

An important insight from the model was the difference in the cost of servicing the customer depending on the channel of distribution. Orders placed electronically, for example, were significantly less costly than orders placed either by telephone or by mail (Figure 10–4).

Further investigation showed that profitable customers in segment 3 typically processed check orders electronically. The less profitable customers used mail and phone ordering.

Based on these insights from ABC, Deluxe started several initiatives to improve profitability, including the following:

FIGURE 10-3

Customer Profitability "Whale Curve" for Segment 3

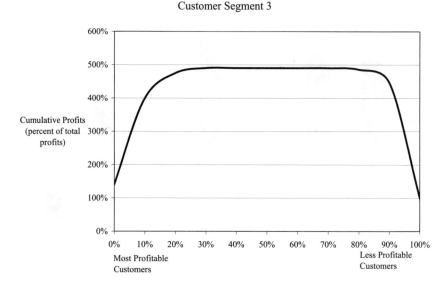

Customer Segment 3

Note that the first customer accounts for 120 percent of the segment's profits, and the last 10 percent account for a negative 400 percent of profits.

- Customers were encouraged to switch to electronic order processing. This program was so successful that the number of orders processed electronically increased by over 50 percent in the first year.
- ABC information was used in customer bidding and contract negotiation. For example, customers were offered discounts for switching to electronic ordering.
- Services that offered little or no value to the customer were eliminated. Custom services were still offered to customers, but at prices that covered the cost of providing them (including the cost of capital).
- Marketing initiatives were evaluated using ABC to determine their likely contribution to shareholder value.

Deluxe followed through on each of these initiatives to make sure that the cost savings were realized. Cost savings would not be realized unless the

FIGURE   10-4

Cost per Order for Different Ordering Channels

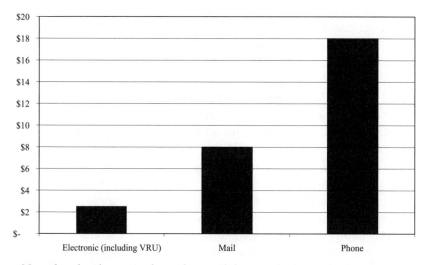

Cost per Order by Channel

Note that the electronic channel is much less costly than either mail or telephone.*

resources that had been freed up were redeployed to better use. The director of profitability commented on the importance of follow-through:

> We had a customer that typed orders for checks using a customer-specific form. When we received these forms, we had to retype them before we could process them. ABC demonstrated how costly this was for us, and also for the customer. We shared our analysis with the customer, who agreed to change the process. This allowed us to eliminate multiple activities and the equivalent of 30 full-time positions. However, I found that the field office had redeployed these people to other activities, leaving costs at the same level. We had to follow up with the field office to make sure that the cost savings were realized.

Deluxe extended ABC analysis to customer costs incurred outside of Deluxe. The company looked at three customer processes: demand creation, order submission, and exception processing. These processes were

*The costs shown are not the actual Deluxe costs. They illustrate the magnitude of difference in channel costs.

affected by changes in the relationship, such as the switch to electronic order processing. The analysis showed how much cost the customer would save by improving the process, fixing quality problems, and changing the method of order entry (Figure 10–5).

The analysis of cost savings in the customer's processes was used in the contract negotiation process. If Deluxe could show that the customer would reduce its internal cost by contracting with Deluxe, this increased the value of the contract to the customer.

Deluxe's financial performance improved significantly over the period 1998 to 2002. By 2002 the company's return on sales had increased to 26.9 percent (from 2 percent in 1997). In his letter to the shareholders in the 2002 Annual Report, the chairman attributed much of this success to Deluxe's business alignment model, which included activity-based costing.

In summary, Deluxe adapted because of the shift in the way it competed in a maturing market. Its existing cost system provided little help in understanding customer profitability and the cost-to-serve activities that underlay profitable customer relationships.

ABC allowed Deluxe to separate the profitable from the unprofitable customers and to understand the reasons for the differences. The insights from ABC were the basis for developing new—and more profitable—customer programs.

FIGURE 10-5

Customer and Deluxe Processes Involved in Selling, Processing, and Fulfilling an Order for Checks

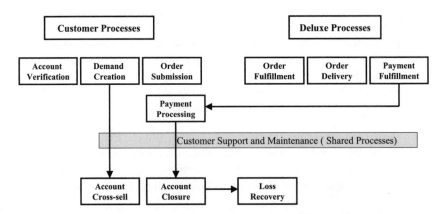

This analysis recognized the value to the customer of looking at the entire customer-supplier process.

PERCIVAL FOODS²

Percival Foods, Inc. (Percival) is a leading supplier of packaged and bulk organic food products. Founded in 1893, its 2003 revenues topped $1.7 billion from more than 200,000 products and 500,000 customers.

Percival's strategy was to be the leader in providing nutritious and environmentally safe food products. Factors that differentiated Percival from its competitors included its brand name, its close relationship with growers and suppliers of organic produce, and its large customer base of small health-food stores, large specialty superstores, and catalog subscribers.

The Percival brand name stands for a high level of trust on the part of the end consumer, as well as for the freshness, pureness, and quality of the firm's products. Percival's customers viewed the company as knowledgeable about the needs of the end consumer, and as a supplier of fresh, high-quality products delivered just in time to meet their specific needs.

Percival's business was highly complex. In addition to its large number of products and customers, there were several other factors that contributed to the complexity:

- The large number of suppliers (products are purchased from over 8,000 growers and other vendors)
- Products grown and packaged by suppliers franchised to use the Percival brand versus those from third-party suppliers
- Products grown and packaged by Percival versus those sourced from an outside supplier
- The large number of distribution centers (products were distributed from approximately 15 major distribution centers in the United States)
- Differences in product size and weight
- Different product packaging options
- Whether or not products were included in the Percival natural foods catalog
- Whether products were exclusive to Percival or also sold by others
- Perishable products that needed special handling and/or refrigeration
- Orders placed via the Internet, electronic data interchange (EDI), or the telephone
- Products shipped by the Percival transportation fleet versus those shipped by regional carriers

- Products shipped from a Percival warehouse versus those shipped directly to customers by a supplier
- Regular processing versus expedited shipping service for urgent orders

The diversity and complexity of Percival's business made it a good candidate for an ABC system. A senior finance manager explained the need for ABC:

> Our business is extremely complex, and we need the sophistication of the ABC tool to manage the data and contribute our analyses and decision making. For example, we are able to slice the data to understand profitability by business segment, by customer, by product line, and even down to an individual product. These data provide for better decisions, which ultimately allow us to drop more profit to the bottom line.
>
> The diversity of our business creates very different cost-to-serve models across our customer base. Given the high levels of complexity combined with different customer, product, and service offerings, we need a sophisticated way of understanding these different business models. If we don't do the analysis up front, we will be scratching our heads and wondering why customers, suppliers, and products later become unprofitable in our business.

The ABC initiative began in 1999. The first step was the completion of an activity analysis. A pilot ABC model was completed in 2000, focused primarily on activities in the Percival warehouses.

The ABC team expanded its focus in 2002 to view profitability multidimensionally—customers, suppliers, and products, in addition to warehouses. The objective was to understand the drivers of profitability and cost complexity, and to use this knowledge to improve profitability for customers, suppliers, and Percival.

A second change was to build the model using a different software technology. The team believed that this new software was better suited to the processing requirements of a complex business model with millions of profit components.

The ABC team revised the model in 2003 to address these concerns. The ABC model was simplified, validated, and modified to report profitability for customers, products, and vendors. The team developed a process for closing the model within five days of the general ledger close at the end of each month. The team also set validation procedures and priorities for model updates and changes.

The 2003 efforts to improve the ABC model enhanced the data integrity and "directional" accuracy of the information. In addition, the model was capable of processing large amounts of data on a monthly basis. In a typical month, the ABC model processed transactions for 400,000 orders, 600,000 shipments, and 800,000 invoice history transaction lines. The model included 9,000 general ledger lines and about 350 activities.

The ABC model was designed to process large amounts of data efficiently. The team used modeling techniques to reduce the number of activities and to leverage the data in the company's transactional systems.

The ABC model took costs from the general ledger and invoice history and assigned them to activities and cost objects. The model computed profit and loss by order line item, and it allowed reporting along multiple profit dimensions. Available reports included profit and loss by customer, supplier, product, distribution center, order, shipment, and line.

One of the reports was the customer profitability "whale" curve (Figure 10–6). This curve shows the cumulative profit earned from

FIGURE 10-6

Percival's Customer Profitability Whale Curve

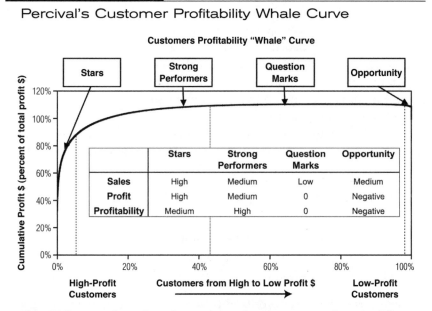

Customers Profitability "Whale" Curve

	Stars	Strong Performers	Question Marks	Opportunity
Sales	High	Medium	Low	Medium
Profit	High	Medium	0	Negative
Profitability	Medium	High	0	Negative

This ABC report shows how four groups of customers contribute in different ways to company profits. Each group presents unique challenges and opportunities for increasing profitability.

Percival customers, starting with the most profitable customers on the left of the graph. This graph reveals four groups of customers; Stars, Strong Performers, Question Marks, and Opportunity.

Stars were high-sales, medium-profitability customers. These customers represented a relatively small percentage of the customer base, but they accounted for a significant portion of operating income. The key issues for Stars were how to retain these important customers, and what lessons could be learned from their success and applied to other customer groups.

Strong Performers had smaller sales volumes, but were highly profitable. Strong Performers were considered the Stars of tomorrow, customers that should be migrated to a larger sales platform.

Question Marks was a large customer group that earned little or no operating income. The issues for this group were how important these customers were to Percival, and how much should be invested in growing them.

Opportunity was the least profitable customer group, accounting for a small percentage of customers. The question for this group was what actions could be taken immediately to improve the profitability of these customers.

"What if?" analyses were performed to examine different ways of improving cost recovery when serving customers. For example, two options being examined for a customer are shown in Figure 10–7. One option was to reduce the number of small orders, and to charge the customer for special handling on perishable orders and those requiring refrigeration. The second option was to increase sales to achieve the same impact on operating income.

The ABC analysis revealed significant differences in the cost to serve for profitable and unprofitable customers. These differences included

- Small versus high order size
- Unpredictable versus predictable order arrivals
- Manual versus automated and scheduled order processing
- Changes versus no changes in shipping requirements
- Large amounts of sales support versus little or no support
- Slow versus rapid payment

The analysis of customer profitability was affected by supplier and product profitability. A finance manager explained the interplay between customers, suppliers, and products:

FIGURE 10-7

Simulation of Options for Increasing the Profitability of a Customer

Cost Recovery Options Tool—What-If Analysis

Example A—Customer A Unrecovered Cost >>> $23K

- Scenario 1—Recovering Operating Costs through Improved Services

Options	2003 Total	2003 Cost Recovery	What If	$ Recovered	Customer Action
1. Order < $150	2,625	8%	100%	$23,009	Reduce < $150 Orders
2. Perish Orders	394	96%	100%	$285	Bundle/Bill Perish Orders
3. Refrig Orders	0	0%	0%	$0	Bundle/Bill Refrig Orders
4. Sales	$814,899		0%	$0	Increase Sales
				$23,294	

You have the option to recover operating costs by increasing order size and consolidating perishable and refrigerated orders or billing.

- Scenario 2—Recovering Operating Costs through Increased Sales

Options	2003 Total	2003 Cost Recovery	What If	$ Recovered	Customer Action
1. Order < $150	2,625	8%	8%	$0	Reduce < $150 Orders
2. Perish Orders	394	96%	96%	$0	Bundle/Bill Perish Orders
3. Refrig Orders	0	0%	0%	$0	Bundle/Bill Refrig Orders
4. Sales	$814,899		20%	$23,294	Increase Sales
				$23,294	

We would need a 20% increase in sales at Customer A to recover operating costs.

ABC analysis helped management assess alternative ways of addressing customer profitability issues.

In addition to customer profitability, we also review supplier profitability by segment. The important issue to remember is that profitability is multidimensional. For example, a customer may be unprofitable because of supplier issues, and vice versa. As a result, we first review customer and supplier profitability, then seek to understand the common denominator—product profitability—in order to make targeted decisions for improving profitability.

The ABC team's analysis divided suppliers into the same four groups as customers. Stars were the most profitable suppliers. The questions asked about this group were whether the current supplier retention program was adequate, and what could be learned from these suppliers' success that could be applied to other suppliers.

Strong Performers were profitable suppliers that contributed modest revenues to Percival. The key was to identify the best suppliers from this group and turn them into Stars.

The Question Mark group was the largest in numbers, but low in revenues and breakeven in profits. The key question for the suppliers in this group was why they were suppliers to Percival. Did Percival care about these suppliers, and did the suppliers care about Percival?

The fourth group contained the Opportunity. These were the suppliers that contributed low revenues and were unprofitable. The analysis prompted immediate action to eliminate losses and to expand purchases of profitable products supplied by these suppliers.

Analysis of product profitability revealed a similar distribution to that of customers and suppliers. It showed whether profitability was being affected at the product level, the supplier level, the customer level, or some combination thereof. If the problem was at the product level, actions might include increasing the price, changing the supplier, or changing the unit of measure.

Based on the ABC analysis of customers, suppliers, and products, several changes were made in 2004. These included

- Renegotiating customer and supplier contracts to reflect the cost and profitability of the contracts. The changes included increases in price and order size, and the correct charging of transportation costs.

- Changes in the product unit of measure to cover the cost of distributing the product and taking the customer's order. For example, packs of seven-grain muffins were sold by the case rather than individually.

- Increases in customer order size to cover the costs of processing orders. ABC showed that, in most cases, orders of less than $50 were unprofitable. Where possible, customers were offered incentives—such as free shipping with large orders—to increase the size and lower the frequency of orders for nonperishable goods. Percival increased the price on nonfrozen perishable items to reflect the additional order processing cost.

- Eliminating pricing discrepancies. For example, one product out of a product line with 10 products was found to be unprofitable. Analysis showed that the price of this product needed to be increased.

- Properly charging handling costs for perishable products to customers who purchased those products. This change was based on an ABC analysis that revealed that handling costs for perishable products were high relative to the billing of these costs.

> Further analysis showed that the problem was the omission of the charge from some customers' bills.

- Increasing the number of orders processed electronically to take advantage of their lower cost. In addition, errors in the processing of electronic orders were identified during the ABC analysis. These errors created system "kickouts" and required manual reprocessing. Over 50 percent of these errors were eliminated, increasing capacity in customer service activities.

- Including an objective for operating income in the performance statements of sales managers and sales representatives. This encouraged sales to focus on profitability as measured by ABC rather than on revenue or gross margin.

The Percival case is an excellent example of the use of ABC to measure, analyze, and improve customer profitability. It reminds us that profitability is multidimensional—understanding customer profitability requires understanding supplier and product profitability as well.

The Percival ABC model is noteworthy because it successfully models a very complex business. A decade ago it would have been difficult to build and sustain an ABC model covering 700,000 products, 8,000 suppliers, and 500,000 customers. Thanks to advances in ABC software and model design, Percival is able to cost-effectively report useful ABC information to managers monthly.

ACTING ON CUSTOMER PROFITABILITY INTELLIGENCE

The Deluxe Corporation and the Percival Foods models are good examples of the power of ABC customer intelligence. The whale curves, for example, clearly articulate the customer profitability profile. They cry out for action. But just what action is required?

Action to improve profitability involves moving customers upward and left in the 2 × 2 diagram in Figure 10–8. From a profitability standpoint, the worst customers are those in the lower right-hand quadrant—they are the customers making up the tail end of the whale curve. They need to be fixed quickly—either the margins improved or the customers eliminated.

The best customers are the high-margin, high-revenue customers in the upper left-hand quadrant. Ideally, this is where every customer should be. Customers in the upper right-hand quadrant need actions to

FIGURE 10-8

Revenue versus Net Margin

	High Margin	Low Margin
High Revenue	Best ☆	Power
Low Revenue	Build	Worst

The sweet spot is in the upper left-hand quadrant. With the help of ABC, this is your destination.

increase margins. Those in the lower left-hand quadrant need actions to grow revenues.

While the whale curve, the 2 × 2 diagram, and other ABC reports communicate the need for action, determining the specific actions to be taken requires more analysis. For example, for each customer type, we can ask the following types of questions:

- What are the opportunities for revenue enhancement?
- What types of customer partnerships will enhance the relationship and its profitability?
- What are the opportunities for eliminating activities and costs that do not create value for the customer?
- What services can be bundled with the products to enrich the customer experience and enhance overall profitability?
- How can the customer solution be customized in a profitable manner?

In each case, the question is the starting point in the search for the profit drivers that determine customer profitability.

Each profit driver is analyzed for its impact on profitability. For example, is a technology investment to allow Internet order taking justified by the reduction in the cost-to-serve activities? Will a change in product packaging reduce the cost of order taking, picking, packing, shipping, and other activities enough to justify the change?

The value of ABC is not just its attention-getting power. It is its ability to focus decisions on the specific actions that *measurably* increase profitability.

ABC ANALYTICS[3]

ABC is a powerful tool, but it may need a little help in mining intelligence from large customer profitability models. For example, Charles Schwab's ABC model reports profitability on over 8,000,000 customers, with growth to 20,000,000 customers planned. What are the challenges associated with extracting information from a megamodel such as this?

The challenge is to comb the vast array of data in a large model to find the nuggets of information on which action can be taken. Whale curves and other aggregate ABC reports are quite useful, but they may not highlight the interactions of complexity and diversity in a complex ABC model.

The Percival model is a good example of this type of complexity; it reports the profitability of 200,000 products, 800,000 line items, and 8,000 vendors, in addition to 500,000 customers, on a monthly basis. The interaction between these cost objects creates billions of opportunities for analysis—an intimidating prospect for any management team.

The answer is ABC analytics. ABC analytics are statistical and data-mining tools for extracting intelligence from the ABC model. They include forecasting tools, simulation models, and other advanced statistical tools. They are used to pinpoint complexity and other factors that affect differential profitability.

Advanced statistical and data-mining tools are used to generate groups from very large customer bases. These advanced techniques, which use neural nets and other mining applications, can identify complexity factors (from distribution, vendors, manufacturing, and support) to create customer groupings.

While technology today allows companies like Percival to process huge quantities of data, it is the analytical tools that let managers chunk the data into groups and make them manageable. Analytics help managers make sense of the data and focus on action plans. The application of these tools is the next frontier for activity-based costing.

SUMMARY

ABC is a powerful analytic tool for revealing hidden patterns of customer profitability. Used to identify profit drivers, it leads to actions that improve company profitability.

Deluxe shows how this works. It illustrates the value of understanding the detailed costs and activities associated with serving the customer. Armed with insights from ABC, Deluxe developed new and profitable customer strategies.

Percival Foods confirms that ABC can cost-effectively model highly complex businesses. Its ABC model routinely reports profitability on a vast array of products, customers, suppliers, and products.

The ABC model is just the starting point in a program to improve customer profitability. ABC information must be reported to management in a meaningful form and mined carefully to reveal the important profit drivers.

REFERENCES

1 The material on the Deluxe Corporation is drawn from Peter B. B. Turney, Deluxe Corporation (A), (B), (C), (D), and (E) (Charlottesville: University of Virginia Darden School, 1999).

2 The material on Percival Foods is drawn from Peter B. B. Turney, "Percival Foods, Inc., Customer Profitability Improvement" (Portland, OR: Cost Technology, Inc., 2004). While the case is based on an actual company, the name and industry have been changed.

3 This section includes material written by Dr. Manash Ray of Cost Technology, Inc.

PART FIVE

How to Implement ABC and ABM Successfully

By now you're probably convinced that ABC and ABM are valuable tools. You've seen how—and understand why—you should not rely on accounting and cost systems to provide useful management information.

You know what ABC systems look like. You know what ABM can do. Now you need to know how to do it—how to put ABC and ABM to work to create results for you.

Chapter 11 shows you how to win management buy-in to ABC and ABM. This is where you get answers to the following questions:

- How do I create interest in ABC and ABM?
- How do I remove barriers to the acceptance of ABC and ABM?
- How do I obtain management's commitment to ABC and ABM?

Chapter 12 explains how to develop a plan to successfully implement ABC and ABM in your organization. It walks you through the eight steps to a completed system and realized results.

Chapter 13 tells you where to find and gather the data you need if you are to create an ABC system. You learn how to

- Gather accurate information with economy of effort
- Get the data into the ABC model
- Automate a sustainable ABC system

Chapter 14 shows you how to design an ABC system. This is where the structure of the system is created and the intelligence is added. This chapter walks you through the steps of the design process. It provides tried and tested rules for each step of the way.

Building a resource planning model or time-based ABC model is different from designing a standard ABC model. Chapter 14 describes these differences and explains how they affect the design process.

CHAPTER 11

Convincing Management to Change

You're convinced that activity-based costing (ABC) is a valuable tool for fostering positive change. You want to introduce it into your company.

To do this successfully, you must first convince management to make the change. Remember, *ABC is quite different from existing systems.* For a change to ABC to be successful, management must believe in it, must want to do it, and must be willing to commit the leadership, effort, and resources required to do it.

The question is, how do you convince management? How do you make sure that ABC is seen not as just another fancy system, but as a necessary and valuable tool for performance improvement.

Well, there's some good news...and there's some bad news.

First the bad news.

Acceptance of ABC is not always achieved without effort and care.

The problem is, ABC requires change. It's a different way of doing business. And, as with any other change, the path to acceptance, successful implementation, and wise use is not without pitfalls.

- *Management may not be fully prepared for what ABC reveals.* At Schrader Bellows, for example, ABC revealed that more than 80 percent of the products were losing money. However, despite the months of effort spent designing the system and analyzing the results, management still could not accept the changes that were necessary to address the situation.[1]

- *Management may oppose the introduction of ABC.* As an example, one company's approach to management buy-in, planning, and implementation was beautifully "textbook." The ABC system was completed. Everything was ready to go.

  Then the company hired a new chief financial officer.

  As it turned out, this person was adamantly opposed to ABC. Management meetings on ABC were referred to as "the gunfight at the OK corral." Ultimately, the well-wrought ABC system was shot down.
- *The ABC model may be poorly designed.* One company, for example, designed an enterprisewide ABC system. The effort involved 15 to 20 people and cost millions of dollars. But management did not use the information that resulted.

  A review of the situation showed that the model was at too high a level (the information was too aggregated) for most managers to use. In fact, we determined that fewer than 50 managers out of nearly 60,000 employees could use the ABC information.

  Even these 50 managers did not use ABC—they were not involved in the design and had no ownership and understanding of the ABC reports. In fact, they refused to use the ABC reports and returned to using the old reports.

Now for the *good* news.

Many organizations have introduced ABC and put it to good use. From their experiences, a method for successful introduction of ABC has been developed. It begins with three crucial steps:

Step 1: Generate interest in ABC.

Step 2: Remove any barriers to the introduction of ABC that may exist.

Step 3: Obtain management's commitment to embark on an ABC project.

STEP 1: GENERATE INTEREST

You're convinced that ABC is a valuable tool. But are your colleagues also convinced? Has top management been briefed on (and bought into) ABC?

It's important to have support from *ABC champions* at all levels of the company. These champions should include top management, plant man-

---

SUCCESSFUL INTRODUCTION OF ABC
BEGINS WITH THREE STEPS:

Step 1 Generate interest.
Step 2 Remove barriers to acceptance.
Step 3 Obtain management commitment.

---

agement, engineering, finance and accounting, and marketing. Success in a service company, such as a hospital, requires support from both administrators and professionals. Success in a government department requires support from the department head and the executive team. Without broad endorsement, it's unlikely that you'll be able to place ABC at the top of anyone's agenda.

The key issues for top management are what ABC can do for the organization and what it will cost to do it. ABC must be perceived as a strategic and cost-effective tool that yields competitive dividends.

The challenge in manufacturing companies is the change in perception that comes with ABC. Marketing and sales, for example, have a light—the light of conventional cost information—that casts a distorted image on their world. When they get their new precision ABC light bulb, they'll need to make radical adjustments in perception. And they will need to be convinced that this new perception is close to reality.

In contrast, engineering has been completely in the dark. For them, turning on the lights may be perceived as a blessing. Production management may also be so disenchanted with conventional cost information that it is happy to turn off the conventional lights.

Finance and accounting must be handled with kid gloves. These people are the ones who are responsible for the existing cost system (and the distorted images it presents) and who have the knowledge to design it. If their support is not carefully cultivated, ABC can appear to be a threat to both their turf and their expertise. But if they are won over, the members of the finance and accounting staff will be an enthusiastic and invaluable source of technical assistance and support.

Service and government organizations have a different challenge. They typically don't have a cost system; they rely on the general ledger as their source of financial information. For them, ABC replaces darkness with light. This light may be accompanied by revelations about inefficiencies and, in the case of service organizations, hidden losses. These revelations may be threatening.

Regardless of the type of organization, the first step in generating support among your important constituencies is to *expose them* to ABC. They need to be shown the problems that can accompany poorly designed cost systems, and why ABC systems are crucial to their success. You can do this by circulating materials on ABC and by organizing seminars.

You should also look for *benchmarks* to use in this exposure process. Benchmarks are organizations similar to your own that have implemented ABC. Their experiences are valuable for answering proof-of-performance questions.

Circulating Materials

Managers without prior exposure to ABC need a short executive summary that tells them

- *What* ABC is
- *Why* it's superior to conventional costing
- *Why* it's important
- *How* it can be used

You can lay the groundwork by putting together an information package for circulation. A video is a quick and easy means of providing basic ABC knowledge. An Internet search will reveal many short articles and case studies that can be read and digested rapidly. And for those who wish to expand their knowledge even further, you can recommend or provide books such as this one.

In-house Seminars

There's no substitute for the voice of experience. This can be provided via live presentations from ABC specialists. Live presentations can be delivered on-site or over the Internet.

Such presentations are an opportunity to get the key players together in one room for an exchange of ideas and information. The specialist can address concerns about ABC and can lead the group in a discussion of how ABC might be applied in your organization. If the presentation is done correctly, the specialist can instill enthusiasm for ABC and buy-in for a project from your management team.

Benchmarks

"What has ABC done for other organizations?" That's a common question asked by potential ABC converts. It's probably best answered with published case studies. A visit to an organization that uses ABC can be an even more dramatic and convincing experience.

The Schrader Bellows case study is a good place to start. It shows the dramatic changes in reported product costs that can occur when ABC is used. These changes—*which can be in orders of magnitude*—should make anyone who is using a conventional cost system extremely nervous.

The power of the ABC analysis at Schrader Bellows is illustrated by an experience following an ABC seminar. One of the people attending, a manager from a local manufacturing company, rushed up to the speaker. "Your description of Schrader Bellows could have been my company," this person exclaimed. "No question about it. We desperately need ABC."

The experience of the Oscilloscope Group of Tektronix is another good example to use. This example shows how ABC can become part of a continuous improvement program. Specifically, the Oscilloscope Group used ABC to show its engineers the cost of designing products with low-volume components. As a result, the count of different parts used in the division's products decreased by over 50 percent.

For those in service and government organizations, there are many case examples to draw on. A quick Internet check will reveal many cases involving military, government, health-care, financial services, and other organizations.[2]

The most compelling benchmark may be an actual visit to an organization that's using ABC. The people there can tell you firsthand why they adopted ABC, how they implemented it, how they are using the information, and the results they have achieved. Such visits make an excellent follow-up to an in-house seminar.

STEP 2: REMOVE BARRIERS TO ACCEPTANCE

A key decision maker's negative comments can be a major barrier to ABC implementation. Unless these comments are overcome, the entire ABC project can be held up.

The danger of anti-ABC comments is that they typically have a grain of truth. They are true in certain limited circumstances. But they are not general truths for the world of ABC.

MYTHS ABOUT ABC

Myth 1 ABC is too difficult to implement and use.

Myth 2 ABC is a cost accounting system.

Myth 3 We do not need accurate cost information.

Myth 4 Cost systems play a limited role in process improvement.

These myths are beliefs about the cost and value of ABC systems. While they contain grains of truth, they are not general truths. Unless they are addressed, these myths may block the successful introduction of ABC.

Certain comments are heard often enough that they are called myths about ABC. These myths generally involve one of four different themes. Being able to recognize these myths and their themes allows you to remove them as barriers to ABC implementation.

Myth 1: ABC Is Too Difficult to Implement and Use

This myth is the belief that implementing an ABC system requires an excessive amount of time and effort. The concern is that the time and effort required exceed the value that will be realized from the use of ABC information.

In a world that has seen thousands of ABC implementations, it is inevitable that some will have taken too long, required too much effort, and failed to provide the desired results. ABC has had its share of failures, and in this regard it is no different from other management initiatives.

But if ABC is done right, it is a cost-effective source of business intelligence that highlights ways to reduce cost and improve profitability. Organizations as diverse as the Deluxe Corporation, Exxon-Mobil, Charles Schwab, the U.S. Marine Corps, and the South Dakota Department of Transportation have one thing in common: They have successfully implemented and maintained an ABC system that delivers a positive return on investment.

These successful organizations set specific goals for their ABC system, planned on certain results, and applied proven methods for implementing, automating, and maintaining the system. The South Dakota

Department of Transportation, for example, used storyboarding to cost-effectively identify the activities for the ABC model. The department then integrated these activities into its timekeeping system to reduce the cost of system maintenance.

We should acknowledge the progress that has been made in improving the ABC implementation process. A project that took nine months fifteen years ago will take three months today. Project management, methods, and tools have all improved out of recognition. And our two-decade experience with implementing and using ABC in diverse settings helps us take the shortest path to results.

Myth 2: ABC Is a Cost Accounting System

Some people label ABC "just another cost accounting system." Nothing could be further from the truth.

In its earliest days, ABC was used to correct inaccuracies in the reported cost of products in manufacturing companies. We have seen cases—such as Schrader Bellows—where ABC resolved inaccuracies that reached thousands of percent and affected most of the product line.

Even in these early days, however, ABC proved its ability to tackle customer profitability and other strategic applications that were outside the scope of cost accounting. Kanthal-Hoganas is a good example of the use of ABC for customer profitability analysis. ABC can also pinpoint areas of high cost, leading to actions to reduce cost. Nortel is a good example of this.

ABC began its life in manufacturing companies, but it quickly migrated to service, distribution, military, government, and other non-manufacturing organizations. These organizations did not use ABC to replace their cost accounting system—they did not have a cost accounting system (there was no inventory to value). Instead, they saw ABC as a tool that would give them important insights into the performance of their organization.

When you look at ABC today, it is difficult to discern any relationship to cost accounting. It is an analytical tool that draws data from corporate information systems, models these data, and yields business intelligence on products, services, customers, processes, and other strategic and operational factors. It provides analytical support for initiatives such as six sigma, supply-chain management, resource management, and business process engineering. It is a source of performance measures for the balanced scorecard.

Myth 3: We Do Not Need Accurate Cost Information

Some people retort that cost accounting systems report costs that are *sufficiently* accurate. Some add that accuracy is unimportant because managers know intuitively what products cost. Others believe that accuracy is unnecessary because cost information is not used to set prices. These beliefs are important because they challenge one of the major benefits of ABC—*more accurate cost information.*

Managers in manufacturing companies may be able to identify products that are overcosted or undercosted. These managers know, for example, that a product that is difficult to engineer, manufacture, or distribute must cost more than simpler products. They recognize this reality even when their conventional cost system reports that the two products cost the same.

However, *managers often do not realize the size of the cost problem.* Experience has shown that managers typically underestimate product cost distortions. They may believe, for example, that the true cost of a difficult-to-produce item is 50 percent greater than the reported cost. In reality, the true cost may be 500 percent greater.

Some companies use cost to set prices. This is particularly true in regulated industries and for defense contractors. But there are other companies that price to market or price based on what the customer is willing to pay. In these latter cases, product cost may not figure into the pricing equation.

However, it's dangerous to believe that accurate costs are unnecessary even if they are not needed for pricing: *Managers chase profits, and profits can be phantoms of the cost system.* It's only natural for managers to devote their attention and resources to the products that they perceive to be the most profitable. And it's the cost system that reports the absolute and relative profitability of products.

For example, it was quite natural for a printed circuit board manufacturer to emphasize the sale of two-sided circuit boards when the cost system showed that they were profitable. In fact, the majority of its sales were two-sided boards.

But when an ABC system revealed the awful reality that two-sided boards were not profitable at current prices, a new strategy was adopted. The two-sided business was deemphasized, and a market for complex multilayer boards was built up.

Such experiences have shown time and again that improved accuracy is an important benefit of ABC. Managers may be able to identify products that are incorrectly costed, but they need ABC to judge the size of the distortion. Even when pricing strategy isn't based on product costs, ABC allows attention to be focused on those products with the greatest relative profitability.

Documenting case histories like this may be enough to dispel this myth. If not, try completing a short proof-of-concept study to demonstrate the value of ABC. For example, a large chemicals company recently completed a small ABC model to identify profit levers—actions that would increase profitability. The study revealed several key levers and successfully demonstrated the value of ABC.

Service organizations also benefit from accurate cost information. While these organizations may not have cost accounting systems, they suffer just as much as manufacturing companies from hidden losses. For example, an insurance company expanded its offerings from auto insurance to life insurance, homeowner insurance, and personal financial advising. The company worked out a discounted fee structure for customers using two or more of its products.

An ABC analysis later computed total costs of this new service offering. It included the costs of developing the products as well as the cost of unique and additional activities.

The analysis showed that the costs far exceeded the net margins from increased sales. The result was that profits declined as revenues rose. Armed with the ABC intelligence, the insurance company cut back on the range of products in each category and revised its discount structure.

An example from the South Dakota Department of Transportation shows how important accurate cost information is for government agencies. The Right of Way function within the department relied heavily on consultants to perform real estate appraisals. An ABC analysis revealed that the internal costs *were lower* than the fees paid to consultants. ABC also allowed them to focus on activities and improve the process so that appraisers now had more time to conduct appraisals. There was a reduction in consulting fees paid out as well as increased productivity in terms of the number of appraisals completed. The result was a lower cost per appraisal.

In a second example, the Bridge Inspection function within the South Dakota Department of Transportation routinely inspects bridges for safety and overall wear and tear. ABC analysis highlighted high-cost activities related to the actual inspection, which had to be done manually on site. Knowledge of the high cost, along with intangible factors such as safety, allowed Bridge Inspection to make a compelling business case for using a vehicle-mounted radar technology.

Myth 4: Cost Systems Play a Limited Role in Process Improvement

Another school of thought maintains that ABC plays a limited role in fostering process improvement. This school views ABC as a strategic product costing tool, but not as a source of information for improving the performance of activities. For those subscribing to this opinion, any decision to implement ABC must be based on strategic benefits rather than cost reduction.

This school is right—ABC is an invaluable strategic tool. It reports accurate product costs for product mix and pricing purposes. This helps guide companies in their choice of markets and customers.

But ABC also provides useful information for cost-reduction programs. Product designers, for example, can use information about the cost of activity drivers, and products' consumption of those measures, to help them design products that have a lower cost. Hewlett-Packard and Tektronix have implemented ABC systems specifically for that purpose—*to help engineers design products with a lower cost.*

ABC also provides information for simulating cost-reduction alternatives. One company, for example, used its ABC system to determine the cost of engineering change activities. Careful study showed that the engineering change process could be redesigned to reduce the time and cost required to complete an engineering change. The ABC system was used to model the proposed change and to confirm the cost savings that resulted.

ABC also provides a wealth of *nonfinancial* information about activities. For example, information about *cost drivers* provides opportunities to manage the factors that cause work. Information about activity *performance*, such as a measure of the quality of the activity's output, provides feedback on how well the activity is being performed. Designation of activities as *non-value-added* provides opportunities for eliminating waste.

ABC can help prioritize process improvements. By revealing the cost-reduction impact of potential improvements, ABC helps focus six sigma, continuous improvement, and process reengineering efforts on those projects that will provide the greatest return.

ABC also ensures that the cost savings that are identified are realized. It does this by showing which resources will be freed up by the improvements, allowing these resources to be redeployed to other, more value-added activities.

Overall, there is no justification for the myth that ABC plays a limited role in process improvement. ABC is, in reality, a rich source of information for managing activities. In some cases, organizations have implemented ABC solely for that reason. This is particularly true in government agencies.

How to dispel this myth? Try implementing a value analysis similar to the one at General Electric described in Chapter 8. Pick a department where you expect to find waste. If you can cut costs successfully, you will find ready converts to your cause.

STEP 3: OBTAIN MANAGEMENT COMMITMENT

Generating interest in ABC is an important first step. But actual commitment to an ABC project requires evidence that ABC will yield substantial benefits for the organization.

Commitment will be forthcoming if you can demonstrate two things: first, that your organization is the type of organization that can benefit from ABC; and second, that there is evidence that your company's existing cost and accounting systems are not doing the job.

The Type of Organization That Benefits the Most

The truth is, any organization can benefit from ABC—large or small, manufacturing, service, or government. Even if you are making a 20 percent return, 25 percent would be better. Even if you are ahead of the competition today, leadership in a market can change hands quickly.

Organizations with a lot of *complexity* and *diversity* are prime candidates for ABC. The more complexity there is, the more overhead there will be, and the greater the potential for inaccurate costs. More complexity also means more opportunity for waste elimination. Either way, ABC provides improved information.

Diversity of products or volumes also increases the value of ABC. If your product line has products with different designs, chances are that these products will require different activities and will cost different amounts. ABC helps you understand and deal with this diversity.

If your products vary in volume (some high, some low), a conventional cost system will usually overcost the high-volume products and undercost the low-volume ones. If the range of volumes is considerable, the cost errors can be thousands of percent. You definitely need ABC to correct these errors, or you'll leave yourself vulnerable to the competition.

Organizations with only one product or service can still benefit from ABC. This single product may be sold to customers in different ways. For example, a software company may sell a single software program. For $1,000, the customer receives a disk and a manual in a box. For $2,000, the customer receives the box and a service contract. For $5,000, the customer also receives training in how to use the software.

Nonmanufacturing costs in a manufacturing company (and all the costs in a service company or government agency) are outside the scope of conventional product cost systems. However, these costs are likely to be significant. And it's important to understand customer profitability and to improve marketing and other customer-oriented activities.

Then there's the issue of *competitive pressure*. To remain competitive, you must have good information. The more accurate your information is, the more competitive you can be.[3]

In the 1980s and 1990s, the Japanese entered markets with high-quality products priced below competitive levels. This sent shock waves through entire industries and revealed patterns of waste and misallocation of effort—the very targets of activity-based management (ABM).

Every decade has its competitive challenges. Yesterday manufacturing companies faced a threat from Japan; today the threat is from China, India, and other developing nations and impacts service companies as well as manufacturers. The threat for government is from fiscal constraints, increasing expectations, and the loss of key personnel through retirement.

The lesson is not to wait for the competitive challenge that could damage performance and jeopardize the future. Take steps today to improve every aspect of your organization. ABC—and its application in an activity-based improvement program—is an insurance policy for the future.

Symptoms of a Broken Cost System

Manufacturing companies that use a traditional cost system are prime targets for ABC. They often exhibit symptoms of using inaccurate cost information to make decisions. Here are some to look for in your company.[4]

Symptom 1: Management Believes the Cost Information Is Distorted

There's a simple test for this: Ask your key managers what they think. For example, ask your manufacturing manager, "Do you believe that the

---

SYMPTOMS OF A BROKEN COST SYSTEM

Symptom 1 Management believes the cost information is distorted.

Symptom 2 Marketing and sales are unwilling to use the cost information for product pricing, market entry, and product portfolio decisions.

Symptom 3 Sales go up, yet profits go down.

Symptom 4 There's a "bootleg" cost system in the company.

Symptom 5 An improvement project fails to yield the expected cost reductions.

Symptom 6 Customers "cherry pick" your products.

Keep your eyes open for these six symptoms of a broken cost system. If you find any of them in your company, chances are that your cost system is causing real damage.

---

reported product costs accurately reflect the actual work necessary to move those products through the plant?"

The manufacturing manager's answer may surprise you.

Symptom 2: Marketing and Sales Are Unwilling to Use the Cost Information for Product Pricing, Market Entry, and Product Portfolio Decisions

Salespeople, especially those on commission, tend to be sensitive to competitive pricing and quality issues. Ask them how they feel about your company's approach to these issues.

Symptom 3: Sales Go Up, Yet Profits Go Down

This one can be a real shocker. It's a clear sign that reported product profit margins are in error. It's time to check your product mix and prices!

Symptom 4: There's a "Bootleg" Cost System in the Company

A "bootleg" system is an *unofficial* cost system (one that has not been blessed by accounting). It's usually found on a personal computer on the shop floor, in engineering, or in marketing. Its existence is a clear vote of no confidence in the *official* cost system.

Bootleg systems have been found at several companies, including Hewlett-Packard and Tektronix.

Symptom 5: An Improvement Project Fails to Yield the Expected Cost Reductions

When this occurs, it is usually the cost system that gets the numbers wrong. For example, a labor productivity improvement may show a substantial reduction in direct labor cost, but it may be accompanied by increases in engineering and information system costs.

Symptom 6: Customers "Cherry Pick" Your Products

If customers love your low-volume specialty products, but buy their high-volume standard products elsewhere, it's a sure sign of improper pricing. This "cherry picking" strategy can be a problem for anyone who relies on conventional cost information to set prices.

Identifying the symptoms of a broken cost system really drives the message home. It's one thing to observe the predicaments of others. It's quite another to know that your own systems are failing.

If you do all the right things, and if you can pinpoint the value of ABC in your company, management commitment will be forthcoming. But it may take longer in some companies than in others.

Sometimes it's agonizingly slow. At one company, the management team attended an ABC seminar and then spent the next year gaining commitment and completing a plan for their ABC project.

Sometimes it happens very quickly. A similar ABC presentation was given at another company. The management team had full commitment the same week. Beyond that, they also had resources identified and an implementation plan and training completed within one month.

SUMMARY

Creating change in your organization—however positive the eventual results—isn't easy. You must deliberately create an environment in which ABC cannot fail to succeed.

Enough experience has been gained with ABC to establish the initial steps to success:

- *Generate interest* in ABC. Cultivate "champions" everywhere you can, but particularly among top management.

- *Remove any barriers* to the acceptance of ABC that may exist. People can develop many misconceptions about a new tool. Ask them what their concerns are, and be ready with the answers.
- *Seek management's commitment* to embark on an ABC project. It's one thing to support ABC in principle. It's another thing to commit time, money, and reputations to an implementation project. If it takes some time to get this commitment, just hang in there. Nobody can oppose something as valuable as ABC indefinitely. Experience has shown that the most vehement opponents often become the strongest supporters.

KEY TERMS

Benchmark.   An activity that is a *best practice* and by which a similar activity will be judged. Benchmarks are used to help identify opportunities for improving the performance of comparable activities. The source of a benchmark may be internal (such as another department in the same company) or external (such as a competitor).

Myth.   A belief about ABC that is a barrier to ABC's acceptance. Demolishing these myths increases the chances of a successful ABC implementation.

Profit lever.   An action that increases profitability.

Symptom.   A visible sign of a broken cost system. Symptoms provide ammunition to advocates of ABC.

REFERENCES

1 Robin Cooper, "Schrader Bellows," 186–272 (Boston: Harvard Business School, 1986).

2 See, for example, William Rotch, "Activity-Based Costing in Service Industries," *Journal of Cost Management*, Summer 1990, pp. 4–14; Richard Zimmerman, "Health Care—an Industry in Need of Realistic Cost Measurement," *As Easy as ABC* (Portland, OR: ABC Technologies, Inc., Fall 1990), p. 3; Peter B. B. Turney, "The Fast Road to Better Performance at the South Dakota Department of Transportation," unpublished white paper, Cost Technology, Inc., 2004.

3 The impact of diversity and competitive pressure on the need for reliable product cost information is discussed in "The Rise of Activity-Based Costing—Part Two: When Do I Need an Activity-Based Cost System?" *Journal of Cost Management*, Fall 1988, pp. 41–48.

4 Symptoms 1, 2, and 3 are from Robin Cooper and Peter B. B. Turney, "Powell Electronics: The Printed Circuit Board Division," 189–054 (Boston: Harvard Business School, 1989). An example of symptom 4 is Robin Cooper and Peter B. B. Turney, "Hewlett-Packard: The Roseville Network Division," 188–177 (Boston: Harvard Business School, 1989). Symptom 5 is documented in Robin Cooper and Peter B. B. Turney, "Tektronix: The Portable Instrument Division," 188–142, 143, 144 (Boston: Harvard Business School, 1988). An example of symptom 6 is Robin Cooper, "Schrader Bellows," 186–272 (Boston: Harvard Business School, 1986).

CHAPTER 12

Developing the Game Plan

Do you know the rule of the "seven Ps?"

Here it is: Proper Prior Planning Positively Prevents Poor Performance.

Activity-based costing is no exception to this rule. In fact, many ABC failures are directly attributable to poor planning.

Yes, ABC can fail, especially when it's not properly planned to meet the specific needs of your company. And the experience of many organizations during ABC implementation shows that planning the implementation carefully enhances the chances of successful implementation.

Implementing ABC is not overly difficult. But it's not a trivial task, either. It takes time and effort. Approaching it in an organized manner— *the seven Ps*—ensures that the time and efforts are well directed and that results will flow from the effort.

The most important qualification for planning ABC is knowledge about the target organization. This comes from experience and a detailed assessment of the requirements. This assessment will identify the organization structure, resources, major processes, product and service groupings, customer types, and other critical ABC information. It will reveal the sources of information in the computer systems, behavioral dynamics, and prior and current initiatives that may influence the course and success of ABC.

The assessment will also identify the most important reasons for implementing ABC. This will help identify the key focus of the ABC effort, increase support for ABC, and increase the likelihood that results will flow from the use of ABC information.

The *game plan* for ABC planning and implementation varies from one organization to another. Organizations differ in their needs, size, complexity, types of activities and processes, technology, information systems, products, and customers. All of these factors require careful study in order to develop a successful ABC game plan. And, because the factors differ, the specifics of the game plan will differ from organization to organization.

However, the steps in formulating a game plan remain the same regardless of differing factors. Briefly, these seven steps are:

1. *Formulate the objectives.* Define what ABC is to accomplish.
2. *Describe the deliverables.* Describe the improved information that will satisfy each of the objectives.
3. *Set the scope.* Determine how extensive a project you will pursue.
4. *Create the organization structure.* Determine how the project will be organized and who will participate.
5. *Determine the training requirements.* Determine the type and scope of training needed for management, implementers, and users.
6. *Complete a project schedule.* Determine what tasks need to be accomplished and how long the project will take.
7. *Budget the project costs.* Estimate the resources required to complete the project.

Let's take a closer look at each of these steps and how to complete each one successfully.

FORMULATE THE OBJECTIVES

ABC can be used for any of several purposes. It's important to select the specific purpose (or purposes), then design a model that serves those specific purposes or objectives.

Selecting the purpose of activity-based costing requires an *assessment* of the organization's strategic needs for business intelligence. This is the process of identifying where ABC can help. The following are some typical examples:

- *Manufacturing cost is too high.* This results in an inability to make profits at competitive prices. It appears that the company's production costs are higher than the competition's.

Requirement: An ABC system that provides information about manufacturing activities (such as key cost drivers) to motivate and support waste elimination programs.

- *Nonmanufacturing cost is too high.* The culprits in this case are excessive marketing, administrative, engineering, and other nonmanufacturing costs.

  Requirement: An ABC system that provides information about nonmanufacturing activities and cost objects (such as customers and distribution channels) and that supports cost reductions in these areas.

- *Cost to serve is too high.* The cost of serving customers is too high. This may include distribution, order processing, and customer service costs.

  Requirement: An ABC system that provides information about cost-to-serve activities and the customers they serve. The information from this system will provide business intelligence about customer profitability and the opportunities to reduce cost and improve profitability.

- *Products are too complex and too different from one another.* The competitive problem in this case stems from product designs that are too difficult and too costly to produce.

  Requirement: An ABC system that provides design engineers with cost information that guides them in the development of low-cost product designs.

- *Market share is declining or has been lost in several key markets.* You're faced with a declining market share, and you don't know how to respond.

  Requirement: A high-level ABC study of market profitability to guide market focus and the dedication of marketing resources.

- *It's unclear which type of customer is best suited to your way of doing business.* Different customers place different demands on your company. Unfortunately, your pricing strategies or sales efforts make no distinctions among customers.

  Requirement: An ABC system that costs customers, allows calculation of customer profitability, and supports the development of appropriate customer and pricing strategies.

- *Market share and profitability need to be improved in one key market.* Despite continuing efforts to improve your product and service capability, market share and profitability fail to expand.

Requirement: An ABC system that costs products and services, facilitates studies of relative product and service profitability, and guides product and service portfolio decisions.

- *There's uncertainty about which parts to make and which to source from outside suppliers.* This is really an uncertainty about where manufacturing effort should be focused.

   Requirement: An ABC system that costs the parts and sub-assemblies going into products and guides make-or-buy decisions.

- *There is uncertainty about which processes to outsource.* There is pressure to outsource, but no one really knows which processes to outsource.

   Requirement: An ABC system that identifies the costs of processes that are candidates for outsourcing. The information from this system will allow comparison of the cost of key services with the price quoted by an outside supplier. It may also be appropriate to conduct a detailed ABC study of target processes—using storyboarding, for example—prior to outsourcing to find out how much cost can be removed. If a lot of cost can be removed, it may not be necessary to outsource.

- *There is pressure to justify budget increases.* Traditional budget formulations—showing the costs of wages, salaries, travel, technology, etc.—are not easily linked to planned service levels and outcomes. They are hard to justify and encourage political maneuvering.

   Requirement: A resource planning system that computes resource requirements based on planned outputs and accomplishments. This forward-looking version of ABC computes spending requirements under different scenarios. It is an engine for formulating fact-based budget requests.

From these examples, it's clear there are numerous possible purposes that an ABC system can be designed to address. As a result, ABC systems are as different as the purposes they address. This also means that their design and use will require different levels of effort.

An ABC system for cost-reduction purposes, for example, requires detailed information (nonfinancial as well as cost) about activities. In contrast, a system to support strategic marketing decisions needs accurate information about the cost of products and customers, but less detail about activities.

As for effort, a system that reports cost to the lowest part number level may take months to complete. A high-level study that costs a few markets or product lines may be completed in a few weeks.

DESCRIBE THE DELIVERABLES

After determining the objectives of the ABC system, a statement of deliverables should be prepared. This contains the purposes of the system and the improved information that will support each purpose.

For example, "more accurate product costs" is a deliverable that guides product portfolio analysis. Other examples are shown in Figure 12–1, which is also typical of a statement of ABC deliverables.

SET THE SCOPE

There are several choices regarding scope that affect the time and effort required to complete an ABC project. Some choices are related to the degree of management commitment to the project. Others are affected by the project's purpose.

For example, each purpose has a different set of tasks associated with it. A customer-focused ABC study requires analysis of cost-to-serve

FIGURE 12–1

Example Statement of ABC Deliverables

Purpose	Deliverable
1. Help prioritize cost-reduction efforts	• Detailed activities • Key cost drivers • Value-added non-value-added • Performance measures • Bill of activities
2. Facilitate analysis of make-or-buy decisions	• Accurate cost of parts and subassemblies • Bill of activity detail • Bill of costs
3. Guide development of customer strategy	• Customer profitability reports • Cost-to-serve activities • Performance measures

Deliverables vary from one implementation to another. Make sure you know what ABC will accomplish before you begin.

activities. This is quite different from make-or-buy decision studies, which require costing parts at the lowest level of the bill of materials. These two different ABC purposes have different tasks that take different amounts of time and effort to complete.

Project scope will vary depending on the degree of management commitment. A major implementation project is appropriate if management is sold on ABC. Alternatively, if management support for ABC is tentative, ABC should start as a pilot project.

One or More Locations or Processes

Some organizations start with ABC at one location or process only. This is appropriate if that single location or process is similar to other parts of the company. To illustrate, a financial services company could implement ABC in a call center in Toronto. When results and knowledge have been gained in Toronto, the company can then extend the implementation to other call centers across Canada.

Cellular One, for example, chose to implement ABC in the credit department at one location. This pilot project focused on the cost of serving customers through different distribution channels. The results of the pilot project were sufficiently interesting to justify expanding ABC to the rest of the company.

Large companies with many different types of operation, however, may chose to implement ABC in multiple locations. General Motors, for example, implemented ABC in 19 different plants. Each plant was carefully chosen to represent a particular type of manufacturing and was used to test a specific use of ABC (such as design for manufacturability or investment evaluation).

All Cost Objects or a Subset of Cost Objects

It's easy to limit the number of cost objects to be costed. This cuts down development time and effort. It also allows the pilot project to focus on the products, services, or customers that will yield the most interesting—*and convincing*—results.

The Oregon Cutting Systems Division of Blount, for example, selected two representative product lines for its initial implementation of ABC. The particular product lines were chosen because they had competitive problems and their costs were too high. It was also felt that results from these lines would be considerable, given the expected big changes in reported product costs.

All Activities or a Subset of Activities

The most common way to limit the number and range of activities that need to be studied is to focus on one area of the organization. For example, Deluxe Corporation's initial ABC model covered cost-to-serve activities. Only later did Deluxe extend the model to manufacturing activities.

Oregon Cutting Systems limited its ABC analysis to manufacturing activities. This allowed the completion of data collection and modeling within the time limits set by management. However, the plan was to extend the scope to include order entry, marketing, and other nonmanufacturing activities.

It's also possible to focus a pilot project on just part of the plant. For example, the procurement area could be studied intensively. This is appropriate if the objective is to eliminate waste in procurement activities. However, it's not feasible if the objective is to cost products in the plant. For this, it's necessary to study all plant activities.

An Entire or a Partial Accounting Period

A new ABC model usually covers the last accounting period. This makes sense. Most people still remember what they did during this period, so it's easy to get information about their activities. It also provides results for a complete accounting period. In manufacturing companies, it facilitates *benchmarking* the new information against the existing cost system.

In some situations, however, it's better to limit the study to several months, such as the last six months. Consider the case, for example, of a production process or product mix that has changed substantially over the last year. In this situation, only the most recent months reflect the current business and activity.

Once the ABC system is in place, managers may demand information more frequently than once a year. Monthly updates will provide managers with the current reports they need.

Backward-Looking or Forward-Looking

Most companies start by using historical costs in their ABC system. This makes sense. A historical perspective is the easiest way to develop a model of the company.

Once managers get a taste for ABC, they are likely to request decision support. They will ask questions such as, "If we outsource this process, what will be the impact on cost?" These questions are best answered using a forward-looking resource planning model.

A shift to resource planning requires changes in the ABC model. Cost assignments are replaced by resource productivity factors and output quantities. Capacity is defined for each resource. These changes allow the model to be run in reverse in order to compute resource requirements and costs based on decision and planning scenarios.

Some organizations implement a forward-looking model *before* they implement a historical analysis model. This is typically the case where budgeting is the primary reason for implementing ABC. Military and government organizations fit into this category.

Single-Period or Life-Cycle Perspective

Most ABC models focus on a single accounting period, even though activities and cost objects may affect several accounting periods. A single-period focus is easier because existing accounting systems are in single-period form.

Dayton Technologies, for example, chose a single-period perspective for its initial model. This allowed rapid development of its ABC system.

The single-period model, however, didn't provide a complete picture of the company. This was because product and die engineering, as well as die use in manufacturing, extended over several years. Once Dayton Technologies completed the initial model, efforts were focused on developing a multiperiod life-cycle version.

Proof of Concept or a Sustainable System

The type of implementation is affected by the degree of management commitment to ABC. If management is interested in ABC, but is not convinced of its value, it may wish to "dip its toe into the water" with a pilot project. On the other hand, if management is fully committed to ABC, a full implementation is appropriate.

A pilot project allows management to evaluate ABC's potential contributions to the organization. If the pilot can show a positive return on investment, it is likely that skeptical managers will quickly fall in behind ABC. Including a storyboarding session in the pilot is a great way of achieving this positive return.

Once management is committed, ABC can proceed to full implementation. Here the goal can be to create an ABC model or to develop a sustainable production system. In the latter case, the intention is to make

ABC the information choice for all decision making. The intention is also to integrate ABC with other initiatives, such as the balanced scorecard and cost-reduction efforts.

A sustainable ABC system is often implemented in phases. A phased implementation is systematic and encourages learning and growth focused on the development and use of ABC.

The South Dakota Department of Transportation, for example, started with a small proof-of-concept model. A departmentwide ABC model was created in the second phase. The model was validated and linked to the balanced scorecard in the third phase. It was automated in the fourth phase, and monthly updates and reports were added. Value creation—activities designed to provide results—accompanied all phases.

CREATE THE ORGANIZATION STRUCTURE

Structuring the project's organization is more than just identifying responsibilities and reporting relationships. It's an opportunity to enhance commitment to ABC.

First, there are three parts to the project organization structure. As shown in Figure 12–2, these are the project team, the project manager, and the steering committee.

FIGURE 12–2

The Organization Structure of an ABC Project

The size and status (full-time or part-time) of the project team depends on the project requirements.

The *project team* does the actual implementation. Its members serve part-time or full-time, depending on the project requirements. A large project requires full-time commitment from one or more people over an extended period of time. Part-time support will be provided by someone from the information technology department and, in some cases, trainers and facilitators. A small pilot project with a less pressing completion date can be handled on a part-time basis.

The leader of the team is the ABC *project manager*. This person is responsible for successful completion of the project and supports the consultants and other team members. The project manager needs leadership, communication, and technical skills; a solid understanding of ABC; and knowledge of the company's activities, products, services, and customers.

ABC implementation benefits from knowledge and experience. Most organizations do not have this capability internally prior to implementation and rely on outside consultants to provide guidance as well as to do model building, data gathering, system automation, facilitating of storyboarding sessions, and other project tasks.

The project manager reports to a *steering committee*. The steering committee is typically composed of the ABC champion, the ABC sponsor, the project manager, and one or two members of the consulting team. Depending on the scope of the implementation and the need to build support among top managers, directors or vice presidents may also be included on the committee.

At Stockham Valve and Fittings, for example, the marketing vice president was appointed to chair the steering committee. This reflected the marketing VP's strong interest in ABC. It also reflected a desire to *increase the likelihood* that marketing would accept—and respond to—the study's results. This was important because the ABC system's primary objective was to provide marketing with *accurate* product cost information to support product portfolio decisions.

The steering committee oversees planning and implementation of the ABC system and ensures that ABC objectives are met. It should review the project plan prior to its acceptance. It should then meet monthly to review progress.

DETERMINE THE TRAINING REQUIREMENTS

Training is crucial to proper implementation, execution, use, and acceptance of an ABC system. There are different types of training required, depending on the audience:

- *Management* should be exposed to ABC concepts. The objective is to achieve a high level of buy-in.
- *Implementers* need skills that will ensure a successful design. This includes technical design skills, software modeling capabilities, and project organization.
- *Users* should understand what information is available from activity-based costing, how to access the information from the ABC reporting system, and how that information should be used in decision making. The objective is to train them to use ABC in a program of ABM.

COMPLETE A PROJECT SCHEDULE

It's now time to put a project schedule together. This is where you summarize the tasks that must be accomplished to complete the project, the estimated time needed for each task, and the overall time required by the project. Figure 12–3 shows a project schedule.

The tasks needed, and the time required to complete them, differ from project to project. Most projects take from three to six months to create the first model. However, a simple *desk study*, which makes a rough estimate of the cost of a limited number of products, may take only a few days.

Creating an ABC system has its own *cost drivers*. These are factors that determine the amount of effort required to implement the system.

FIGURE 1 2 – 3

ABC Project Schedule

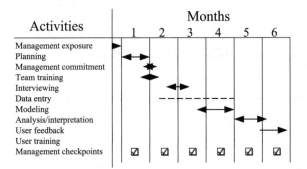

The actual time scale depends on the project's objectives, number of cost objects, number of different activities, number of interviews, and other such factors.

FIGURE 12 – 4

Cost Drivers of ABC Implementation

Number of products
Number of part numbers
Number of customers
Number of bill-of-materials layers
Number of processes
Number of departments
Number of activities
Number of people interviewed
Prior experience
Existing knowledge

These drivers determine just how much effort must be expended to complete the project. If you estimate the magnitudes of these drivers during project planning, you'll have a good idea of how long implementation will take.

This effort, and the associated cost, varies from company to company depending on the cost drivers shown in Figure 12–4.

For example, the number of people interviewed is an important cost driver. In one plant with a limited support staff, a team of two completed interviewing in just two weeks. In another plant, it took more than three months for a team of six to complete the interviews. This latter plant designed and manufactured defense products. It was very complex and had over 200 departments.

The overall amount of time required to complete the project can be reduced if tasks can be overlapped. The task of building the resources module, for example, can proceed during the interviewing phase.

BUDGET THE PROJECT COSTS

Achieving the benefits of ABC requires incurring costs. Internal and external costs should be budgeted up front. This will allow a careful comparison of the costs and the deliverables.

The major *internal cost* is the cost of the people assigned to the implementation team. You need bright, experienced individuals for an important project such as this. Another internal cost is staff time for training, data collection, storyboarding, and participation in the value creation process.

FIGURE 12-5

Example ABC Implementation Budget

Internal Costs		
Salaries and benefits for 3 months:		
• Full-time: 4 staff @$50,000	$50,000	
• Part-time: 1 staff 50% @6,250	6,250	
Other resources	10,000	
Total internal costs		$66,250
External costs		
Seminars	$ 5,000	
In-house training program	20,000	
Storyboarding materials	1,000	
Computer hardware	10,000	
Software	50,000	
Consulting	200,000	
Total external costs		$286,000
Total Project Costs		$352,250

This is for a three-month project in a medium-size organization. The deliverables include an assessment, an ABC model, storyboarding of two or three processes, and the beginning of one or two initiatives to implement cost savings or profit improvement.

The major *external costs* are training, consulting, and software. An in-house training program can cost in excess of $20,000. Consulting costs depend on the scope and complexity of the project, but vary from $100,000 for a pilot to several million dollars for a multiyear project to create a sustainable performance management system. ABC benefits from the use of special-purpose ABC modeling and reporting software. This can add anywhere from $50,000 upward.

To give you a feel for the different cost factors, Figure 12–5 shows the budget for a moderate-size three-month ABC implementation project.

SUMMARY

With a good game plan and some effort, you'll reap the rewards of a successful ABC implementation. The system will be completed, and the information can be used to foster improvement all over the company. But to reach this goal, you need to include all of the eight key steps in your game plan:

- Formulate the objectives of your project.
- Describe what tangible outputs the project will deliver.
- Set the scope of the project.
- Describe the organization structure of the project including the project team, the project manager, and the steering committee.
- Determine training requirements.
- Complete a project schedule that shows what tasks must be completed and how long the project will take.
- Estimate the costs of implementation.

KEY TERMS

Deliverable.   A tangible benefit of activity-based costing.

Pilot project.   A test of the applicability and utility of activity-based costing.

Project team.   The individuals who plan, design, and implement the ABC system.

Steering committee.   An upper management group that oversees the planning, implementation, and results of the ABC system.

Value creation.   Activities that realize results from the ABC project.

CHAPTER 13

Gathering the Information

The information required by an ABC system is defined by the conceptual model described in Chapter 4. From this model, you know that you need information about resources, activities, and cost objects. You also know that you need information about the linkages between those items.

Now you need to find out where to go for this information. As it turns out, there are three primary sources for ABC information:

1. *The accounting department has information about the cost of resources.* This information is in the general ledger account balances. The account balances are the starting point for creating the resources used in ABC.

2. *Information about activities comes from the people who do the work or are knowledgeable about the work.* What are the activities? How do they consume resources? What are the cost drivers and performance measures?

3. *Information about cost objects, activity drivers, and some performance measures is found in the company's information systems.* For example, the number of material receipts (a potential activity driver) is found in the inventory control system.

You'll be surprised at how much of the information needed to design an ABC model is *readily* available. In addition to the official data sources, it's common to find data files in desk drawers or personal computers. These unofficial information sources may be unknown outside of the work area, but they are often useful for ABC.

FIGURE 13-1

Information Checklist

☑ Organization chart
☑ Department head count
☑ Department budget
☑ Job descriptions
☑ Salary by employee
☑ Activities
☑ Cost drivers
☑ Performance measures
☑ Resource drivers
    Effort per activity
    Noneffort resources (e.g., travel)
☑ Activity drivers
☑ Data sources

You need a lot of information for activity-based costing. Make sure you know what you want before you conduct an interview or send out a questionnaire.

The focal point for information gathering is the place where the work is performed (the department or the process). This is where you obtain information about activities and learn where data about cost objects and activity drivers can be found (Figure 13–1). You will also learn where the data are stored.

Knowing the location of data is one thing. Successfully gathering them—and seizing the opportunity to teach their users about ABC—can be quite another. There are, however, some secrets that make the task substantially easier. These secrets cover the areas of

- How to collect the information
- How to conduct an interview
- How to get the data into the ABC system

The goal of this chapter is to reveal those secrets to you.

HOW TO COLLECT THE INFORMATION

You know *what* information you want. That's largely determined by the ABC model you're about to build.

You also know *where* to find the information. You've checked your company's organization chart, and you've identified the departments and processes to be investigated.

The next issue is *how* to collect the information.

There are five major information-collecting techniques: *observation, timekeeping systems, questionnaires, collaborative interviews,* and *manager interviews*. Let's take a closer look at each method.

Observation

Observation is a fast and low-cost way to obtain information about the work that is being done. Just look around. What do you see going on? What conclusions can you draw from your observations?

Observation may be fast, but it's not always easy. It requires experience and knowledge about the type of work going on. It benefits from experience within the organization. And its success depends on an uncanny ability to draw correct and relevant conclusions from what's observed.

Observation won't be enough to obtain everything you need. But it can supplement the information you obtain from other sources.

Timekeeping Systems

Timekeeping systems provide records of the work that is done and the time spent on each activity and cost object. For example, the engineers in one company maintained records of their work and the products they were working on. This information was then used to develop an activity-based model for engineering.

In the past, timekeeping was not popular among workers. This was because managers and support staff weren't enthusiastic about filling in time cards daily—sometimes they were required to log their time in 15-minute increments. This was time-consuming, and its value was not apparent to those filling out the cards.

Today, however, timekeeping benefits from the widespread use of the Internet. Timekeeping systems are maintained online, and each employee can easily enter the day's time electronically at his or her desktop.

The best use of timekeeping is in production ABC systems that require updated time information for the monthly run. Then it is a cost-effective solution.

Questionnaires

Questionnaires can also be used to elicit information about the work. This is done by sending lists of appropriate questions to individual department heads or others who are knowledgeable about the targeted work areas.

In general, questionnaires can be used in three ways.

Preinterview Questionnaires

This type of questionnaire (Figure 13–2) is sent to department heads prior to an interview. It serves as an interview preview. It allows the department heads to gather their thoughts in preparation for the interview. The responses also provide the ABC design team with food for thought prior to the interview.

Questionnaires as a Primary Data Collection Tool

A questionnaire may be used in lieu of interviewing or timekeeping. It is faster than an interview. It is also less intrusive than timekeeping, and it can be filled out by managers at their convenience and in the privacy of their offices. If you have hundreds of managers to interview, questionnaires may be the only feasible alternative.

To be effective, however, such questionnaires must be carefully designed. They must be complete, and they must ask the right questions in the right way. For example, if the question asks for data about cost drivers, but does not make absolutely clear what a cost driver is, the answer may be wrong.

FIGURE 13–2

Example Preinterview Questionnaire

---

1. What are your primary activities?
2. How many employees do you have? Please list your
   employees and the time each spends on his or her specific activities.
3. Do you provide services to other departments? If so,
   please specify the type of activity and the receiving
   department.
4. To perform your activities you need material and supplies:
   a. Where are they obtained?
   b. In what activities are they used?

Questionnaires are efficient ways of obtaining information, but they lack the human touch of an interview.

Questionnaires, unlike interviews, provide no opportunity for feedback. You miss the spontaneous questions and dialogue that often lead to important insights into the department's activities.

Follow-up Questionnaires

Questionnaires can also be used following the interview. One purpose is to confirm the accuracy of the conclusions drawn from the interview. In other words: Have we recognized the right activities? Are our estimates of the effort devoted to each activity reasonable?

If there are disagreements over the correctness of the ABC design, it's better to find out before the design is finished rather than after.

Another use is to update the previous period's design. The questionnaire is used to find out if anything has changed during the intervening period. For example, are there any new activities? Has the relative effort shifted from one activity to another?

Collaborative Interviews

Another possibility is to use collaborative interviews. This involves interviewing a group of key people from a department or process to learn what they do. The information learned is documented on storyboards. As we learned in Chapter 8, storyboards can be used to document, measure, analyze, and communicate process performance. The results from this storyboarding exercise are usually significant, with cost savings of 20 to 30 percent typical in just the first two to three days. Collaborative interviewing is a different application of storyboarding for a different purpose.

The analyst uses the collaborative interviewing session to determine the activities, the relative effort expended on each activity, and other pertinent model data. There is no need to collect process information such as cost drivers and performance measures.

There are three advantages of collaborative interviews. First, data from storyboarding are more accurate than those from interviews. This is because of the group nature of the technique—all the important people from the process can be included in the session.

Second, storyboarding is more efficient. The visual nature of the technique allows for validation of the storyboard information prior to the end of the session. There is no need to go back to the group later and ask the people involved to validate the results.

Third, buy-in to the results and overall enthusiasm for ABC are usually very high. This is because of the participative nature of the technique and the feelings of ownership that result.

Manager Interviews

Interviewing managers is a key element in the ABC process. In fact, many companies use interviews as the primary investigative tool during initial ABC model design.

But interviewing is more than just a data-collection tool. It's a dialogue. Information flows both ways. This provides an opportunity to involve the users of ABC in the design process itself. Users learn about the ABC project—how it works and what it is to accomplish. Such involvement makes it more likely that they'll be supporters of ABC and use it to foster positive change.

In short, interviewing has three key purposes:

- *Gathering information from reliable sources.* It's a tool for collecting much of the data used to build a model of the activities and their relationship to resources and cost objects.

- *Educating users.* It's an opportunity to teach potential users about ABC.

- *Gaining commitment.* Interviewing is an opportunity to answer questions, address concerns, and build commitment for the project.

HOW TO INTERVIEW SUCCESSFULLY

Interviewing managers is the most popular ABC data-gathering method So it's worth spending some time to learn how to do it well. This begins with *determining whom to interview.*

Whom to Interview

The purpose of interviewing is to obtain information. Thus, the first step is to *identify those individuals with the most potential for providing the information you need.*

These people are usually managers or supervisors. They have the broadest knowledge about the activities performed in their departments. True, their subordinates actually perform the activities and usually know more about the fine details. But there are more subordinates than there are managers, and interviewing all of them would take too much time.

You'll find some managers who can't provide the needed information. This is particularly true if the manager is new to the organization. These managers may not know what each subordinate is doing or the time that is spent on each activity. Subordinates may also maintain input and performance data that aren't used by managers. To obtain information from such areas, you'll need to schedule additional time for follow-up interviews with selected subordinates.

How to Prepare for the Interview

There are two aspects to preparing for an interview. One is to prepare yourself. The other is to prepare the interviewee. The objective in both cases is to increase your chances of gaining all the information you need in the shortest possible time.

Remember, people are busy. They may not have time to grant you a second interview. Also, it'll probably take several weeks to interview all the people on your list. A second round of interviews will delay the project that much more.

Preparing to Conduct the Interview
You can prepare yourself by doing some advance research. For example:

- Learn what you can in advance about the department's operations.
- Make sure you know what information you are looking for, and formulate your questions in advance.
- Know what level of detail to ask for (if the ABC system is to be used for value analysis, for example, you will need detailed activity information).
- Understand the project's objectives and scope (you are an ambassador for the project, and you will inevitably be called on to talk about it).
- Be familiar with the concepts of ABC and activity-based management (so that you can teach people about ABC and pave the way for positive change).

Preparing the Interviewee
The interviewee needs to know what ABC is, what the project is to accomplish, and what information is needed. This knowledge can be communicated in the three following ways:

1. *Kickoff meeting.* A kickoff meeting is a good forum for presenting information to the interviewees. At Oregon Cutting Systems, for example, the design team invited all the interviewees to a presentation that covered the basic concepts of ABC, discussed the project, and described the purpose of the interview. This

eliminated the need to brief each interviewee individually at the start of the interview.

2. *Interview orientation.* An alternative to the kickoff meeting is to do the orientation during the interview itself. While this may take more time, the interview is a *private meeting,* and the interviewee may be more willing to express concerns about the project. Orientation can also be tailored to the particular background of the interviewee. If the interviewee has attended an ABC exposure program or has participated in the planning or design process, the orientation will be quite short. If the interviewee has scant knowledge of ABC, a half hour or more may be required.

3. *Material distribution.* Distributing materials in advance is valuable—if you can get the interviewee to read the information. A brief executive summary of ABC concepts, the project, and the interview guidelines are most likely to be read.

Articles, books, and videotapes are useful sources for those who are willing to take the time. The Fort Riley U.S. Army base, for example, purchased copies of *Common Cents* for each manager. Fort Riley used *Common Cents* to guide its ABC implementation effort.

Other materials that should be distributed are

- A preinterview "to do" list for the interviewee. This may include preparing or copying relevant material, such as a staff list, an organization chart, a data source list, and so forth.

- A questionnaire that should be filled out and returned to the design team prior to the interview.

- A notice stating the time and place of the interview. If possible, arrange to have the interview in the interviewee's office. This interviewee will be more relaxed there. A second choice is the safe, neutral ground of a conference room.

How to Conduct an Interview

The goal is to make the interview a positive experience. It's an opportunity to ensure quality design of the ABC model *and* to pave the way for positive change.

Success is most likely when the interviewer plays the role of coach. The ABC coach is a teacher, a motivator, and a facilitator of the ABC model's design and successful use.

Playing the role of a coach helps communicate to interviewees their ownership of ABC, their responsibility for its success, and the help they can expect to receive from the ABC team. A coaching role creates an atmosphere of trust in which open communication is possible.

Substantial experience in conducting interviews for designing ABC models has already been gained. This experience has yielded a recommended series of ABC coaching steps:

INTERVIEWING GUIDELINES

1. Explain the purpose.
2. Review the benefits.
3. Describe the project.
4. Explain the process.
5. Ask key questions.

6. Facilitate the answers.
7. Provide feedback.
8. Communicate responsibility.
9. Offer support.
10. Express appreciation.

1. *Explain the purpose.* Begin the interview by explaining why you are there. You want to brief the interviewees about ABC and the ABC project. You want a chance to address any concerns they may have. And you want to help them gather the data and design the model.

2. *Review the benefits.* Here's a chance to sell the ABC concept. Show how activity-based information can help focus strategy and improve operations. Give examples of how ABC may benefit the interviewee's own work area.

3. *Describe the project.* Talk about the ABC project and its importance to the company. What will be the deliverables? What's the scope? Who is involved? What is the role of the interviewee? Who is supporting the project? What progress has been made? And when will the project be completed?

4. *Explain the process.* Tell the interviewees about the data requirements of ABC. Go over the process of model design, emphasizing its dependence on the knowledge and input of the interviewees. Make it clear that you are not looking for absolute precision, just good-quality information that meets the needs of ABC users (such as themselves) at a reasonable cost.

5. *Ask key questions.* Ask a set of questions designed to yield all the data you need about each process. What work is done? What resources are required? How should the use of resources be

measured? Why is the work done? How well is it done? Which cost objects or other activities benefit from the work, and how should this benefit be measured? Where are the data located?

You may need to supplement this list of questions depending on the project's deliverables. For example, you may want to know the level of each activity or whether it is value-added or non-value-added.

6. *Facilitate the answers.* Help the interviewees answer the questions. Ask follow-up questions if you sense that an answer is incomplete or reflects a misunderstanding of the original question. Provide technical assistance if the interviewees cannot respond because of a lack of knowledge of ABC. Keep the interview on track (it's easy to go off on a tangent).

7. *Provide feedback.* Tell the interviewees what you have learned about each key discussion area. This gives them feedback on what has been communicated and a chance to correct any misunderstanding. It also gives them a chance to change their mind.

   As a matter of procedure, explain that a copy of the finished model of the process will be forwarded to all interviewees for review. This provides further opportunities for feedback and reinforces the notion that each interviewee owns a part of the model.

8. *Communicate responsibility.* The interviewees have primary responsibility for the design of the model of the process and for updates. They are also responsible for explaining ABC to other members of the department, for ensuring that department members are trained to use the information, and for fostering positive change.

9. *Offer support.* Make it clear that the interviewees are not alone in carrying out their responsibilities. Offer them software and information systems support. Offer technical support to resolve model design and data analysis issues. And describe how you can help them train their staff.

10. *Express appreciation.* Don't forget to thank each interviewee for the time and support that she or he is providing to the ABC project. Remind the interviewees how important they are to the success of the project. Congratulate them on their contributions to the improvement of the organization.

What Documentation to Request

Background documentation serves as reference material during the modeling process. Examples are organization charts, budgets, position descriptions, transaction tracking reports, head-count listings, and salaries by employee.

Interview documentation is a summary of what was learned during the interview. It's part of the design process record and is available to subsequent designers or users.

What an Interview Schedule Should Look Like

An interview schedule should allow time to absorb, document, and model the results of each interview. A reasonable schedule includes no more than two or three interviews per day with one to two hours per interview (Figure 13–3).

FIGURE 13–3

Take Care in Setting the Interview Schedule

	Interview Schedule					Date Page of
No.	Interviewee	Date	Time	Day	Interviewers	Comments
14	Sandra Booth	8/10	8:30 a.m.	Mon.	Peter/Mary	Check data sources
15	John Kershaw	8/10	1:30 p.m.	Mon.	Peter/Mary	
16	Brian Hutton	8/12	9:30 a.m.	Wed.	Vic/Nancy	
17	Susan Moody	8/12	3:00 p.m.	Wed.	Vic/Nancy	
18	Bob Edwards	8/14	8:30 a.m.	Fri.	Peter/Vic	Interfaces with Sandra Booth dept.
19	Mike Roberts	8/14	2:00 p.m.	Fri.	Mary/Vic	
20	Roy Peterson	8/17	9.00 a.m.	Mon.	Peter/Nancy	
21	Kathy Smith	8/17	2.30 p.m.	Mon.	Peter/Mary	

Don't set too fast a pace—leave time for modeling and evaluation. Having two interviewers at each interview is recommended.

Time should be set aside for modeling the results of the interviews. Time should also be available for follow-up interviews with subordinates or repeat interviews with managers.

Interview assignments should be based primarily on knowledge of the department. A secondary consideration is the availability of people on the design team.

It's always wise to have two people conduct each interview. This ensures proper coverage of the important issues. One person can do the job, but two people can reinforce each other and exchange notes.

GETTING THE DATA INTO THE ABC SYSTEM

How you get data into the ABC system is always a *practical* design concern. Also, there is a cost associated with data entry. This cost varies with the design of the system and the source of the data.

Basically, there are two ways to get data into the system: *extract, transform, and load (ETL)* and *hand entry*.

Extract, Transform, and Load (ETL)

ETL is the electronic transfer of data from one computer system to another. Most data required by ABC exist in an electronic form, whether in a legacy or a modern database. Electronic transfer is the ideal way to move these data into the ABC system.

ETL involves the extraction of the data required by ABC from the source system. These data are transformed into a format that is compatible with the ABC software. Automatic load programs are created to move the data into the ABC system.

Setting up ETL requires a technology consultant and ETL software. Most of the effort takes place during the initial setup. If ETL is properly automated, system maintenance will be minimal.

Stockham Valve and Fittings, for example, completed an ABC system with 58 activity drivers. This design matched the complexity and diversity associated with the large number of products and wide range of activities in the company. Implementation of the design required the import of millions of data elements.

Thanks to a well-developed information system, Stockham Valve found that data for 57 of the activity drivers were stored electronically. This allowed the bulk of the data to be transferred from the transactional database to the ABC system electronically (Figure 13–4).

FIGURE 13-4

Electronic Transfer of Data

MIS System		
Purchasing Module	**Shop Floor Control Module**	**Inventory Control Module**
# purchase orders	# of times run	# of receipts
	# of operations	# of issues
	# of molds	
	# of setups	
	# of inspections	

Electronic transfer of data is essential if you have many cost objects. There are just too many pieces of data to enter by hand. For example, Stockham Valve and Fittings' ABC system costed about 80,000 different parts, but most of the data for the activity drivers and cost objects were transferred electronically from Stockham's computer system.

Manufacturing companies are not alone in their need for the electronic transfer of data. ABC systems in government and service organizations also have significant data requirements. For example, the ABC model at the South Dakota Department of Transportation uses data that come directly and indirectly from several sources. These include the equipment management, general ledger, time card, inventory, accounts payable, payroll, and highway systems. Automating the extraction, transformation, and loading of these data is crucial to the efficient update of the ABC model each month.

Hand Entry

The time-consuming alternative to electronic entry is hand entry. This is necessary when the data are not available in electronic form. It may also be the easiest method when building a small pilot ABC model.

However, entering data by hand is not recommended for a sustainable ABC system. This is because there are just too many pieces of data to enter by hand each time the model is updated. Stockham Valve and Fittings did hand-enter data for one activity driver. However, this driver affected fewer than 50 products during the year, and the data took only a few minutes to enter.

SUMMARY

Information gathering can be the most time-consuming aspect of building an ABC system. It involves scouring the company for information about resources, activities, and cost objects. This is done by learning

1. *How to collect the information.* There are five ways to collect information:
   - *Observation* is a quick way to learn what's going on. Take a walk around the plant and see what's happening. But this does require good observational skills.
   - *Timekeeping systems* are convenient sources of time data, but are not usually available during a pilot project. Web collection tools make this method quite easy to implement, however, and it is cost-effective for sustainable ABC systems.
   - *Questionnaires* are packages of questions soliciting information. They can be used before interviews to obtain preliminary information, or they can be used in lieu of the interview. They can also be used following the interview to confirm the ABC model's quality. Questionnaires are efficient, but they lack the *personal* touch of interviews.
   - *Storyboards* use a group process to create a picture of each department's activities and related information. This process is relatively fast and accurate, and it elicits a positive response from the participants.
   - *Interviewing* is a common ABC information collection technique, even though it is time-consuming. It allows two-way communication—the interviewer gathers knowledge about activities, while the manager learns about activity-based costing.
2. *Whom to interview.* The rule is, interview those who are most likely to have the information you need. Department managers are the usual choice under this rule—they generally have the broadest knowledge of the activities in their departments.
3. *How to prepare for the interview.* The interviewer prepares for the interview by doing homework about ABC, the ABC project, and the department in question. The interviewer also prepares the interviewee by supplying information on ABC concepts, the project, and the information required.
4. *How to conduct an interview.* Success in conducting an interview

requires basic communication skills and careful attention to the dos and don'ts of interviewing.

5. *What documentation is required.* Important documentation includes material that guides the modeling process and summarizes what was learned during implementation.

6. *What an interview schedule looks like.* An interview schedule should set a pace that allows time to absorb the knowledge acquired and create a model from that information.

7. *How to get data into the ABC system.* The data can be electronically transferred from the organization's information systems or from spreadsheets, or they can be entered by hand. Electronic transfer is recommended for sustainable ABC systems, but it requires information technology expertise and software.

Information gathering gives you knowledge of your company's activities and people such as you have never had before. It's also fun once you get the hang of it. If you learn to ask the right questions and get the right information, it makes the ABC modeling process that much easier.

KEY TERMS

Collaborative interviews.   A group process that creates a picture of each department's activities and related information on storyboards. An accurate and efficient data-gathering technique, it helps create buy-in for the ABC initiative.

Extract, Transform, and Load (ETL).   The extraction of data from legacy or modern databases, the transformation of the data into a format that is compatible with the ABC software, and the loading of the data into the ABC system.

Interviews.   In-person question-and-answer sessions. This is the traditional information-gathering method of choice in ABC. Interviews must be planned and conducted carefully; otherwise they can be time-consuming, inaccurate, or not well received.

Questionnaire.   A compilation of questions about the work that goes on in the company. Questionnaires don't have the personal touch of interviews, but they can be an efficient way to collect data.

Timekeeping system.   A record of the time devoted to activities or cost objects. Not commonly used in pilot projects, it is cost-effective as a way of gathering time data for sustainable ABC systems.

CHAPTER 14

Designing the Model

Designing an ABC model is a critical stage of the implementation process. It's where the structure of the system is created and the *intelligence* is added.

This is similar to playing chess. Each piece of the model has a specific purpose, and there are some clearly defined rules to follow. But many judgments are also involved, and it's often difficult to measure the impact of each decision immediately.

The designer's job is to meet the system objectives at minimum cost and with a minimum of complexity. At the same time, the system should provide the *right kind of information* at the *right level of detail*. This is necessary if the ABC system is to be successful in supporting strategic and process improvement decisions.

The model should be as simple as possible—*but no simpler*. If it's too simple, it will report inaccurate costs. The model's activity information may also be insufficient to support improvement processes.

At the same time, the model should be as complex as necessary—*but no more complex*. If it's too complex, it will be too costly to design, implement, and maintain. It will also burden users with unnecessary detail and possibly be less understandable.

The key is to strike a proper balance. To help you do this, let's look at some tried-and-true rules for success and how they can be applied in following the major steps of the design process. Briefly, these steps are

- Identifying activities
- Reconstructing the general ledger

- Creating activity centers
- Defining resource drivers
- Determining attributes
- Selecting activity drivers

Designing a resource planning model or a time-based ABC model is somewhat different. They require different data, and the number of activities will also differ. These differences are covered at the end of the chapter.

IDENTIFYING ACTIVITIES

It is unusual for an organization to have a clear list of its activities identified prior to building an ABC model. Process flowcharts may exist, along with other functional definitions. But ABC has a different purpose and structure from these tools, and the correct list of activities will also be different.

There are four main rules to follow in identifying activities for ABC. These rules are listed briefly in the accompanying box entitled "Rules for Identifying Activities." Let's take a closer look at each of these rules and how they are applied in building a standard ABC model.

Rule 1: Match the Detail to the Purpose of the Model

The task of identifying activities is governed by the chosen purpose, or purposes, of the ABC system. If the purpose is strategic (e.g., choosing how specific markets or customers are to be served), the primary job is to accurately assign costs to cost objects. Strategic models typically contain enough activities to report accurate costs—but no more.

The Deluxe Corporation strategic model, for example, contained 150 activities. This was enough to report accurate customer costs, but the model did not provide detailed process information (this detail was not required for Deluxe's strategic purpose).

If the purpose is to improve the process (e.g., to better meet customer needs), the ABC model should report useful information about activities as well as cost objects. ABC models with a process purpose typically have more activities than a purely strategic model.

For example, a strategic model for a military organization had an activity called "maintain tanks." There was a lot of cost assigned to this activity—many millions of dollars—but the name communicated nothing

RULES FOR IDENTIFYING ACTIVITIES

Rule 1 Match the detail to the purpose of the model.
Rule 2 Use macro activities to balance conflicting objectives.
Rule 3 Combine insignificant items.
Rule 4 Describe activities clearly and consistently.

about the underlying process. Only when it was broken into its constituent activities could inferences about the process be drawn.

Whether the model is strategic or process in nature, activities must be defined. This is done during the data-gathering stage (covered in Chapter 13).

Information about activities is typically received in more detail than can (or should) be used in the ABC model. For example, an interview of a manager of operations in a department of transportation might reveal that the work includes treating cracks, filling potholes, and chip sealing. The ABC model builder, however, might determine that only one activity—"repair road surfaces"—is necessary to account for all three types of work.

As a further example, examine the list of customer service activities in Figure 14–1. The first four activities are just different aspects of processing

FIGURE 14−1

Activities in a Customer Service Process

Activity	Cost	
	$	%
Receiving orders	$21,455	15
Processing orders	21,811	16
Scheduling shipments	31,292	22
Invoicing customers	15,409	11
Maintaining customer files	3,144	2
Maintaining inventory files	4,905	4
Processing returns	9,744	8
Preparing reports	12,825	9
Administering	12,825	9
Filing	6,190	4
Total	**$139,600**	**100**

customer orders. Do you want all four of these activities in your model? Or do you want just one activity called "processing customer orders"?

Suppose the model's primary purpose is to determine the cost of servicing customers. For this, the single activity "processing customer orders" is sufficient. This activity allows you to compute the cost of a customer order and assign it to customers based on the number of times each customer places an order.

But suppose the model's primary purpose is to provide information for performance improvement. Now the four activities involved in processing a customer order become important. Each of these activities represents a separate unit of work in the customer service department. Each has its own problems and its own opportunities for improvement. So each activity should be included in the ABC model.

The model builder has to be careful not to take this reduction process too far. Using too few activities could compromise the accuracy of cost.

For example, let's say you found that three activities are performed in the receiving department: receiving raw materials, receiving bar stock, and receiving supplies. You also learn that the activity "receiving bar stock" varied depending on the type of bar stock received. What should the activities be?

From a process standpoint, there is only one activity, "receiving bar stock." However, if the difference in effort required for each type of bar stock is material, the correct answer is to recognize two receiving activities—one for each type of bar stock. Using just one activity will compromise the reported accuracy of the cost to serve for different customers. (It is possible to reduce the number of activities without compromising accuracy. This is done using the techniques of time-based ABC, which is covered later in the chapter.)

Rule 2: Use Macro Activities to Balance Conflicting Objectives

What do you do if your system has both process improvement *and* strategic objectives?

Process improvement requires detailed information about activities. Supplying this amount of detail in the system, however, may confuse strategic users.

The solution is to use *macro activities*. Macro activities are aggregations of related activities, and they have their own additional set of rules:

Macro Rule 1: The activities are at the same level.

Macro Rule 2: The activities use the same activity driver.

Macro Rule 3: The activities have a common purpose.

In the example of the customer service department, the four activities associated with processing a customer order can be assigned to a single macro activity. They are all customer service activities (the same level). All use "number of customer orders" as the activity driver. And all are part of the customer order process. This satisfies all three macro rules.

Using macro activities creates two tiers of activity, with each tier meeting a different need. At the lower tier, information about the four activities supports improvement of the process. At the higher tier, strategic users can ignore the detail and focus on the single macro activity.

Rule 3: Combine Insignificant Items

Activities that are too small to be worth recognizing individually should be combined. This helps reduce system clutter.

The activities listed in Figure 14–1, for example, include "maintaining customer files" and "maintaining inventory files." These two activities could be combined in the ABC system.

This combination is possible—and usually desirable—because the cost of these activities is insignificant. The cost assigned to each is about 2 percent and 4 percent, respectively, of the customer service department costs. Also, the cost of both activities can be traced to customers using the same activity driver ("number of customers").

Rule 4: Describe Activities Clearly and Consistently

How you describe activities determines the effectiveness of the system and the information it provides. A *clear description* of activities enhances the ability to communicate the work that each activity represents. A *consistent definition* of activities makes it easy to find activities of the same type or process.

The key to describing activities clearly is to use short, understandable, and descriptive labels. In one company, for example, an activity involved loading finished goods onto truck trailers. This was described in the ABC system as "M/H-load f.g.-semi." Such a description has meaning only for the people working in the material handling department. In contrast, "loading finished goods" is short, understandable, and fully descriptive of the work done.

Labels chosen for activities should contain a verb and a noun. This has the advantage of avoiding confusion.

For example, is "setup" the activity or the activity driver? Actually, "set up machine" is the activity, and "setup time" is the activity driver.

Activity labels should also be consistent across the entire company. Like activities should be described in a like manner no matter where they are performed.

At National Semiconductor, for example, a *patterning* activity was performed in the manufacture of integrated circuits (ICs). In this activity, an image was exposed onto photosensitive material. This image allowed the creation of electric circuits on the ICs.

The description of the patterning activity was inconsistent from one location to another. It was variously called "stepping," "aligning," and "exposing."

Despite these inconsistencies, the activities were essentially the same. They differed only in the resources used and the age and type of technology.

This lack of consistency in description would have inhibited prioritization of improvement efforts. Each separate activity would have appeared less significant in a Pareto analysis than the overall activity.

A set of common definitions and descriptions of activities is called an *activity dictionary.* This activity dictionary sets a standard for ABC within functions and across plants and companies. Its use improves system design and has helped large, diverse companies such as National Semiconductor benchmark activities across multiple sites.

NATIONAL SEMICONDUCTOR CORPORATION

National Semiconductor Corporation designs, manufactures, and markets high-performance semiconductor products. Headquartered in Santa Clara, California, the company is a global leader in mixed, analog, and digital technologies.

RECONSTRUCTING THE GENERAL LEDGER

After identifying activities, the next step is to establish activity costs. This begins with the general ledger, which is the starting point for establishing the flow of costs in ABC.

The general ledger is where you find the financial information about company resources. For example, how much was paid in salaries so far this year? How much depreciation did we have? How much did we accrue in taxes? How does all this compare with the budget (what we should have spent)?

In short, the general ledger is a useful data source for ABC system designers. It provides, in one place, a summary of all important (and unimportant) financial data about the company.

Unfortunately, in looking for activity cost information, the general ledger is also a source of frustration and difficulty. This is because

- General ledgers are usually organized around the type of expenditure, such as rent or interest (the *line items*), rather than the activity.

- General ledgers are often full of excruciating detail of the wrong kind. The chart of accounts for a medium-size company or division may run to hundreds of different items. There may be dozens of different accounts, for example, detailing the many elements of employee benefits. In addition to pensions, there may be vacations, health care, dental care, and insurance of various types.

- Despite the many detailed accounts, general ledgers are sometimes aggregated at too high an organizational level. For example, line items of expenditure, such as salaries or building depreciation, may be available only at the division level.

- Costs are collected in the general ledger for time periods that may not be consistent with economic life cycles. The general ledger follows the accounting period, with account totals accumulated by month, quarter, and year. Resources, however, such as those in engineering, may benefit several years of product and process life.

- Costs in the general ledger may comply with generally accepted accounting principles but lack economic sense. Depreciation, for example, is often computed using lives that are shorter than the true economic lives. As a result, depreciation fails to parallel actual consumption of the asset.

- In some government agencies, costs in the general ledger may not match operational data for the same time period. This will be the case when the government agency uses cash-basis accounting. For example, an agency's time card and work data are recorded in the time period in which the work is done. The

> general ledger, however, picks up the payroll cost only in the
> following period, when the wages and benefits are accrued. This
> lack of matching must be resolved if the agency wishes to
> update its ABC model each month.

The basic problem is that most general ledgers are not designed around
activities. Instead, they are well designed for one specific purpose: preparing financial statements. For the general ledger accounts to be useful in
determining activity costs for an ABC system, they must be reconstructed.
This reconstruction is governed by three rules.

RULES FOR RECONSTRUCTING THE GENERAL LEDGER

Rule 1 Combine related accounts.
Rule 2 Decompose to the department level.
Rule 3 Adjust uneconomic items.

Rule 1: Combine Related Accounts

A fact of life for most companies is that the general ledger is not activity-based. This is not surprising, since general ledgers are designed for financial reporting and control and not for ABC.

It's common to find hundreds of accounts in a general ledger, even in relatively small companies. This amount of detail may satisfy an accountant's need to pinpoint the type of expenditure. But it also creates a burden of excruciating detail for ABC.

Numerous accounts create clutter in the ABC system. They also create additional work because each account's cost must be assigned to activities.

The solution is to combine accounts that are related. Related accounts share a common purpose and are assigned to activities in the same way.

For example, salaries, health insurance, and pension costs can be combined into an account called, let's say, "personnel costs." This title is descriptive of all its constituent accounts, and it can be assigned to activities using a single resource driver (typically an estimate of effort expended on each activity).

Combining accounts in this way reduces clutter in the model. It also reduces system design effort, since there are fewer paths for assigning costs. If it is done within the ABC model, it is still possible to verify the sources of each cost element.

If the model is a resource planning model rather than an ABC model, the information about resources will be different. It will include definitions of activity skills and productivity (for each class of worker, for example, it could be minutes to process a unit for each activity). This information is maintained in a *resource dictionary*.

Rule 2: Decompose to the Department Level

Once you've combined related accounts, you need to subdivide them to obtain department costs. For example, if costs are maintained at the division level, assign costs to the plant level first, then to departments within the plants. If the general ledger already maintains cost data at the department level, no assignment is required.

The department is a convenient level for the assignment of costs to activities. This is because most activity data are obtained directly from the departments. For example, the percent of department effort expended on each activity can be applied to the department's personnel cost as a resource driver.

Rule 3: Adjust Uneconomic Items

There's no need to follow generally accepted accounting principles in ABC. This is because ABC's primary purpose is business improvement, not financial reporting.

Thus, it makes sense to adjust general ledger items that aren't economically realistic. For example, depreciation can be recomputed on a *consumed* basis. Development costs can also be collected in a special holding account and assigned to production over the product's life.

There could just as well be a rule 4: build an activity-based general ledger. This involves assigning costs to activities in the general ledger. It is a recommended step in building an ABC-based performance management system that supports activity-based budgeting and monthly analysis of activity performance. It is accompanied by steps to resolve general ledger issues and automate data transfer to the ABC model—both of which reduce the cost of ABC system maintenance.

CREATING ACTIVITY CENTERS

Activity centers are clusters of activities. They give structure to the activity information in the system and facilitate reports about related activities.

RULES FOR CREATING ACTIVITY CENTERS

Rule 1 Put activities into departmental activity centers first.
Rule 2 Use attributes to create activity centers *on demand*.
Rule 3 Use nested activity centers to create hierarchies of activity information.

Rule 1: Put Activities into Departmental Activity Centers First

The simplest way to organize activities is by department. This is familiar, since departmental activity centers parallel the organization chart.

Rule 2: Use Attributes to Create Activity Centers *on Demand*

Activity centers can be formulated *on demand* for users who want information about various groups of activities. A user may be interested in a process that cuts across department lines. This could be the engineering change process, for example. Or the user may be interested in a specific type of activity, such as one associated with detecting poor quality. In both cases, it's possible to prepare an *on demand activity center report* that provides the desired information.

Attributes make it possible to create activity centers on demand. Attributes are labels describing the type of activity. Their virtue is that they allow you to locate activities with identical characteristics easily.

Dayton Technologies used this approach by labeling each activity associated with preventing, detecting, and correcting poor quality (Figure 14–2). This facilitated activity center reports that highlighted information about the three types of activity.

F I G U R E   1 4 – 2

Using Attributes to Create Reports

Preventing	Detecting	Correcting
Training	Inspecting	Inspecting returns
Preparing quality reports	Checking line work	Grinding
	Trying out	Trouble-shooting
	Evaluating shrinkage	

Dayton Technologies labeled activities associated with preventing, detecting, and correcting defects. This allowed it to prepare reports about *poor quality*.

Rule 3: Use Nested Activity Centers to Create Hierarchies of Activity Information

Nested activity centers are centers that are contained within other centers. This is illustrated by Figure 14–3, which shows a single activity center for a company's procurement process.

Within the procurement activity center, there's another activity center for each department in the procurement process. In turn, each of these

F I G U R E   1 4 – 3

Nested Activity Centers

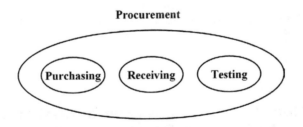

The individual support departments are *nested* in the procurement process. They're part of an activity-information hierarchy that can be accessed at different levels for different purposes.

lower-level activity centers contains various activities and may even contain other activity centers. For example, the "testing" activity center would contain various testing activities. It could also contain a "calibration" activity center covering those activities associated with calibrating the test equipment used by the "testing" activity center.

The value of nesting is that it creates hierarchies of activity information. This allows users to focus easily on different levels and breadths of information. A process-level activity center, for example, provides a high-level view. From this, each nested activity center and its constituent activities take you progressively deeper into the bowels of the organization.

DEFINING RESOURCE DRIVERS

The fourth step in designing an ABC model is defining the resource drivers. The resource drivers, in turn, define the consumption of resources by activities. For example, the activity "tapping parts" uses electric power to run the tapping machines. The driver for the consumption of this resource might be "number of machine hours." A more accurate driver is "kilowatt hours used," but this is only possible if a meter is used to measure the power consumed by the tapping machines.

Attaching cost to activities often requires multiple steps, with a resource driver for each step. The process of cost assignment starts in the accounts in the general ledger. Cost is then moved progressively downward or sideways until it reaches the activities.

RULES FOR DEFINING RESOURCE DRIVERS

Rule 1   Assign the cost of enabling activities to primary activities.
Rule 2   Use tracing wherever possible.
Rule 3   Use common sense to determine how you assign cost.
Rule 3   Separate effort and noneffort costs.

Rule 1: Assign the Cost of Enabling Activities to Primary Activities

One of the activities in the order processing department in Figure 14–4 is "administering." This activity includes tasks such as evaluating employee

FIGURE 14-4

Enabling Activities

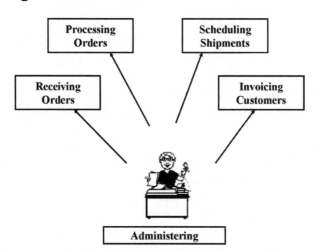

Enabling activities are those that support other activities. Their costs should be assigned to the activities that they benefit. In this case, "administering" the order processing department benefits several customer-related activities, and its cost is assigned based on the proportion of time spent on each activity.

performance and supervising employees. It also supports other activities in the department, such as "receiving customer orders."

"Administering" is an *enabling* activity, one that benefits other activities. It does not, however, directly benefit cost objects.

In contrast, "receiving customer orders" is a primary activity. It directly benefits cost objects (the customers in this case).

The cost of enabling activities is assigned to the primary activities that they benefit. This is preferable to trying to find an activity driver for an activity that has no direct link to cost objects. (What is an appropriate activity driver for "administering"?)

Rule 2: Use Tracing Wherever Possible

Cost should be traced wherever possible and allocated only as a last resort. The cost of "administering," for example, can be traced to the primary activities based on measures of time spent by the administrator on each primary activity.

Tracing is the assignment of costs based on specific data. For example, supplies consumed in machine maintenance can be traced directly to this activity (assuming that records have been kept). This creates an unambiguous assignment of cost.

Allocation is the indirect assignment of cost. For example, the cost of administering can be allocated to the activities that benefit from it. A common allocation method is to use the relative effort devoted by nonadministrative employees to the primary activities.

Keep in mind, however, that allocation is a "dirty word" in cost systems—something to avoid if possible. It connotes arbitrariness of measurement and a limit to the meaning of the resulting information.

Knowing whether a cost is allocated or traced is important to users. For example, allocated costs, such as the cost of space, are unlikely to go away if the activity is eliminated. In contrast, traced costs, such as the cost of supplies, often disappear if the activity is no longer performed.

You should use allocation only when direct tracing is impossible or doesn't make sense. This will generally be the case in the following three situations:

1. *Resources are shared by activities.* A building may be shared by many activities, for example, but the cost is incurred for the entire facility. It's impossible to attach a portion of a jointly incurred cost directly to an activity. As a result, the cost must be allocated using a resource driver such as the percent of floor space occupied.

2. *Measurement is impractical or costly.* It may be possible to measure the use of a resource directly. But the data for the driver may be unavailable, costly, or intrusive. You can ask the janitors to record how much time they spend cleaning the areas occupied by each activity, for example, but they may balk at filling out the time cards.

   Tracing may not be possible simply because records have not been maintained. The cost of supplies, for example, cannot be traced if records of usage have not been kept by the activities.

3. *The information is not material.* It's possible to measure the use of a resource directly, but the additional information is not justified by the amount of cost involved. For example, you could measure the amount of waste generated by each activity. However, the cost of waste disposal may be too low to justify the additional measurement cost. Thus, it's more economical to allocate this cost than to trace it.

Sometimes, however, allocations can be converted to tracing with justifiable additional measurement cost. For example, the cost of power is often allocated to machines based on machine hours. This may not be accurate when a variety of machines are used. However, if meters are installed on the machines, power cost can be traced directly to each machine.

Rule 3: Use Common Sense to Determine How You Assign Cost

Look at the resource, look at how it's shared by the activities, and do what makes the most sense. You may not be able to prove you are right, and you will still need to use the results with care.

THE ALLOCATION CONUNDRUM

The problem with allocation is that you cannot prove that one method is better than another. You also need to be very careful how you interpret allocated costs.

Here's an example using two alternative allocation methods:

Cost of facilities (e.g., building depreciation and property taxes) = $100,000

Alternative 1		Alternative 2	
(Resource driver = % of space occupied)		(Resource driver = same per activity)	
Activity 1	Activity 2	Activity 1	Activity 2
10,000 sq. ft.	5,000 sq. ft.	50%	50%
$67,000	$33,000	$50,000	$50,000

A building may be shared by many activities, for example, but the cost is incurred for the entire facility. Should we allocate using floor space? This commonly used approach assumes that each square foot costs the same. This may be a reasonable assumption in some cases, but it's still an assumption. In other cases, the assumption is clearly wrong. A plant with clean and nonclean rooms, for example, will not comply with this assumption (a weighted cost per square foot makes more sense in this case).

The solution is to use common sense when you allocate—and use the results with care.

For example, many companies use *percent of occupied floor space* to assign facility costs. Does this make sense? It does if you believe that the cost of space is equal per square foot.

But what if the plant was built to eliminate vibrations in certain key processes? Does an equal cost per square foot make sense here? Should the purchasing activity, for example, bear part of the additional structural cost that really benefits only some other process?

In this case, the cost per square foot is not equal across the facility. A different resource driver—such as a *weighted cost per square foot* that assigns more cost to the key processes—makes more sense.

Rule 4: Separate Effort and Noneffort Costs

Assignment of cost differs for effort costs and noneffort costs. Effort costs are those that are associated with people doing work. Primarily, these are the salaries and benefits that people receive. Noneffort costs are resources other than salaries and related costs.

The resource driver for effort costs is a measure of the effort expended on each activity. This measure is derived from information gathered through interviews, time cards, or questionnaires. It's summarized on an *effort analysis worksheet* such as that shown Figure 14–5.

Figure 14–5 shows how each person in the department spent his or her time. Helen Small, for example, spent 90 percent of her time implementing changes to bills of materials and 10 percent of her time testing products.

The simplest resource driver for this effort is to take the sum of each column (or activity), divide this by the total department effort, and multiply this ratio by the department's total salaries and benefits. Scheduling, for example, would receive 105/500 of this total cost.

Implicit in this resource driver is the assumption that each person in the department receives the same salary. If Helen Small is paid less than the department average, this driver will assign too much cost to the activities she works on.

A more refined method is to adjust the estimates of time to reflect the relative salaries. This can be done using approximate weights or by tracing the cost of each person directly to the activities performed. For example, you can assign Helen Small's salary and benefits to the two activities she performs. Implementing changes to bills of materials receives 90 percent of this total, and testing receives the other 10 percent.

FIGURE 14–5

Effort Analysis Worksheet

Activity Dept:Production Int date 8–17	Setting up	Scheduling	BOM Chg*	Testing	Running Machines	Moving Material	Must Equal 100%
Name							
Henry Carter		30	70				100
Karen Lu			90	10		100	
Bob Gray	10			5	5	80	100
Jack Zimmer	25				75	100	
Khalid Khan	10	75	15				100
TOTAL	45	105	175	15	80	80	500
Activity drivers	Setup hours	# Batches	# ECNs*	# Tests	# Machine hours	# Movements	

BOM Chg* = Changing bill of materials
#ECNs* = Engineering change notices

This worksheet summarizes information about who does what and the time spent on each activity. The percentages are used to trace effort-related costs to activities.

The additional cost of adjustment may not be worthwhile or even possible. This may be because the differences in salaries are minimal or because the design team does not have access to information on individual salaries.

As for noneffort costs, they should be traced to activities wherever possible. Costs such as travel, entertainment, training, and utilities are susceptible to tracing.

The overall problem is finding records of cost consumption. General ledger systems, for example, typically do not record cost consumption by activity. It is common, however, for departments to keep such records. At TriQuint, for example, department managers maintained detailed records of the use of supplies by each activity.

Remember, your primary goal is to choose resource drivers that accurately measure the consumption of resources by the activities. But be careful of the cost of doing this. Don't spend valuable time and money to achieve marginal gains in accuracy.

DETERMINING ATTRIBUTES

Determining attributes is the fifth step in designing an ABC system. Attributes are labels that enhance the meaning of the information in the ABC model. For example, you could attach the attribute "customer" to an activity to signify that the activity supports customers and not products.

RULES FOR DETERMINING ATTRIBUTES

Rule 1 Let the objective of the model govern the choice of attributes.

Rule 2 Let the user assign sensitive or judgmental attributes.

Rule 1: Let the Objective of the Model Govern the Choice of Attributes

ABC models vary in the objectives they support. Different objectives require different reports, and attributes facilitate the preparation of these reports.

To expand on this, consider an ABC model that supports process improvement. The model uses attributes to identify value-added and non-value-added activities. This enhances the ability to identify improvement targets. Other attributes, such as cost drivers and performance measures, facilitate judgments about the way the work is carried out and how it may be improved.

Process attributes allow a functionally organized model to report activities and cost by process. In a department of transportation, for example, activities can be tagged according to which key process they belong to: planning and design, operations, business support, or finance.

Strategic models also benefit from attributes. For example, customers in a particular distribution channel can be identified using a channel-specific attribute. This allows the preparation of reports based on the cost of products sold through this distribution channel.

ABC models can be linked to balanced scorecards using attributes. Each activity can be tagged with an attribute for the scorecard perspective it supports. The activity "conduct landowner meetings" (related to appraising condemned property) is attributed to the customer dimension. The activity "conduct safety training" is attributed to the organizational health perspective.

Rule 2: Let the User Assign Sensitive or Judgmental Attributes

Some attributes are best left for the user to create. Examples are attributes that are too user-sensitive to be defined by the designer or those that cannot be specified in advance.

Designating an activity as *value-added* or *non-value-added*, for example, can be a sensitive issue. The ABC designer may be an outsider and should be cautious in making judgments about the work done by someone else. Would you feel good being told that your work is non-value-added?

By all means, help people arrive at a conclusion about whether an activity is value-added or non-value-added. And support their efforts to eliminate waste. But it may be counterproductive to impose any judgment on them.

Also, some attributes cannot be specified in advance or are unique to the user. For example, does the cost of salaries and benefits assigned to a receiving activity vary with the number of receipts?

The cost is variable if the change in the number of receipts is large enough and the time frame is long enough for the resources to be redeployed or increased. The designer cannot make this determination in advance, however, because these factors are unknown at the time the system is designed.

SELECTING ACTIVITY DRIVERS

Activity drivers capture demands placed on activities by cost objects. It's important to pick activity drivers carefully so that products, customers, and other cost objects are costed accurately.[1]

RULES FOR SELECTING ACTIVITY DRIVERS

Rule 1 Pick activity drivers that match the type of activity.
Rule 2 Pick activity drivers that correlate well with the actual consumption of the activity.
Rule 3 Minimize the number of different drivers.
Rule 4 Pick activity drivers that encourage improved performance.
Rule 5 Pick activity drivers with a modest cost of measurement.
Rule 6 Don't pick activity drivers that require new measurements.

Rule 1: Pick Activity Drivers That Match the Type of Activity

Activity drivers should match the type of activity. For example, scheduling the production of a batch of parts is a batch activity. It's best suited to a batch activity driver such as the number of production runs. (You schedule the batch each time it's run.)

In this situation, it's not acceptable to use a unit activity driver such as direct labor hours. This is because the number of units (and direct labor hours) varies from one product to another with little regard to the number of batches produced.

Rule 2: Pick Activity Drivers That Correlate Well with the Actual Consumption of the Activity

Simply matching the level of activity driver and the level of the activity does not always assure accuracy. The activity "setting up," for example, requires a choice between the number of setups and the number of setup hours. The question is, which correlates best with the performance of the activity?

The correct choice actually depends on the circumstances. Using "number of setups" is adequate if the effort per setup does not vary from one type of part to another. But if the time required differs from part to part, then "number of setups" doesn't correlate well with the variation in effort from one part to another. This variation in effort is better measured by using "number of setup hours" as the activity driver.

Rule 3: Minimize the Number of Different Drivers

The cost of measurement is affected by the number of activity drivers you choose. You need just enough drivers to assign cost to the cost objects accurately. Additional drivers beyond this point increase the cost of measurement but not the value of the model.

The number of activity drivers in ABC models varies from two to hundreds, depending on the complexity of the situation. In some cases, however, 20 to 30 drivers is sufficient.

Rule 4: Pick Activity Drivers That Encourage Improved Performance

Activity drivers are often used as performance indicators. Because of this, designers should try to choose activity drivers that encourage performance improvement.

The Oscilloscope Group of Tektronix, for example, used "number of part numbers" as an activity driver to communicate the cost of component proliferation to product design engineers. The engineers responded to this activity driver by dramatically reducing the number of different parts used in products.[2]

Also, activity drivers that are detail-specific are more likely to encourage improved performance. For example, the driver "time spent in first-piece inspection" focuses attention on the time and cost required by the inspection activity. In contrast, "number of production runs" as a driver may yield accurate product costs, but it doesn't focus attention on the inspection activity.

Rule 5: Pick Activity Drivers with a Modest Cost of Measurement

Different activity drivers incur different measurement costs. Measuring "number of setup hours" is usually more difficult and costly than just simply counting "number of setups." Moreover, "number of setups" may already be counted for you by the existing information system. In contrast, measuring setup hours may require establishing a new timekeeping system.

Rule 6: Don't Pick Activity Drivers That Require New Measurements

Try to avoid picking activity drivers that will require new measurements. Numerous useful drivers often already exist in the company's current information systems. Using these existing drivers avoids the cost of making new measurements.

Always take a careful look around. Even if the data are not in the information system, you may find what you need in someone's desk drawer or personal computer.

If not, you can come up with a "wish list" for next year. This should identify areas where new measurements will improve the quality of the system. If ABC is an important tool in your company, then it deserves its share of information systems support.

DESIGNING RESOURCE PLANNING AND TIME-BASED ABC MODELS

Designing resource planning and time-based ABC models is somewhat different from designing standard ABC models. The differences in these models include the following:

- Practical capacity is defined for as many activities as possible.
- Productivity rates for each resource type are used instead of percentage resource drivers. For example, a rate of five minutes per order determines how much of the order entry resource is used each time an order is processed.
- Activity drivers are defined as quantities of outputs or processing time per unit for each cost object. Activity drivers that assign activity cost indirectly—such as the number of part numbers for procurement activities—don't measure the use of resource capacity.
- Diversity is modeled in the time equations used in time-based ABC models. This reduces the number of activities needed to report accurate costs.

Data gathering for resource planning and time-based ABC models reflects these differences. Less time is spent on surveys to determine activities. More time is spent estimating practical capacity, determining productivity rates, and building time equations.

Resource planning and time-based ABC models are usually hybrid models. That is, some parts of the model are similar to a standard ABC model, while other parts are built to the new rules. This is because some parts of an organization are susceptible to the measurement of time and capacity, while others are not. For example, it is difficult to estimate time per transaction for some administrative activities.

Standard ABC models can reside on a stand-alone PC, whereas resource planning and time-based ABC models should be connected to corporate databases. In particular, time equations in time-based ABC models are dependent on transactional data.

S U M M A R Y

Designing an ABC system is a typical managerial task. You apply some basic rules, and you use a lot of judgment to achieve your objective. As discussed in this chapter, the following six major steps will help you complete a successful design:

1. *Identify activities.* In this step you decide how much detail you need about the activities and how you are to describe and define the activities.

2. *Reconstruct the general ledger.* The second step is to reconstruct the general ledger. This reduces the amount of detail as well as the work required. It also adjusts the financial data to fit ABC needs, such as assigning development costs over the life cycle of products.

3. *Create activity centers.* This third step groups (and reports) activities in ways that are more meaningful to the user. This includes departmental and cross-functional reports of activities.

4. *Define resource drivers.* The fourth step is to attach costs to activities. This uses resource drivers that define the costs consumed by activities. The goal is to use resource drivers that accurately measure the consumption of cost without requiring an excessive amount of time and incurring excessive cost.

5. *Determine attributes.* The fifth step is to attach attributes to the data in the system. Attributes are labels that enhance the meaning of the activity-based information.

6. *Select activity drivers.* The sixth step is the selection of activity drivers to capture the demand placed on activities by cost objects. The goal is to pick activity drivers that cost products and customers accurately, but at a reasonable cost themselves.

For resource planning and time-based ABC models, identify the areas of the model that will be built according to the principles of predictive modeling. Then estimate the data required for these areas (productivity rates, practical capacity, and transaction volumes) and build the time equations.

K E Y   T E R M S

Activity dictionary.   A common set of definitions and descriptions of activities in an ABC model. It includes a description of each activity and the tasks associated with that activity. It is used to set standards of consistency for ABC system design. Also referred to as the *dictionary of activities*.

Allocation.   Indirect assignment of costs, usually in a manner that spreads costs arbitrarily across multiple benefiting activities or cost objects.

Enabling activity.   An activity that supports a core (mission critical) activity. Preparing paychecks for workers in core activities is an example of an enabling activity. See also *secondary activity*.

Macro activity.   An aggregation of related activities. This helps manage detail in an ABC system without reducing the amount of useful information available.

Nested activity center.   An activity center contained within another activity center. This is part of a hierarchy of information within an ABC system that allows users a choice as to the level of detail and organization of information that they prefer.

Tracing.   Assignment of costs based on specific activity-related data.

REFERENCES

1 Rule 1 was first described in Anne Riley and Peter B. B. Turney, *TriQuint Semiconductor* (Portland: Cost Technology, Inc., 1990). Rule 1 is also discussed in Peter B. B. Turney, "Ten Myths about Implementing an Activity-Based Cost System," *Journal of Cost Management*, Spring 1990, pp 24–32. Rules 2, 4, and 5 were discussed by Robin Cooper in "The Rise of Activity-Based Costing—Part Three: How Many Cost Drivers Do You Need, and How Do You Select Them?" *Journal of Cost Management*, Winter 1989, pp. 34–46. Rule 3 is discussed in Peter B. B. Turney and James M. Reeve, "The Impact of Continuous Improvement on the Design of Activity-Based Cost Systems," *Journal of Cost Management*, Summer 1990, pp. 43–50.

2 Robin Cooper and Peter B. B. Turney, "Tektronix: The Portable Instrument Division," 188-142/3/4, (Boston: Harvard Business School, 1988).

PART SIX

How to Sustain the Success of ABC and ABM

Common Cents isn't just about building ABC models or creating systems. It's about results.

Results provide a positive return on the investment incurred to create the ABC system. They measure the contribution of ABC and ABM to the success of the organization.

The question for the final chapter of the book is how to sustain these results over time. How do ABC and ABM, and the results associated with them, continue long after implementation is complete?

Chapter 15 describes three ways of sustaining the success of ABC and ABM. First, the ABC model adapts as the organization changes. Second, a value creation process transforms analysis into action, and action into results. Third, ABC and ABM are plugged into the organization's performance management system.

These three steps *institutionalize* ABC and ABM and lead to *continuous results*. They allow ABC to power the financial performance of today's and tomorrow's organizations.

CHAPTER 15

Continuous Results from ABC

ABC is business intelligence for all types of organizations. It reveals the hidden opportunities to improve cost and profitability. It directs improvement efforts to their highest value.

Gaining these benefits requires effort and care. Needs must be assessed, plans prepared, data gathered, models built, reports prepared, managers trained, and so on.

With the right mix of planning, methods, skill, and experience, ABC provides a positive return on investment for any organization. Cost savings and profit improvements can be measured and compared with the cost of implementation to quantify ABC's value.

The ABC systems with the highest returns are those that are sustained over time. One-time savings from an ABC initiative can be significant. The results are multiplied, however, when ABC's impact is sustained.

Organizations that practice business process management expect continuous process improvement over time. Is it not reasonable—and achievable—to expect continuous results from ABC?

The question for this concluding chapter is this: How do you sustain the positive impact of ABC over time?

Organizations achieve continuous results from ABC in three ways. First, it is important to cost-effectively keep the model up-to-date to reflect new management uses of ABC, changes in the business, and the results of each reporting period. Second, a value creation process consistently delivers results from ABC. Third, ABC—along with resource planning— is integrated into a comprehensive performance management system.

KEEPING THE MODEL UP-TO-DATE

An ABC model is a representation of a living organization. It is descriptive of what the organization does, and it measures how well it does it. To represent the organization over time, however, the model must adapt. The information it reports must be accurate and up-to-date—even in the face or rapid and extensive change.

There are three parts to keeping a model current. The first is to keep the model relevant when strategic focus and operational needs change. For example, a model that was designed to report customer profitability will not have the right information to support a new cost-cutting initiative. Cost-cutting decisions require different and more detailed information about activities.

Second, it is necessary to update the model to reflect organizational changes, additions and deletions to the product line, new markets, and so on. These changes have a big impact on the model—the activities will be different; the structure of the model will change; different resources with different costs will be deployed; and the type, mix, and volume of outputs and customers will also change.

Third, it is important to cost-effectively automate the regular updating of ABC data and the reporting of ABC information. Depending on the type of ABC system, automation may include

- *Electronic reporting of time spent by staff on activities.* Ideally, this involves simple and timely Web reporting on a daily or weekly basis.
- *Electronic links from source data systems to the ABC model.* Source systems will include the general ledger, the time-reporting system, operational systems, and sources of key data. In some cases the data are staged in a data warehouse prior to entry into the ABC model.
- *Activity-driver equations in the ABC model.* Activity-driver equations use data from transactional systems. They are used in time-based ABC models to reduce the time and effort required to update the system. (See Chapter 6 for a discussion of time-based ABC).

- *Access by managers to updated ABC information.* Ideally, managers will access ABC information over the Web, using software tools to analyze and report the information in the ABC model. Managers use preformatted ABC reports that match their decision requirements. They also use software to probe the ABC model to answer specific queries.

THE VALUE CREATION PROCESS

Results of any kind—let alone continuous results—don't happen by chance. They are the outcome of a systematic process that increases the probability of measurable, positive, and continuous results.

A successful value creation process includes the following components:

- *Defined roles and responsibilities.* Responsibilities are defined for the overall success of the ABC program, and also for the success of each part of the program. For example, someone is responsible for the cost-reduction goals of each process team.
- *Change management program.* ABC is no different from any other management initiative—it runs into barriers to change. People are often slow to warm to a new and unproven technique. Indeed, they may feel threatened by the transparency that ABC creates. This is resolved by a change management program that includes leadership, communications, and training.
- *Analytical tools and techniques.* Opportunities to reduce cost or improve profitability are found through the application of analytical tools and techniques. These include storyboarding for identifying cost reduction and statistical tools to generate additional intelligence to find profit improvements.
- *Structured process.* Value creation relies on a structured process for creating results. This process ensures that improvement opportunities are turned into realized cost savings or profit improvements.
- *Decision support.* ABC is useful for many different decision-making purposes. These purposes include lowering the total cost of ownership of equipment, reengineering the supply chain, and managing the capacity of human resources. Value is realized from ABC when it is used extensively in management initiatives.

- *Linkage to scorecards.* The results targeted by the value creation process should be linked to the scorecards in a performance management system. This ensures that someone is responsible for the results and increases the visibility of success or failure.

PERFORMANCE MANAGEMENT SYSTEM

Organizations that successfully institutionalize ABC embed it in their performance management system.[1] This simultaneously increases the value proposition associated with ABC and increases the likelihood that strategic planning efforts will succeed.

The purpose of a performance management system is to help execute strategy. It communicates the strategic plan to the organization. It identifies the outcomes and measurements associated with success. It creates resource and activity plans to accomplish the planned outcomes and target performance measures. It analyzes performance to provide feedback on current performance. And it creates learning that influences future plans and performance.[2]

How do ABC and resource planning help in the execution of strategy? First, ABC is an indispensable source of performance measures. Second, ABC reveals disconnects between planned outcomes and current performance. Third, resource planning helps place resources and activities where they have the greatest positive impact on the achievement of strategic goals.

Performance Measures from ABC

The balanced scorecard includes two dimensions that benefit from ABC-derived performance measures. ABC is the source of measures of activity cost for the process dimension. It is also the source of measures of profitability by customer type for the customer dimension. Where will these measures come from if you don't have ABC?

The South Dakota Department of Transportation, for example, linked ABC to its Balanced Scorecard. Over 20 percent of the department's performance measures—primarily in the process dimension of the scorecard—came from the ABC model. In addition, each division, program, region and area of the department had a performance measure for cost savings obtained from storyboarding.[3]

Linking ABC to the scorecard helps keep the spotlight on results. If people are responsible for performance measures of cost and profitability, they will pay very close attention to cost and profitability.

Scorecarding is a repetitive process. Performance measures are kept up-to-date, with new targets set each period. ABC allows these targets to be compared with actual results at the end of the period. This sustains the importance of—and interest in—ABC over time.

Performance Disconnects

An ABC model is a model of current resource deployment and activity performance. When each activity in the model is linked to the goal it supports, ABC reveals the appropriateness of this current deployment.

At ABC Technologies, for example, ABC revealed two types of deployment disconnects. The first disconnect occurred when an activity was not associated with a goal. Resources were deployed to perform an activity that had no relationship to strategically important goals. This discovery prompted management to ask the question, "Why are we performing this work?"[4]

The second disconnect occurred when goals were not associated with activities. Presumably these goals were important—they were included in the scorecard—but no work was planned that would ensure that the goals were completed. This discovery prompted the question, "How can we be successful with these goals when no one is working toward their accomplishment?"

Correcting these disconnects requires an adjustment to the business model. Activities with no purpose are discontinued, and the resources devoted to them are deployed to better use. Goals with no activities require the deployment of resources and assignment of activities for their completion.

Deployment of Resources and Activities

Resource planning helps create the resource and work plan to accomplish strategy-based scorecard goals and performance measures.[5] Resource planning is used in the following ways:

- Identification of performance gaps
- Simulation of alternative ways of achieving the desired performance

- Capacity planning
- Identification and resolution of performance bottlenecks
- Identification of resources that need to be redeployed
- Preparation of a performance budget that reflects strategic requirements

Resource planning is the analytical engine for integrated performance management systems. It fills critical measurement needs, reduces the time required for analysis, and increases the quality of the plan and its defensibility.

SUMMARY

A sustainable ABC system provides a positive return on investment. It delivers results in diverse ways. It offers easy access to information and low cost of data update, model revision, and system maintenance.

The continuous results ABC will adapt and grow over time as management finds new ways of putting it to work. Other management initiatives will come and go, but ABC will continue in its role of powering the financial performance of tomorrow's organizations.

KEY TERMS

Continuous results.   The relentless and ongoing application of ABC to yield profit improvement and cost reduction over a sustained period of time.

Performance management system.   A method of executing strategy that integrates strategy mapping, resource planning and budgeting, activity-based costing, and value creation into a management system.

Sustainable ABC system.   An ABC system that is kept up-to-date and used to create results indefinitely.

Value creation.   Activities that realize results from the ABC system.

REFERENCES

1 Some government organizations refer to these systems as performance budgeting systems, the term used by the Government Performance and Results Act (GPRA).

2 Peter B. B. Turney, "Collaborative Performance Management Systems," Cost Technology, Inc., 2004.

3 Peter B. B. Turney, "The South Dakota Department of Transportation: The Fast Road to Better Performance," Cost Technology, Inc., 2003.

4 Peter B. B. Turney, "ABC Technologies, Inc., Linking Activity-Based Information to the Scorecard," University of Virginia Darden School Foundation, 2000.

5 Resource planning is covered in Chapter 6.

GLOSSARY

ABB   Activity-based budgeting.

ABC   Activity-based costing.

ABM   Activity-based management.

Activity   A unit of work performed within an organization. A description of the work that goes on in the organization and consumes resources. Testing materials is an example of an activity.

Activity analysis   The evaluation of activity performance in the search for improvement opportunities.

Activity-based budgeting (ABB)   Preparation of cost budgets using resource planning to help estimate workload and resource requirements.

Activity-based costing (ABC)   A method of measuring the cost and performance of activities, products, and customers. It assigns costs to activities based on their use of resources, and assigns costs to cost objects based on their use of activities. ABC recognizes the causal relationship between cost drivers and activities.

Activity-based management (ABM)   A discipline that focuses on the management of activities as the route to improving the value received by customers and the profit achieved by providing this value. This discipline includes cost-driver analysis, activity analysis, and performance analysis. ABM draws on activity-based costing as a major source of information.

Activity center   A report of pertinent information about the activities in a function or process.

Activity cost pool   The total cost assigned to an activity. The sum of all the cost elements assigned to an activity.

Activity dictionary   A common set of definitions and descriptions of activities in an ABC model. It includes a description of each activity and the tasks associated with that activity. It is used to set standards of consistency for ABC system design. Also referred to as the *dictionary of activities*.

Activity driver   A factor used to assign cost from an activity to a cost object. A measure of the frequency and intensity of use of an activity by a cost object. If performing custom engineering work for a customer is an activity, the number of engineering hours could be the activity driver.

Allocation   Indirect assignment of costs, usually in a manner that spreads costs arbitrarily across multiple benefiting activities or cost objects.

Attributes   Labels attached to data in an activity-based cost system to signify the meaning of the data and to facilitate the reporting of information.

Balanced scorecard   Goals and performance measures derived from the organization's strategic plan and strategy map. Goals and performance measures are grouped into perspectives, including financial, customer, internal business process, and organizational health and learning.

Batch activity   An activity that is performed on a batch of a product. Inspecting the first piece of each batch is a batch activity.

Benchmark   An activity that is a *best practice* and by which a similar activity will be judged. Benchmarks are used to help identify opportunities for improving the performance of comparable activities. The source of a benchmark may be internal (such as another department in the same company) or external (such as a competitor).

Bill of activities   A list of the activities and costs associated with a cost object. The bill may include additional information such as which activities are non-value-added.

Business process management (BPM)   A method of improving the performance of business processes by combining information technology with management methods such as Six Sigma and activity-based costing.

Collaborative interviews   A group process that creates a picture of each department's activities and related information on storyboards. An accurate and efficient data-gathering technique, it helps create buy-in for the ABC initiative.

Continuous improvement   The relentless and ongoing search for ways to improve business performance.

Continuous results   The relentless and ongoing application of ABC to yield profit improvement and cost reduction over a sustained period of time.

Conventional cost system   An older, traditional cost system that uses direct material and labor consumed as the primary means of apportioning overhead. This was adequate when the overhead cost of indirect activities was a small percentage of the direct labor consumed in actually making products. But today, automation has reduced direct labor substantially, leaving indirect activities as a far more significant cost factor. For this and other reasons, using direct labor as a primary apportioning device can cause significant costing distortions and poor strategic decisions.

Core activity   An activity that directly supports the mission of the organization. Repairing a pothole in a road is an example of a core activity for a transportation department.

Cost accounting system   A financial accounting method for costing manufactured products to allow the proper recording of cost in the inventory and cost of sales accounts. See also *conventional cost system*.

Cost analysis   Simulation of cost-reduction opportunities. Cost analysis helps you select the opportunities that yield the greatest improvement. It also helps build commitment to improvement actions and helps communicate the knowledge gained through the improvement.

Cost assignment view   The part of ABC in which cost is assigned to activities and the cost of activities is assigned to cost objects.

Cost driver   An event or causal factor that influences the level and performance of activities and the resulting consumption of resources, elapsed time, and quality. For example, defective materials that lead to low product quality are a cost driver for procurement and production activities. An activity may have multiple cost drivers associated with it.

Cost element   The amount paid for a resource and assigned to an activity. Part of an activity cost pool.

Cost object   The reason for performing an activity. Products and customers are reasons for performing activities. Cost objects include products, services, customers, projects, and contracts.

Customer activity   An activity that provides value to external customers. Providing technical assistance is an example of a customer activity.

Customer value   The difference between customer realization and sacrifice. Realization is what is received by the customer. It includes product features, quality, and service, and also the cost to use, maintain, and dispose of the product. Sacrifice is what is given up by the customer. It includes the amount paid for the product plus the time spent acquiring the product and learning how to use it. To maximize customer value, it is necessary to maximize the difference between realization and sacrifice.

Customer value analysis   Study of customer activities directed at finding ways to improve customer value and reduce the cost of delivering that value.

Death spiral   The sequential outsourcing or dropping of products in response to inaccurate cost information.

Decision simulation   Analysis of the cost and profit impact of alternative decision scenarios using resource planning.

Deliverable   A tangible benefit of activity-based costing.

Dictionary of activities   See *activity dictionary*.

Enabling activity   An activity that supports a core (mission critical) activity. Preparing paychecks for workers in core activities is an example of an enabling activity. See also *secondary activity*.

Extract, Transform, and Load (ETL)   The extraction of data from legacy or modern databases, the transformation of the data into a format that is compatible with the ABC software, and the loading of the data into the ABC system.

Flexibility   The ability to respond to changing customer needs quickly.

Focused factory   The organization of production around a narrow range of products to provide low cost and high throughput.

Full absorption   A requirement in financial accounting that all overhead costs, even those associated with unused capacity, be assigned to existing products.

Functional silos   Vertical dimensions of an organizational hierarchy where functional considerations override organizational considerations.

General ledger   A database of financial accounting information. The general ledger classifies financial information according to rules such as generally accepted accounting principles (GAAP), government accounting standards, or utility reporting standards.

Goal seeking   The search for ways to improve the competitiveness of a product or service. The search starts with identification of high-cost activities in the bill of activities. It then proceeds through the causes of high cost and finishes with actions to reduce or eliminate the effect of these causes.

Interviews   In-person question and answer sessions. This is the traditional information-gathering method of choice in ABC. Interviews must be planned and conducted carefully; otherwise they can be time-consuming, inaccurate, or not well received.

Investment management   The use of ABC to manage capacity for maximum profitability and to direct capital spending to the most profitable improvement targets.

Just in time (JIT)   (1) the determination of workload based on the use of output by the next activity; (2) continuous improvement.

Lean organization   A customer-focused organization with high standards of quality, service, response, and value.

Life-cycle costing   Costing products over their entire life cycle rather than for a single accounting period. The product life cycle spans development, introduction, growth, maturity, decline, and abandonment. Life-cycle costing helps assess product profitability.

Macro activity   An aggregation of related activities. This helps manage detail in an ABC system without reducing the amount of useful information available.

Myth   A belief about ABC that is a barrier to ABC's acceptance. Demolishing these myths increases the chances of a successful ABC implementation.

Nested activity center   An activity center contained within another activity center. This is part of a hierarchy of information within an ABC system that allows users a choice as to the level of detail and organization of information that they prefer.

Non-value-added activity   An activity that is judged *not* to contribute to customer value. Also, an activity that can be eliminated without reducing the quantity or quality of output. An example is the activity of moving parts back and forth.

Pareto analysis The arrangement of activities or activity drivers in descending order of cost. The activities or drivers accounting for the majority of the cost are targeted for cost reduction.

Performance budgeting An integrated system of strategic planning, performance measurement and budgeting. Mandated by the U.S. Government Performance and Results Act (GPRA), it uses resource planning to formulate the budget.

Performance management The use of ABC to improve financial performance. It includes searching for low-cost product designs, identifying cost-reduction opportunities, guiding efforts to improve quality, and measuring performance.

Performance management system A method of executing strategy that integrates strategy mapping, resource planning and budgeting, activity-based costing, and value creation into a management system.

Performance measure An indicator of the work performed in an activity and the results achieved. It is a measure of how well an activity meets the needs of its customers. Performance measures may be financial or nonfinancial.

Pilot project A test of the applicability and utility of activity-based costing.

Practical capacity A realistic estimate of the amount of time available to do work after deducting breaks, sick leave, staff meetings, and other nonproductive uses of time.

Primary activity An activity that has an output that directly benefits external products, services, or customers. Providing a consulting service to a client is an example of a primary activity.

Process A series of activities that are linked to perform a specific objective.

Process view The part of ABC that provides operational information about activities.

Product activity activity that benefits all units of a type of product. Changing engineering specifications on a product is a product activity.

Profit lever An action that increases profitability.

Project team The individuals who plan, design, and implement the ABC system.

Quality function deployment (QFD) The design of products and processes based on customer requirements.

Questionnaire A compilation of questions about the work that goes on in the company. Questionnaires don't have the personal touch of interviews, but they can be an efficient way to collect data.

Real time Rapid reporting of data from an activity or process. It provides the ability to change the performance of the activity while the work continues.

Resource dictionary A compendium of attributes of individual resources such as job positions, types of equipment, and other resource elements. Attributes include skills, capacity, activities performed, and other performance information.

Resource driver   A measure of the cost of resources used by activities. It takes the cost of the resource and assigns it to the activities.

Resource planning   An activity-based model that predicts resource requirements based on forecast levels of demands.

Resources   Economic elements applied or used in the performance of activities.

Resources available   Resources currently deployed to the process and available to meet customer needs.

Resources required   Resources required to process the forecast outputs.

Scorecard   A list of goals and associated performance measures for an area of activity such as a division, department, or process. See also *balanced scorecard*.

Secondary activity   An activity that (1) has an output that benefits an internal customer or (2) has only a general benefit and no measurable benefit to internal or external customers. Career counseling is an example of the first type of secondary activity. Public relations is an example of the second type of secondary activity. See also *enabling activity*.

Service activity.   An activity that benefits all units of a type of service. Designing a new retirement plan for a group of external customers is a service activity.

Six sigma   A method used to design or redesign processes to remove the sources of variability and increase quality. Sigma (σ) is a statistical term used to denote the amount of variability in a process, product, or service.

Steering committee   An upper management group that oversees the planning, implementation, and results of the ABC system.

Storyboarding   A structured method of applying ABC analysis to processes. It is a team-based visual approach to cost reduction, process improvement, process reengineering, and best practices development. (Storyboarding is also used to gather activity data for use in the ABC model. See also *collaborative interviews*.)

Strategic analysis   Analysis of products, services, and customers for strategic opportunities. Strategic analysis may point out opportunities for repricing, redirecting resources to more profitable opportunities, and changing product strategy.

Strategic management   The use of activity-based analysis to set and implement strategic priorities.

Strategy map   A visual cause-and-effect representation of an organization's strategy. Used to communicate strategy effectively, it helps guide the development of scorecards.

Supplier management   The use of ABC to identify waste (in terms of cost, time, and poor quality) in supplier relationships and to help build strong customer-supplier partnerships that can eliminate this waste.

Sustainable ABC system   An ABC system that is kept up-to-date and used to create results indefinitely.

Symptom   A visible sign of a broken cost system. Symptoms provide ammunition to advocates of ABC.

Target costing   Setting cost targets for new products based on market price. The analysis starts with an estimate of the selling price and subtracts profits and distribution costs to arrive at the target cost. Engineers then use ABC to help design a product at this cost.

Theoretical capacity   Total time available to do work before deducting nonproductive time.

Time-based ABC   A method of implementing ABC and resource planning using time equations. It may be more accurate than standard ABC models and costs less to build and maintain.

Time equation   A compound equation combining time estimates from several activities into a single activity driver.

Timekeeping system   A record of the time devoted to activities or cost objects. Not commonly used in pilot projects, it is cost-effective as a way of gathering time data for sustainable ABC systems.

Tracing   Assignment of costs based on specific activity-related data.

Unit activity   An activity that is performed on a unit of a product or service. Attaching a resistor to a printed circuit board is an example of a unit activity.

Value analysis   Intense study of a business process with the intent of improving the process and reducing cost. Its goal is to ensure that you perform the right activities in the right way.

Value creation   Activities that realize results from the ABC system.

Variance reporting system   A system designed to flag costs that are higher than standard, allowing management to take action to correct the underlying problem.

World class   An organization that has achieved high standards of business performance and is continuously improving its ability to meet its customers' needs.

Index

ABOUT THE AUTHOR

Peter B.B. Turney, Ph.D., is the president and CEO of Cost Technology and an adjunct professor at the Darden Graduate School at the University of Virginia. Dr. Turney is a founder of ABC and ABM, and has led successful implementations of the programs in manufacturing, service, and government organizations throughout the world. A frequent presenter to management groups, he has written for the *Harvard Business Review, Sloan Management Review, Cost Management*, and other leading journals.